# Library Surveys

NUMBER SIXTEEN
*Columbia University Studies in Library Service*

# Library Surveys

Edited by
Maurice F. Tauber
and
Irlene Roemer Stephens

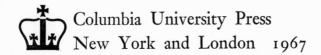 Columbia University Press
New York and London  1967

*Maurice F. Tauber* is Melvil Dewey Professor of
Library Service at Columbia University.

*Irlene Roemer Stephens* is Chief Librarian and
Professor at Richmond College of the
City University of New York.

Copyright © 1967 Columbia University Press
Library of Congress Catalog Card Number: 67-25304
Printed in the United States of America

# Columbia University Studies in Library Service

# The Conference

T HE Conference on Library Surveys, held at Columbia University, June, 14–17, 1965 and sponsored by the Committee on Library Surveys of the Association of College and Research Libraries of the American Library Association and the School of Library Service, Columbia University, was organized to review present-day knowledge in the conduct of surveys of various types of libraries. The committee had long expressed an interest in a conference which might crystallize the widespread interest in the survey as an approach to providing library services, thereby encouraging increased support of libraries. Thus, the Conference on Library Surveys had two major objectives: to provide an opportunity for registrants to increase their knowledge of the uses of the survey method in seeking solutions to library problems, and to provide opportunity for discussion of problems and techniques of library surveys in relation to particular situations.

The conference attendance included not only the experienced consultants who participated in the program, but individuals who had been involved in surveying responsibilities or situations, as well. Consequently, it was possible to achieve the objectives of the conference.

In the organization of the program, it was considered worthwhile to include a background paper on the application of the survey method to library operations. In his paper on the origins and evolution of the survey, Guy R. Lyle has discussed certain aspects of library surveys which have been carried over from the survey approach as applied in other fields. He has also described important landmark surveys which have influenced the development of the survey method in library situations.

Among the most elusive areas in library development and service to survey is that of the resources of libraries. The assessment and evaluation of book collections and other resources is of vital importance. Auspicious development of library resources, in support of the goals and in fulfillment of the functions of the library, involves continuing scrutiny and evaluation of collections, with concurrent revision and modification of acquisition policies. Edwin E. Williams and Lewis Leary, presenting the librarian's and the professor's standpoints, respectively, have sought to review procedures and measuring instruments used in the evaluation of resources. It is apparent that, in the evaluation of resources, surveyors are dealing with one of the most sensitive areas in libraries for diagnosis and recommendation. The criteria applied in the assessment and evaluation of collections should be defined and reexamined to insure their validity. The reliability of instruments applied in the evaluation of library resources should be reviewed with reference to specific situations. Williams and Leary have raised questions which require the attention of consultants and the librarians of libraries being surveyed. The variations in purpose, program, personnel, operations, and clientele are intricate and should be examined carefully in any survey of library resources. Further research relating to description of collections, the use of lists for checking purposes, and the quantitative and qualitative examination of books, periodicals, and other holdings has been suggested.

The prompt acquisition of selected library resources and the adequate and scheduled processing of these materials are among the more important responsibilities of librarians in all types of libraries. In an age when the volume of publication and distribution of books and other materials from all parts of the world is overwhelming, processing (including acquisitions, cataloging and classification, and preservation) has expanded greatly in terms both of costs and complexity of operations. The increase of centralized and regional processing, along with the introduction of mechanized approaches to the organization of materials, has been one of the dramatic developments in the last decade. Actually, the contributions of the national processing centers, as well as cooperative and commercial enterprises, should be evaluated in terms of the extent to which these centralized services meet the specific requirements of the several types of libraries. The editors of this book have discussed the basic approaches to the study of technical services operations. Although some of the prescriptions recommended for the efficient organization of materials may appear similar within the various functional units of technical services divisions, it should be apparent that the prompt and economic acquisition and organization of materials and maintenance of collections are dependent on systematic operations and procedures, intelligent division of responsibility between professional and clerical personnel, and coordination of operations with emphasis on a scheduled flow of work. Possibilities for saving money and time through centralized and cooperative activities should always be considered by the surveyor.

Critical reviews of studies of the use of libraries have resulted in doubt as to the validity of use studies in establishing criteria for the improvement of library services. Efforts to summarize the value of use studies have resulted in what might be called negative conclusions. Leon Carnovsky, who has been a student of them over the years, has summarized the issues involved and has discussed potentially applicable patterns of procedure. Admittedly, one of the crucial aims of surveys is to determine the extent to which user needs are satisfied, since the surveyor seeks to learn what constitutes achievement in library service. All surveys are concerned with the effectiveness of services, whatever these services may be. Library service has often been examined using subjective approaches; the findings of such studies should be examined carefully. The application of use studies in determining adequacy of library resources and services should be further evaluated.

Lowell Martin has explored some of the major areas requiring examination in surveys of personnel, using penetrating illustrations of observations made in surveys. Evaluation of staff adequacy and competence is a pressing problem in libraries. With the shortage of well-qualified personnel, the pace has slowed in many libraries, and the need has been steadily growing for consultants to assist librarians and administrators in reorganizing personnel so that the abilities of all staff members can be fully utilized in surroundings promoting high morale. The refinement of instruments for evaluating personnel and job assignments is certainly an area which requires continuing attention.

The increasing amount of library construction has brought with it the demand for library building consultants on a widening scale. Though many working librarians and library school faculty members continue to serve as consultants in the writing of programs and in planning new library buildings, there are now several experienced full-time building consultants. Donald E. Bean selectively organizes teams of librarians to serve as consultants on library buildings. In his chapter on library building consultation, Bean describes the issues involved in writing library programs and in preparing library building plans. Many of the observations reported have not been similarly synthesized before. Bean not only includes directions for making certain that a proper program and plan will be drawn up, but he also cautions librarians in regard to problems which may arise during specific aspects of planning a new library building.

Library administration, in terms of budget and finance, with regard to organization and management, is discussed by John A. Humphry and Stephen A. McCarthy, respectively. Although they have found it desirable to discuss these matters in connection with specific types of libraries, the variables are similar in all types of libraries and, thus, the discussion might well prove useful to library administrators generally. The budget and financial support of libraries are obviously the foundation on which all services are built, and the experiences of Humphry are directly applicable. The constant pressure on libraries to expand services in new directions, without increase in budgetary allocations, results in problems of organization and management, many of which are discussed by McCarthy. More automation in libraries and the emphasis on productivity have resulted in changes in library organization and an increased awareness of the economics of library operations.

Although these areas of library operation were regarded as of major importance for consideration in the conference, it became clear as the program was developed that it would be interesting to include a discussion of special approaches and problems in surveys of libraries of different types. Thus, with Morris A. Gelfand as moderator, academic and research libraries were discussed by Mark M. Gormley, public libraries by Andrew Geddes, school libraries by Frances E. Henne, special libraries by Janet Bogardus, and state libraries by Walter T. Brahm. These papers, with the added comments by Gelfand, provide guidance with respect to special approaches which might be used in surveying different types of libraries. Certainly, there are important differences in surveys of the various types of libraries; the special approaches in individual types of libraries have been discussed by the contributors. Variations in approach are also referred to in the discussions of surveys of particular library functions.

The final paper of the conference was prepared by E. W. Erickson, who earlier had examined a number of academic library surveys as a doctoral project at the University of Illinois. Erickson has enlarged on his earlier work, and his consideration of the value, effectiveness, and use of the library survey as an instrument of administration is concise and practical. His effort to learn something of the use of the survey as a teaching instrument in library schools and in library administration is cited since library surveys, as a body of literature, have sometimes been neglected as a source of information pertinent to solving problems currently faced by practicing librarians.

The conference director and his colleagues at the Columbia University School of Library Service express their gratefulness to all participants, to the various librarians who served as moderators on quick notice, and to the members of the audience who actively participated in the discussions. Moderators, in addition to those on the program, included George M. Bailey, Richard H. Logsdon, Harold L. Hamill, and A. Frederick Kuhlman.

Gratitude is especially expressed to Mr. George M. Bailey, executive secretary of the Association of College and Research Libraries, for his help in preparing the program, and to the members of the ACRL Committee on Library Surveys for their direct interest and suggestions.

The conference director is especially indebted to Dean Jack Dalton, and Carlyle J. Frarey, assistant to the dean, in helping to develop the program and for aiding in the conference generally. Mrs. Molly Herman, Mrs. Marilee Martel, Mrs. Ruth Pelner Donnelly, Miss Cynthia Kessel, Miss Jessica Spadola, and Mrs. Gail Levine, all of the School of Library Service, and Dr. Seoud Makram Matta, Cairo, Egypt, a graduate of the doctoral program of the school, assisted in many ways in making the conference pleasant for the participants and the audience. Philip Weimerskirch, a student at the school, assisted with tape recordings of various portions of the proceedings. Irlene Roemer Stephens assisted the director from the outset in the planning and conduct of the conference, and in editing the papers. Mrs. Nathalie C. Batts, Mrs. Marianne Cooper, and Miss Emma Lou Kopp assisted in the proofreading.

Finally, a word of thanks is owed Cody Barnard, editor at the Columbia University Press, for his help in improving the entire manuscript for publication.

MAURICE F. TAUBER
*Director*
*Conference on Library Surveys*
IRLENE ROEMER STEPHENS

*March, 1967*

# Contributors

DONALD E. BEAN, *Library Management and Building Consultants, Inc., Glenview, Illinois*

MISS JANET BOGARDUS, *Librarian, Federal Reserve Bank of New York, New York, New York*

WALTER T. BRAHM, *State Librarian, Connecticut State Library, Hartford, Connecticut*

LEON CARNOVSKY, *Professor, Graduate Library School, University of Chicago, Chicago, Illinois*

E. W. ERICKSON, *Head Librarian, Eastern Michigan University, Ypsilanti, Michigan*

ANDREW GEDDES, *Director, Nassau Library System, Hempstead, New York*

MORRIS A. GELFAND, *Librarian, Queens College of the City University of New York, Flushing, New York*

MARK M. GORMLEY, *University Librarian, The University of Wisconsin, Milwaukee, Wisconsin*

MISS FRANCES E. HENNE, *Professor, School of Library Service, Columbia University, New York, New York*

JOHN A. HUMPHRY, *State Librarian, and Assistant Commissioner for Libraries of the State of New York*

LEWIS LEARY, *Professor and Chairman, Department of English and Comparative Literature, Columbia University*

GUY R. LYLE, *Director of Libraries, Emory University, Atlanta, Georgia*

STEPHEN A. MC CARTHY, *Executive Director, Association of Research Libraries*

LOWELL A. MARTIN, *Vice President and Editorial Director, Grolier, Inc., New York, New York*

MRS. IRLENE R. STEPHENS, *Chief Librarian and Professor, Richmond College of the City University of New York, Richmond, New York*

MAURICE F. TAUBER, *Professor, School of Library Service, Columbia University, New York, New York*

EDWIN E. WILLIAMS, *Assistant Director of Libraries, Harvard University, Cambridge, Massachusetts*

# Participants in the
# Conference on Library Surveys

THE following people, in addition to the contributors, participated in the conference:

Kenneth S. Allen, Associate Director, University of Washington
Libraries, Seattle, Washington

Lee Ash, Project Director, Survey of Medical Library Resources,
New York City

George M. Bailey, Executive Secretary, Association of College and
Research Libraries, Chicago, Illinois

Mrs. Delma H. Batton, Acting Librarian, Library Commission for
the State of Delaware, Dover, Delaware

Miss Florence E. Biller, Library Consultant, California State Library, Sacramento, California

Miss Polley Bignell, Department of Library Science, The University
of Mississippi, University, Mississippi

Miss Ruth E. Blanchard, Liaison Librarian, Smithsonian Institution,
Washington, D.C.

Ralph Blasingame, Jr., Associate Professor, Graduate School of Library Service, Rutgers University, New Brunswick, New Jersey

Larry Bone, Librarian, Shelby County Libraries, Memphis, Tennessee

Irene Borys, Head Cataloger, New York University School of Law,
New York, New York

Jack W. Bryant, Director, Greenwich Library, Greenwich, Connecticut

James H. Burghardt, Assistant Librarian, Library Association of
Portland, Portland, Oregon

Miss Frances L. Carey, Assistant Director of Libraries, Naval War College Libraries, Newport, Rhode Island

Morris L. Cohen, Librarian, Biddle Law Library, University of Pennsylvania, Philadelphia, Pennsylvania

Miss Carolyn Crawford, Director, School Libraries and Instructional Materials, State Department of Education, Honolulu, Hawaii

Miss Mavis Cariou, Consultant, Etobicoke Board of Education, Islington, Ontario, Canada

Jack Dalton, Dean, School of Library Service, Columbia University, New York, New York

Mrs. Marguerite Densky, Chief Librarian, Université de Montréal, Montréal, Canada

Jacob S. Epstein, Assistant Librarian, Public Library of Cincinnati and Hamilton County, Cincinnati, Ohio

Miss Sallie Farrell, State Librarian, Louisiana State Library, Baton Rouge, Louisiana

Rev. Paul-Emile Filion, S.J., Chief Librarian, Laurentian University, Sudbury, Ontario, Canada

Miss D. Nora Gallagher, Director of Libraries, Adelphi University, Garden City, New York

Guy Garrison, Director, Library Research Center, University of Illinois, Urbana, Illinois

Arthur Goldzweig, Assistant Librarian, Hunter College, New York, New York

Mrs. Margaret Graig, School Librarian, Stamford Central School Library, Stamford, New York

Miss Gloria Grieco, Assistant Librarian, College of New Rochelle, New Rochelle, New York

Mrs. Elaine Haas, Director and Library Consultant, Technical Library Service, New York, New York

Harold L. Hamill, City Librarian, Los Angeles Public Library, Los Angeles, California

Mrs. Mary A. Huffer, Acting Librarian, Smithsonian Institution, Washington, D.C.

Mrs. Lillian C. Irons, Assistant Executive Secretary, Vermont Free Public Library Service, Montpelier, Vermont

Robert Dale Jaccaud, Assistant Head of Extension, Lima Public Library, Lima, Ohio

Sidney L. Jackson, Associate Professor, Department of Library Science, Kent State University, Kent, Ohio

Osman G. Jama, Student from the Somali Republic, Eastern University, Ypsilanti, Michigan

Miss Hazel A. Johnson, Librarian, Connecticut College, New London, Connecticut

Harold D. Jones, Assistant Librarian, Brooklyn College Library, Brooklyn, New York

Leon Karpel, Director, Mid-Hudson Libraries, Poughkeepsie, New York

A. Frederick Kuhlman, Director Emeritus, Joint University Libraries, Nashville, Tennessee

Samuel A. Lacey, Assistant Chief, Extension Services, Queens Borough Public Library, Jamaica, New York

Miss Katherine Laich, Assistant City Librarian, Los Angeles Public Library, Los Angeles, California

Miss Jean M. Legg, Consultant, Michigan State Library, Lansing, Michigan

Miss Alberta Letts, Director, The Nova Scotia Provincial Library, Halifax, Nova Scotia, Canada

Mrs. Doris Lewis, Chief Librarian, University of Waterloo, Waterloo, Ontario, Canada

Miss Dinah Lindauer, Director, Public Library/School Relations Project, Nassau Library System, Hempstead, New York

Winifred B. Linderman, Professor, School of Library Service, Columbia University, New York, New York

Richard H. Logsdon, Director, Columbia University Libraries, New York, New York

Mrs. Constance M. Lyle, Public Relations/Extension Department Head, Lima Public Library, Lima, Ohio

Miss Isobel Phelps Lynch, Chief, Extension Division, Enoch Pratt Free Library, Baltimore, Maryland

Robert R. McClarren, Director, Indiana State Library, Indianapolis, Indiana

Seoud M. Matta, Graduate Student, School of Library Service, Columbia University, New York, New York

Ellsworth Mason, Director of Library Services, Hofstra University, Hempstead, New York

John J. Miniter, Teacher, School of Library Science, Texas Woman's University, Denton, Texas

Mother M. de Montfort, O.S.U., Head Librarian, College of New Rochelle, New Rochelle, New York

Joseph Myers, Supervisor of Library Construction Grants, Pennsylvania State Library, Harrisburg, Pennsylvania

Bruce Peel, Chief Librarian, University of Alberta, Edmonton, Alberta, Canada

Dominic A. Persempere, Administrator, Andrew Warde Branch, Fairfield Public Library, Fairfield, Connecticut

Miss Ruth H. Phillips, Public Library Consultant, Virginia State Library, Richmond, Virginia

S. Gilbert Prentiss, State Librarian, New York State Library, Albany, New York

Miss Helen E. Rodgers, Head Librarian, El Camino College, California

William A. Roedde, Director, Provincial Library Service, Ontario Department of Education, Toronto, Canada

Harold L. Roth, Library Director, East Orange Public Library, East Orange, New Jersey

Mrs. Sylvia K. Sentner, Circulation Librarian, Cornell University Medical Library, New York, New York

Robert Shaw, Assistant to the Executive Secretary, Library Administration Division, American Library Association, Chicago, Illinois

Mrs. Marie Shultz, Assistant Director, Field Services Division, Texas State Library, Austin, Texas

Walter D. Shih, Administrative Assistant, Prince George's County Memorial Library, Hyattsville, Maryland

Morton Snowhite, Chief Cataloger, Newark College of Engineering, Newark, New Jersey

Miss Eleanor F. Street, Director, Westport Public Library, Westport, Connecticut

Miss Elizabeth Stroup, Information Research Assistant, Library of Congress, Washington, D.C.

Ray R. Suput, Assistant Director, University Libraries, Western Reserve University, Cleveland, Ohio

Mrs. Natalie Tsonev, Administrator, Southern Maryland Regional Library Association, Leonardtown, Maryland

William J. Van Beynum, Librarian, Russell Library, Middletown, Connecticut

Mrs. Joan Warnow, Librarian, American Institute of Physics, New York, New York

Paul A. Winckler, Associate Professor, Graduate Library School, Long Island University, Brookville, New York

Donald E. Wright, Chief of the Bureau, Bureau of Library Services, State Department of Education, Hartford, Connecticut

# Contents

PART ONE

# Use of the Survey Method

# 1 An Exploration into the Origins and Evolution of the Library Survey

GUY R. LYLE

For the purpose of this paper, a library survey is a specialized type of investigation whose goal is the improvement of library service.

The concept of the library survey is by no means new. An exhaustive research would probably show examples as far back as one cared to go, to Socrates, for example. Since this paper is limited to the library survey in the United States and since my enthusiasm for the subject is moderate, I have gone back somewhat less than a hundred years.

One hundred years of the library survey movement in one hour is a tall order by any standard. But, then, Dr. Tauber might well retort, university library administration in 641 pages was even more remarkable—and Wilson and Tauber's attempt was generally hailed as a success.

The analogy is not without greater significance than the merely numerical, for Wilson and Tauber are almost as synonymous with the library survey as they are with university library administration. However, in this paper, I shall limit myself to that aspect of the library survey which we ordinarily associate with origins and history. I eschew any attempt at summarizing the contents or classifying the various types of surveys, a job which has already been done satisfactorily by others. Instead, my interest is to select a half dozen or so landmark surveys of the past hundred years, to summarize their accomplishments and methodology, to expose some of the undercurrents which were at work beneath the surface of librarianship, and to hint at the manner in which they affected or were influenced by, or simply provided the setting for, surveys and the development of survey technique.

## PHILADELPHIA CENTENNIAL OF 1876

In every great movement there is a long, slow growth till the idea ripens and some special step is taken which marks an epoch. We date the new library movement from August, 1876, when, taking advantage of the Centennial, a hundred leading librarians were called together in a four days convention where it was found that the time was ripe and the American Library Association was founded to carry on that important part of the movement which demanded national organization of librarians.[1]

Melvil Dewey was right. The Philadelphia Centennial of 1876, with its appeal to the pride and patriotism of Americans, was the occasion rather than the cause of the library explosion of 1876.[2] But it was also the cause rather than the occasion for the first landmark survey of the state of the library profession. I refer, of course, to the special government report on *Public Libraries in the United States*,[3] published in 1876. Even though the American public library of 1876 had not yet proliferated into the ever-widening services of its modern contemporary, the Centennial commission recognized the importance of libraries as a part of the educational representation at the Philadelphia exhibition. By identifying library services with education, the commission sought to raise the public esteem in which these services were held.

Hardly had the printer's ink dried on the first copies of *Public Libraries in the United States* when its editor-in-chief, Samuel R. Warren, rushed copies to the assembled librarians at the Philadelphia library conference—a splendid gesture, though hardly the sort of thing that should be brought before a group of librarians on a holiday. *Public Libraries in the United States* is a large fat volume weighing five and a half pounds. It purports to offer "as full a survey as time and means would permit of all classes of public libraries, from the time of establishment of the first public library in the colonies to the present." [4]

The methodology was extremely simple. Each American town which had a population large enough to accommodate a public library was contacted, and if a local library did indeed exist there, library officials and other interested persons were asked to submit material. Statistics were gathered and edited. When enough data became available in a specific field, they were used as a base for special essays—some exceptionally good—on the history and current condition of library service in law, theology, medicine, colleges, government, prisons, and in the public library. Facts were seen to be a primary requirement, not merely to show the present condition and extent of library service but also to provide information which would help to awaken the interest of all engaged in educational work to the need of libraries. The report laid basic descriptive groundwork for the improvement of library administration and as such made a useful contribution to librarianship.

Progress in librarianship has always proceeded at two levels. On the workaday level it accumulates piecemeal, by a sequence of small steps, and by what might be described as the experience school of trial-and-error. Like an advancing tide, the limit of professional knowledge at this level edges slowly forward, and each generation of librarians adds a little to the contributions of library science. At another level, some say a higher level, there are those who stand back and view library development in longer perspective. They see growth not merely as quantitative, a matter of adding new information and new ways of doing things; their ideas transform the whole vision of the profession, so that in time we come to interpret all our experience within the framework set by a new constellation of ideas. The work of the "Committee of Five on Library Service," appointed by American Library Association president William Warner Bishop in 1918, is characteristic of the first level; the energizing force of Frederick P. Keppel and the Carnegie Corporation, of Louis R. Wilson and the Chicago Graduate Library School, illustrate the second.

## THE SURVEY OF THE "COMMITTEE OF FIVE ON LIBRARY SERVICE"

Let us look first at the work of the "Committee of Five on Library Service" whose *Survey of Libraries in the United States*[5] stands out in my mind as another landmark in the origin and evolution of the library survey movement. The committee, of which Arthur E. Bostwick was chairman, was created in 1919 to make a comprehensive study of library methods and practices and to publish its findings. It spluttered and sputtered until 1924 when the magic of a Carnegie Corporation grant turned the crank.[6] The committee was well aware that no thorough investigation of library practices had been made since the Centennial report and that the fiftieth anniversary of the American Library Association was scarcely two years away. The time was ripe. Libraries, especially public libraries, were now going concerns. There was need to know what the other fellow was doing and how he was doing it. The task of the committee was not to discover new methods and principles but "to present an accurate description of the most generally prevailing forms of practice . . . to describe, likewise, the important variations from the prevailing forms; and to cite, wherever possible, some of the most interesting illustrations both of the prevailing forms and of the less usual."[7] A detailed questionnaire was sent to 3,034 libraries. Replies were received from 49.5 percent, but the omission of "so many notably efficient libraries" probably limited the effectiveness of the survey.[8] Verification of information received was made by checking replies and asking for further information on anything which might be misinterpreted by the editors. The final report was published in four volumes, without extensive comment, criticism, or evaluation. The first volume dealt with the administrative aspects of college and public library work; the second with public services in college and public libraries; the third with extension work, children's services, and school library service; and the fourth with technical processes. In spite of the fact that some important librarians dragged their feet and others failed to contribute, the four-volume *Survey of Libraries in the United States* afforded an intensive and useful study of libraries as they existed in the 1920s. It is true that there was no attempt to evaluate or persuade in this work, but looking back one is aware that such a survey is significant of a period when public library service was greatly expanding and when librarians were hopefully looking for ready answers to tomorrow's tasks. The essential facts turned up in the survey were helpful to many librarians in directing their operations.

## THE INFLUENCE OF FREDERICK P. KEPPEL AND THE CARNEGIE CORPORATION

The next major development in the library survey movement sprung, as has already been suggested, from the energizing force of Frederick P. Keppel, Louis R. Wilson, and a new school of librarianship. Actually, the new school arose because Sarah Bogle, Theodore Koch, Carl R. Roden, George Utley, and a number of other members of the Chicago Library Club believed that librarians were not getting a proper library education, or enough education, or the kind of education they should have.[9] These people felt strongly enough about their convictions to do something about them. On April 20, 1923, they conveyed their ideas to the newly appointed president of the Carnegie Corporation, Frederick P. Keppel, who at the time was seeking ways of translating his own conclusions about two other important studies—C. C. Williamson's *Training for Library Service* (1923) and William S. Learned's *The American Public Library and the Diffusion of Knowledge* [10]—into a program to further the cause of library training.

Frederick Keppel was the kind of man who felt that in order to do something really worthwhile, one had to take the long view. When he recommended to his board setting up a new and different kind of library school, he was not uttering the usual platitudes. He had back of him a foundation with a long record of experience in library philanthropy. He had made a thorough study of Williamson and Learned. He had sought advice far and wide, and finally, "by endless repetition of his constant and often embarrassing question, 'Well, what do you want us to do?' reduced the situation to the specifics of his widely heralded 'Ten-Year Program in Library Service.'" [11] According to his own statement, he visualized the new school of librarianship as one that would "occupy for the librarian's profession a position analogous to that of the Harvard Law School or the Johns Hopkins Medical School." [12]

## STUDIES IN READING

The Chicago Graduate Library School opened in 1928. At the end of twelve short but exceptionally busy years, it could reflect with some satisfaction that it had already directed the attention of the library profession toward a more objective a d critical approach to the solution of library problems. In no area was this new approach, this new recalculation of the course of librarianship, more evident than in the library survey movement. Whereas criticism and evaluation in surveys had previously been studiously avoided, the stage was now set for the critical light of scientific evaluation. "What was also needed," according to Chase Dane, "was someone who would or could approach library problems from the point of view of the sociologist. And in Douglas Waples the Graduate Library School had this person." [13] I need hardly remind this audience that the lead-off survey was *What People Want to Read About* (1931), wherein Douglas Waples and Ralph W. Tyler anatomized the reading interests of adults. William S. Gray and Bernice E. Leary followed in 1935 with *What Makes a Book Readable*, while Douglas Waples again, in 1938, surveyed the social aspects of reading during the depression years in *Books in Print*. I read all these books at the time. Before reading them, I was naïve enough to think there were straightforward answers to why people read and what they read. But after reading these books, I discovered that the what, why, and how of reading is a much more complicated affair. I remember wishing that I might make a study of those who *don't* read.

The year 1938 witnessed the publication of what I have chosen for my third landmark survey, Louis R. Wilson's survey of the general pattern of reading in the United States, *The Geography of Reading*. Wilson was assisted by a Carnegie Corporation grant, the aid of the Illinois Emergency Relief Administration, which provided expert statistical and cartographic assistance, and two doctoral research assistants in librarianship. His presentation has all the earmarks of a modern scientific and educational survey. The problem is clearly defined, all the data are assembled, and the interpretation is surrounded by a veritable hailstorm of statistical proof, tables, maps, graphs, and figures. The method of investigation comprised principally the examination of an overwhelming mass of statistical reports, government publications, surveys, and special studies; they are enumerated in hundreds of page footnotes and a fifteen-page bibliography. Careful and exact measurement checks are introduced to insure valid comparisons. Wilson has been interested all his professional life in four things. How evenly are library resources distributed in the United States? How does this distribution compare with that of other social and educational agencies for the dissemination of ideas? If there are disparities, does it matter? If it does matter, what can be done about it? The first two questions were answered once and for all in his book; the third is wisely sidestepped by the assumption that "through [the library] freedom, equality of educational opportunity, and preparation for participation in a democratic government might be achieved";[14] an answer to the fourth is found in the final chapter of recommendations. These recommendations have a peculiar quality of prescience, as though in some way Dr. Wilson had heard about the Great Society and sneaked in before the gate was open to proclaim the need for the extension of library planning in each state and region, the importance of state recognition that library support is of equal consequence with support to schools, and the suggestion that the equalization of library service can best be done through state and federal participation rather than through complete dependence upon local support.[15]

For me, at least, one of the fringe benefits of reading *The Geography of Reading* in the 1930s was its unequivocal demonstration that library problems do not exist in splendid isolation from one another or from other agencies of communication. Dr. Wilson showed that they are as interwoven as the strands in a spider's web.

## MANAGEMENT ENTERS THE SURVEY PICTURE

The Chicago school did not confine itself to studies in reading and surveys of the social effects of print. Nothing, indeed, was more striking about the new school, especially in its heyday in the 1930s and 1940s, than its diversity. When Dean Wilson spoke of objectives, he stressed first the importance of a philosophy of librarianship and of the search for guiding principles. For those who read Pierce Butler's scientific philosophizing, *An Introduction to Library Science,* and still lacked the faith, there were other facets to explore. Studies in library management stressed the importance of utilizing the findings of such recognized experts as Gulick, Urwick, White, and Dimock on the general theory of administrative organization. If this seemed to some librarians to be a rather temporary fad whose long-run promise hardly justified the enthusiasm produced by the Chicago summer institute of 1936, the fact remained that the functions of library management were studied intensively for the first time with results that had a marked effect on library surveys of the period. The brilliant, skillful interpreter of *The Government of the American Public Library*, Carleton B. Joeckel, was the figure that really dominated the surveys of this period.

This application of management principles and research to library evaluation is perhaps best illustrated and certainly most characteristic of the next landmark survey, *A Metropolitan Library in Action* (1940), prepared by Joeckel and Leon Carnovsky and said to be the most ambitious study of an individual library yet made. Both men were associated with the Chicago Graduate Library School. They were assisted by a substantial grant, eleven research assistants, consultants in and outside the profession, and took a year for the accumulation and analysis of data. Some of the elements which made this survey of the Chicago Public Library distinctive may be gleaned from these abbreviated quotations from library administrators and students of library administration. E. W. McDiarmid: "Administrative organization and management are [shown to be] of greater importance to library service than many librarians have realized in the past"; Carl Vitz: "Its great value to library trustee and administrator and to the student of library administration lies in its detailed and careful consideration of the varied problems involved in the management of the public library. . . . Theories of organization and administration are discussed in the light of the Chicago Public Library situation and considerable reorganization is recommended"; John S. Cleavinger: "Findings [are] of significance to libraries generally. An instance is the discussion of the importance of a plan of administrative organization under which there will be adequate distribution of administrative authority and responsibility . . . or the difficult situation that has resulted from operation under civil service and the application of the local-residence requirement." [16] A most interesting by-product of the general treatment of management procedures to me was the surveyors' recommendation for the establishment of a research and planning division and the development of an experimental branch for the testing of new techniques and services.

## THE PUBLIC LIBRARY INQUIRY

The public library during the depression decade proved a good force in the making of a better social order. Under multiplying handicaps of increased demand for service and retrenchment in local support, the leadership of the profession sought ways and means to hold steady and at least keep their library operations on the same scale as they had in the past. The American Library Association had a planning committee, as had most of the states, made up of leading citizens as well as librarians, and out of the deliberations of this committee came standards, short-term objectives, and long-time programs.[17] Virtually all of this planning proceeded from three contemporary facts: the inability or reluctance of local authorities to support a rising scale of library use; the general public demand for a careful scrutinizing of costs in education and government in order to discriminate between the essential and nonessential; and, the growing recognition of the need to extend library services to the 37 percent of the population without such services. In an effort to determine objectively and by approved modern investigative methods what were the actual facts about the operations and problems of the American public library, the American Library Association invited the Social Science Research Council to make "an appraisal in sociological, cultural, and human terms of the extent to which librarians are achieving their objectives and an assessment of the public library's actual and potential contribution to American society."[18] This survey, termed generically the Public Library Inquiry, comprised nineteen projects and was published in ten volumes and special reports during a three-year period, 1949 to 1952.

Although instigated by librarians and advised by a committee on which librarians were a minority, the Public Library Inquiry was an investigation by specialists in the various fields of the social sciences who made widespread use of the techniques of the social psychologist, sociologist, and student of public administration. A staff of twenty-four workers prepared special studies on the public library's public, library government, the book industry, government publications, and work measurement, the last being one of the first studies to my knowledge in which a management consultant firm was brought in to examine library procedures. The studies were generally restricted to a group of sixty libraries chosen as representative of systems of all kinds out of 7,408 units in the nation. Because of the way in which this sampling was constructed, Carnovsky concluded that "it is probably safe to say that it gave a fairer picture of the [1926 ALA] American library scene than did the much larger sample used in the Survey." [19] Field studies and extensive questionnaires were substantially supplemented by numerous conferences with a selected group of key librarians.

A volume prepared by the director of the Inquiry, the late Robert D. Leigh, and entitled *The Public Library Report* (1950) brought together the conclusions and recommendations of the separate studies. Since the findings have been amply reported elsewhere, there is no need to go into them here. The entire project constituted an effort foreshadowed in previous studies to analyze on a nationwide scale a sociocultural institution and an entire occupational group. Subjects such as the need for state and federal aid, the library's role in a communications revolution, the minimum financing needed to give proper library service, and larger units of service were very much in the air at the time. The Inquiry reports brought these subjects closer to ground. Garland Taylor's criticism of the *Report* is well founded:

> It is somewhat repetitious, and sometimes indulges in the bright bustling manner of bringing platitudes to light as though they were gems of wisdom. . . . Of such measuring devices as the ALA Classification and Pay Plans the author appears to be entirely unaware. He greatly distorts the problem of acquisitions by exclusive attention to current materials, to the total neglect of out-of-print and antiquarian books.[20]

Another distinguished librarian said bluntly: "The total result of the survey was to bring Leigh and Bryan up-to-date on what the Graduate Library School had been doing for a decade and a half. And it pushed almost everything else off the boards while its surveyors held forth on the library platforms of the nation." All in all, however, the Inquiry received high praise and is commendably free of social science jargon. Carl Roden, librarian of the Chicago Public Library, called it "an impressive undertaking, well planned and exceedingly well carried out."

## THE UNIVERSITY LIBRARY AND THE SURVEY

State and public libraries were not the only ones subject to scrutiny in the 1930s and 1940s. For one reason or another the university library of this period had been left out of budget priorities when funds were being allocated to an ever-widening program of university studies and services. While the library was left to stagger along on a college library budget, the university was expanding its faculties, Ph.D. programs, and research far beyond what present and foreseeable library financial means could support. In this incipient stampede the library was in grave danger of being trampled. University officials were aware of the library problem but now for the first time they began to sense that something had to be done about it if their programs of graduate work and research were to be successful. Many turned to surveyors from outside the university to evaluate their library program and operations and to make suggestions for improvement. The earliest of the institutional library surveys prepared by outside experts was the *Report of a Survey of the University of Georgia Library*, published by the American Library Association in 1939. I well remember the discussions with Louis R. Wilson, who set up the machinery of the Georgia survey and served as its senior surveyor. While an institutional survey is primarily a product of reflections about the individual problems of a particular institution, Wilson believed that there were certain essential components of any good university library which established the framework of the Georgia survey. These related to collections adequate for carrying out the objectives of the university, a staff large enough and sufficiently well trained to afford a high level of library service, materials effectively organized, a good physical plant and modern equipment, close library integration with the administrative and educational policies and practices of the university, integration of library resources and services with state and regional library resources, and adequate library finances. Whatever the reason, this sevenfold concern contributed substantially to shaping the pattern of future university library surveys. Georgia was followed by library surveys at the universities of Florida (1940), Indiana (1940), South Carolina (1946), Stanford (1947), Cornell (1948), Texas A. & M. (1950), and Notre Dame (1952), to name but a few. Surveyors of surveys passed favorable judgments on the results.[21] The surveys had the stamp of authority, afforded a relatively complete view of the library as seen through the eyes of objective though sympathetic observers, and, since several surveyors were usually involved in each survey, provided a kind of collective diagnosis of the problems to be studied and of suggested solutions. On the other hand, the surveys produced no new survey methodology. The Georgia survey may have inadvertently even been a disservice in this regard. It established a pattern from which few subsequent surveys endeavored or cared to deviate. Instead of devising new approaches or responding to new situations with a new dynamic, the surveyors tended to follow the established pattern. This is not to suggest, of course, that all university library surveys are carbon copies. But as busy, practicing librarians, university library surveyors usually take a greater interest in the measurable and organizational problems of finance, physical plant and equipment, and operational problems than they do in some of the more intangible problems of policy, relationships, and library use.

THE SELF-SURVEY

It is impossible to conclude this excursion into the history of the library survey movement without reference to the self-survey. From the 1930s to the 1950s, self-surveys flourished and left some notable blueprints to guide future surveyors. There was *The University Libraries*, by M. Llewellyn Raney, Director of University Libraries at the University of Chicago, one of a series of twelve volumes published in 1933, presenting the results of a complete survey of the University. The purpose of the survey was to evaluate the book collections and to calculate what additions would be necessary in the years ahead. The Raney survey was a pioneer in developing bibliographic checklists and procedures for ascertaining the periodical literature fundamental to each discipline.

There was *A Faculty Survey of the University of Pennsylvania Libraries,* published by the University of Pennsylvania Press in 1940, and perhaps best remembered by librarians for its often-quoted libel: "This survey differs from most surveys of the same sort in that it was made, not by the distributors of books, but by the users of books; not by librarians, but by scholars." Again we have an attempt at a thorough faculty assessment of the weaknesses and strengths of the book collections. A unique feature was the use of a pilot survey of library holdings in English history, prepared especially for the survey as a model to be used by the other departments of the university.

There was the *Report of the Harvard University Library* by Keyes D. Metcalf and his collaborators in 1955. This survey dealt with acquisition, cataloging, service, interlibrary cooperation, space, personnel, organization, and finance. Its great virtue was its careful marshaling of relevant facts, precise and lucid analysis, frankness in facing up to unsolved problems, good common sense, and complete avoidance of the sin of self-glorification.

Finally, there is *The Columbia University Libraries,* prepared by Tauber and his colleagues and published by the Columbia University Press in 1958. One of the most comprehensive of the self-surveys, it dealt with administrative organization, resources, cataloging, facilities and equipment, photoduplication services, personnel, reader services, interlibrary cooperation, and financial support. A special feature of the Columbia survey was the battery of skillfully worded questionnaires used to obtain the views of administrators, faculty, library department heads, professional school students, undergraduates, and select librarians from the city. These data occupy fifty-two pages in the appendices. The Columbia survey differed from the Raney survey in the evaluation of the book collection. Instead of checking bibliographies to test the quality of the collection, the surveyors sought an editorial opinion from the faculty on the quality of collections according to an evaluation scale ranging from basic information to exhaustive collections.

In recent years the self-survey has gained considerable popularity in colleges and universities because of the institutional self-study and periodic visitation program of the regional accrediting associations. While the techniques of the self-survey in this program have been studied,[22] it is too early to assess the success and significance of the self-survey itself. It would be easy to make much of its weaknesses such as the limitations in depth and the extra load placed upon a staff already overburdened with professional duties. Nevertheless the requirement of the institutional self-study and periodic visitation program has provided one great boon to the library. It has opened up lines of campus communication which no other motivation short of a sizable foundation grant could accomplish. Any undertaking as important as a basic plan for the development of the college and university must of necessity require wide faculty and administration involvement. As a participant, the library has had an unequaled opportunity to clarify its role and to assess its position in the college or university organization.

## SUMMARY

This concludes my study of the origins and evolution of the library survey movement in the United States. As "history," it is, of course, incomplete. I have not discussed many types such as the state-wide cooperative, or management-consultant survey, not simply because of lack of time but because it would be terribly tedious to cut out any more cookies from this great mass of dough in one lecture. Scholars in library history might do worse than consider the origins and evolution of the library survey as a suitable topic for a dissertation. A great deal has been written about the types and techniques of library surveys, but the history of the survey has been neglected.

What can one learn from this modest exploration into the history of the library survey? I believe the first point to make is that the library survey has contributed substantially to the improvement of library service and the status of the profession. It has helped to clarify the purposes which librarians and libraries are trying to serve. It has helped to explain to trustees, administrators, faculty members, and the public what the library does, where it is going, and what means are appropriate to carry out its mission. It has provided students of library science and library textbook authors with some of the essential source material on major library problems—finance, legal, accounting, personnel, and organization. It has exerted a broadening influence, on library services by showing the impact of libraries on society and vice versa. It has contributed most perhaps to individual library progress and improvement. The old taunt of John Cotton Dana that "the passion for the survey, which has toured our country like a plague for a number of years, has at last laid hands on this group of my fellow library workers" [23] would scarcely find an echo in a council of librarians today. Indeed the library survey could not have survived unless it had made a substantial contribution to the improvement of libraries and librarianship.

The second point to make is that the survey has contributed to the movement toward a scientific evaluation of libraries and their services. Starting with the simplest form of questionnaire and statistical tabulation, the survey has, over the years, utilized and tested most of the surgical tools of the research process and popularized them: documentary analysis, questionnaries, checklists, visits, interviews, observation, modern methods of statistical analysis, machine tabulation, and scientific assessment. It has demonstrated the value of standards, tested them, and pointed the way toward their revision. It has helped to teach pragmatic librarians about theoretical concepts of library government, book selection policies, and administrative principles even though some of these same librarians, immediately after learning their lesson, confessed that they regarded these theories as a lot of baloney anyway, confirming once again their belief that librarianship is mostly a matter of common sense. I doubt very much if the library survey has helped to discover any new principles or new survey techniques. After all, this is not the task of the survey. Unlike research in the laboratory or stacks, the library survey must deal with a going enterprise, and usually with many problems in combination, and not with any single isolated item. It would not surprise me indeed if the survey techniques of today were pretty much the same as those in use a decade ago. In no small part, the development of survey technique has been a problem in applying the research methodology of science and the social sciences to the study of library problems.

Having paid my respects to the library survey's contribution to research methodology in librarianship, let me hasten to add that once one goes beyond a study of the landmark survey it is apparent that what is needed more than a knowledge of survey techniques is assistance in identifying important and relevant problems of genuine professional concern in a given situation. A checklist of survey techniques does not appear to me to be of much value in deciding what are the crucial problems requiring a solution nor in comprehending what is to be done after the problems are identified. For example, I have examined dozens of survey reports of college and university libraries in which departmental evaluations by faculty have revealed serious gaps in the library's book collections in each field. In each case the surveyor has recommended a sizable arrearage fund to close the gaps. If the institutions surveyed are to become what they aspire to be, they will eventually acquire such materials. But it is questionable whether a crash program of acquisition is wise or practicable. If the library has not made definite progress in the last twenty years in building its collections, is it likely that it will reach the promised land in the next three or five years? Quite frankly, a careful reading of the evidence on which the arrearage recommendation is made displays an unrealistic faculty attitude that may seriously affect the orderly process of development of the collections. As one of my faculty colleagues so aptly put it: "I can admire a forward look in planning, but it doesn't take an optician to point out that farsight may be a serious defect of vision."

Finally, I should say that an historical review of the landmark surveys, as well as subaltern works, enables one to identify the components of a good survey. These qualities would appear to be essential: 1) The purpose is clearly defined; 2) the data are well organized so that the reader gets a clear picture of what the problems are, how they came about, and what steps can be taken to improve them; 3) the assertions and conclusions are tested by a variety of methods; and 4) the interpretation is sensitive, imaginative, and human. I think many surveys fail on the fourth point. The facts are all marshaled, the data are tested, and the findings and recommendations are in; yet for the reason indicated above, the survey fails to get near its subject on intimate terms. I do not want to be too offensively specific, but let me illustrate from one of the surveys. On the subject of personnel, it summarizes as follows:

> The "modal" librarian . . . is an unmarried woman in her middle thirties. . . . She entered the library service in her early twenties. Her professional training is limited to the Library's own Training Class. . . . She has never attended a library school. . . . She has little expectation of finding a position in another library. She belongs to the American Library Association . . . but she is not particularly active. . . . In her community activities, she is not much of a "joiner."

Now, I maintain that this statement in a library survey is not only indefensible, it is libelous. It distorts the whole image of librarianship. It is the impression that remains in the mind of the public long after the tables and graphs are forgot. However true in detail, it is totally false in the round. The library owes everything to its staff and has become what its staff has made it. Libraries have been, and are, understaffed, and the staffs are underpaid. Consequently, the quality has not always been what it should be. The improvement, however, is not merely a matter of administrative organization, classification and pay plans, or the application of modern office procedures to library procedures, but of greater encouragement of the staff. All honor, I say, to the men and women who have done so much with so little. Let the ladies be called "models" but not "modals," speak of what they *have* and not of what they *have not*, and if the only thing they tell the surveyor they read regularly is the *Wilson Library Bulletin* and the *Saturday Review*, remember there is no subject on which librarians manifest such duplicity as on the subject of what they read.

REFERENCES

1. "Development of the Modern Library Idea, the Association, Journal, Bureau and School," *Library Notes* 1:47 (June 1886).
2. The American Library Association was founded at Philadelphia, October 4–6, 1876; the Library Bureau was established by Melvil Dewey in 1876; *Library Journal*, Vol. 1, No. 1 appeared September 1876; and the *American Catalogue*, author and title entries of books in print, began with July 1, 1876.
3. U.S. Bureau of Education. *Public Libraries in the United States; Their History, Condition, and Management.* Special Report. Washington, D.C., U.S. Government Printing Office, 1876.
4. U.S. Commissioner of Education. *Report for the Year 1875.* Washington, D.C., U.S. Government Printing Office, 1876, p. CIV.
5. American Library Association. *A Survey of Libraries in the United States.* 4 vols. Chicago, American Library Association, 1926–27.
6. "Carnegie Corporation Grants for Library Service," *Library Journal* 49:424 (May 1, 1924).
7. American Library Association, *Survey*, I, 11.
8. Lowe, John Adams. "Snapshots of Library Administration," *Library Journal* 51:900 (October 15, 1926).
9. *New Frontiers in Librarianship:* Proceedings of the Special Meeting of the Association of American Library Shools, December 30, 1940. Chicago, Graduate Library School, n.d., p. 6.
10. Learned, William S. *The American Public Library and the Diffusion of Knowledge.* New York, Harcourt Brace, 1924. Williamson, Charles C. *Training for Library Service* New York, Merrymount Press, 1923.
11. Carnegie Corporation of New York. *Annual Report*, 1926, pp. 9–10.
12. Keppel, F. P. "Carnegie Corporation and the Graduate Library School," *Library Quarterly* 1:23 (January 1931).
13. Dane, Chase. "Library Survey Literature," *Iowa Library Quarterly* 17:35 (January 1954).
14. Wilson, Louis R. *The Geography of Reading: a Study of the Distribution and Status of Libraries in the United States.* Chicago, ALA and University of Chicago Press, 1938, p. 429.

15. *Ibid.*, pp. 440–42.
16. McDiarmid, E. W. *College and Research Libraries* 3:71 (December 1941); Vitz, Carl. *Library Journal* 65:343 (April 15, 1940); Cleavinger, J. S. *Library Quarterly* 10:417 (July 1940).
17. "National Plan for Libraries." *ALA Bulletin* 29:91–98 (February 1935); A.L.A. *State Plans for Library Development as Adopted by State Library Associations.* Chicago, ALA, 1937; Ridgeway, H. A. "State Plans and Surveys of Public Library Service," *ALA Bulletin* 44:463–68 (December 1950).
18. Leigh, Robert. *The Public Library in the United States: the General Report of the Public Library Inquiry.* New York, Columbia University Press, 1950, p. 3.
19. Carnovsky, Leon. "Public Library Surveys and Evaluation," *Library Quarterly* 25:24 (January 1955). Dr. Carnovsky refers here to the ALA *Survey of Libraries in the United States, 1926–27*, 4 vols., which sent out some 3,000 questionnaires.
20. Taylor, Garland F. "The Public Library Sits for Its Portrait." Louisiana Library Association *Bulletin* 14:37 (Spring 1951).
21. Wilson, L. R. "The University Library Survey; Its Result," *College and Research Libraries* 8:368–75 (July 1947); Erickson, E. W. *College and University Libraries Survey, 1938–1952.* ACRL Monograph 25. Chicago, ALA, 1961.
22. Gelfand, Morris A. "Technique of Library Evaluators in the Middle States Association," *College and Research Libraries* 19:305–20 (July 1958).
23. Dana, John C. "Mr. Dana's Criticism," *Library Journal* 49:828 (October 1, 1924).

# 2 Surveying Library Collections

EDWIN E. WILLIAMS

MOST of my remarks on surveying library collections will deal with one or another of three major topics: purposes, methods, and results. Why are library collections surveyed? How are they surveyed? What is known (and what can be guessed) about the results?

Before these questions are approached, however, something should be said of the source materials that have been available and of the kinds of survey that are to be considered. The literature that I ought to have read is of three kinds. First, there is the related or potentially relevant material, which has no clear boundaries and is enormous in extent. Something useful might have been discovered in almost any work dealing with communication, the methods of research and teaching, reading, and statistical techniques, to say nothing of works on librarianship treating topics such as accreditation, acquisition policy, book selection, fund allocation, library statistics, storage, and weeding. My preparation in this vast area of related materials is no more than fragmentary and haphazard.

Second, there are works directly concerned with surveying library collections—the surveys of surveying. These are not very numerous; they consist of only a few chapters or subsections in a few books, and a few journal articles or portions of articles.[1] Here, at least, I can hope that I am reasonably well prepared.

Finally, there are the accounts and reports of surveys themselves. Hundreds have been published, and hundreds more in manuscript could undoubtedly be turned up by a resourceful scholar. I must plead guilty to having sampled only; Harvard does not have a good collection of surveys except for university libraries, and I have had no time for work elsewhere aside from two days at the headquarters library of the American Library Association, where there are at least thirteen shelves tightly packed with slender surveys. Fortunately I know that the other speakers at this conference are well qualified to make up for my deficiencies. It would be unreasonable to suppose that anything I say will be new to them, but I can urge them to listen because I hope they will correct my mistakes and close the gaps that I leave.

It might be easier to avoid mistakes and gaps if surveys of library collections were less diverse than they are. Some surveys deal with collections only; many more deal with them in the course of a more inclusive study, and the extent to which collections are considered varies enormously in these general surveys. At one extreme, while the University of Chicago survey of 1933 was ostensibly a general survey, something like 85 percent of the volume was devoted to the library's collections.[2] On the other hand, while it might seem safe to assume that any general survey would have something to say of the collections that libraries contain, nothing of the sort is to be found in the four-volume *Survey of Libraries in the United States* that appeared nearly forty years ago.[3]

Most published surveys are made by outsiders, but a few are self-surveys. Many deal with collections of a single library, but perhaps as many more are multilibrary studies, some of them covering hundreds of collections. Most surveys attempt to cover all collections of the library or libraries with which they are concerned, but a few are restricted to specified subjects. Libraries of every size and species have been surveyed, and there are also surveys covering all collections in a given area or on a given subject regardless of the type of library in which they are to be found.

Many of the varieties theoretically possible do not, however, seem to be exemplified by published surveys. The survey of an individual school library is not likely to be published; excellent and detailed advice on how to survey such a library is available,[4] but the published school-library surveys that have been examined were all general, multilibrary studies. Published surveys dealing with individual public libraries are plentiful, but they are nearly all surveys covering the institution as a whole rather than its collections only, and nearly all are made by outsiders.[5] This is true also of published college-library surveys; [6] in the university and research field, however, the self-survey is more common, as well as the survey dealing only with collections. It can hardly be said that published special-library surveys of any kind are common,[7] unless one counts those covering departmental libraries in universities.[8] Finally, three varieties of survey covering more than a single type of library can be distinguished: those concerned with other aspects of libraries in addition to collections, those that deal with collections only but cover all subjects, and those restricted to collections in specified subjects.

A few strays do not fit into any of the categories that have been suggested. There is Marjorie Plant's *The Supply of Foreign Books and Periodicals to the Libraries of the United Kingdom,*[9] as well as the surveys of American research library acquisitions that preceded the inauguration of the Farmington Plan,[10] and the surveys of Farmington Plan receipts that have followed.[11] All of these, however, may be classified as surveys of acquisitions, and so left for the third session of this conference. Surveys have also been made in connection with weeding projects,[12] and surveys at Chicago [13] and Yale [14] have sought to test principles governing the retirement of books to storage. These, on the basis that they are essentially surveys of use rather than of the collections as such, may be left for later discussion.[15]

It is difficult indeed to see how to draw any clear line of demarcation between surveys of collections and guides, handbooks, or descriptions. These descriptive works are very numerous; they make up most of the nearly 8,400 items listed in Downs' *American Library Resources* and its *Supplement.*[16] Titles cannot be counted upon to make the distinction: If the *Survey of Special Collections in New Jersey Libraries* [17] is a survey, so is

Gilder and Freedley's *Theatre Collections* [18] (subtitled "An International Handbook") and so too, perhaps, is the *American Library Directory*.[19]

## PURPOSES

Though an author may select a misleading title, it would seem that his intent should provide a basis for distinguishing between the true survey of collections and the guide or handbook. This, consequently, may be the appropriate point at which to begin a review of the purposes of surveys. The first of these purposes to be considered—the dissemination of information that will help scholars to locate materials they need—may be the sole purpose of a guide or handbook; it has also been a major purpose of many surveys. For example, the stated aims of Professor Tauber's Australian survey included these:

> to make known the strength of general libraries in special subjects;
>
> to discover unsuspected or little-known collections of real importance;
>
> to acquaint scholars and other research workers . . . with the collections likely to be most useful to them;
>
> to assist in spreading library use, with possible relief to some large libraries;
>
> to facilitate interlibrary lending, especially in advance of a retrospective union catalogue
>
> to assist in spreading interlibrary lending, with possible relief to certain libraries;
>
> to supplement permanently the use of a union catalogue, both current and retrospective.[20]

These are all purposes that would be served by descriptions, guides, or handbooks; they would also, of course, be served by printed catalogues and union lists, which clearly are not surveys.

It might seem reasonable to say that the survey never has these as its sole purposes, but always has in view the improvement of collections, and hence is always concerned to some extent with what is lacking as well as with what is available. This would provide a basis for distinguishing many of the descriptions, guides, and handbooks from surveys, but doubtful cases would remain. Karl Brown's monumental *Guide to the Reference Collections of the New York Public Library*,[21] for example, calls attention to weaknesses as well as to strengths. The subtitle, "A Survey of Facilities for Advanced Study and Research," would have been as appropriate for Brown's work as it was for Downs' *Resources of New York City Libraries*,[22] which frequently refers to Brown for further information.

It may be prudent, then, to retreat in as good order as is possible from the excursion into classification. The guide is always meant to be useful to the scholar in search of material (and, of course, to the reference and interlibrary loan librarians who serve him); the survey of collections is always meant to assist those responsible for building up these collections. Some works are useful for both purposes. We do not have to assign call numbers at this conference, so there may be no reason why we should not call such works both guides and surveys. After all, some men are scholars, some are librarians, and a few at least are both.

Two purposes of surveys have been mentioned; many surveys seek to collect, organize, and disseminate information useful to the scholar, and all of them attempt to further the improvement of collections, which almost inevitably calls for providing evidence that deficiencies exist. In some cases the survey merely indicates that additions are needed; at the other extreme, a survey may describe gaps minutely and list desiderata. Under the overall heading of improvement, therefore, the purpose may be only to demonstrate need in the most general terms, or it may be to provide detailed guidance in building up the collection.

Multilibrary surveys—particularly, of course, those dealing with research collections—normally also have explicit purposes in the area of library specialization and cooperation. A plan for specialization, it is usually assumed, ought to build on existing strength. Hence the Library Survey Committee of the National Conference of Canadian Universities and Colleges, believing that it might be desirable "to persuade the larger universities to select certain limited subject fields, and to build up collections in those fields systematically, year by year," engaged a surveyor to "visit the larger universities, and give his candid opinion upon the existing collections that could be raised to research level in the way proposed." [23] Likewise, in Australia, Professor Tauber was called upon "to describe, evaluate and arrange in classified form the major collections in the country." [24] Surveys preparatory to specialization are also concerned with discovering weaknesses in collective resources that may be remedied by specialization in acquisition.[25] In addition, multilibrary surveys of collections have been made in order to obtain evidence of the need for union catalogues and information on their probable magnitude.[26]

Theoretically, of course, it would be possible for either a single-library or a multilibrary survey of collections to conclude that a simple redirection of collecting effort would be sufficient —that the desirable economies and cutbacks in overdeveloped fields would release funds sufficient to make up the deficiencies found in other areas. In practice, however, a published survey of collections almost invariably finds that more books and other library materials—and hence additional funds—are needed.[27] It would seem to follow that the purpose of a survey of collections is not solely to suggest action by librarians; the surveyor must hope also to influence academic administrators, legislators, private benefactors, and perhaps others, as well as to enlist support by those who use the collections. Something more of this and other purposes will be said when results are considered; first, however, it seems desirable to look at the methods used by surveyors and the sources from which they obtain the information on which their reports are based.

## METHODS

Statistics, it seems safe to say, are used in surveys of collections more consistently than anything else; if a general library survey says anything at all about library collections, it is almost sure to mention their size. In some cases there are good reasons for doubting that further information would contribute very much. There are widely accepted standards for minimum sizes of school, college, and public libraries, below which, in the judgment of professional organizations or accrediting bodies, it is impossible to provide the variety of materials required for adequate service. If the surveyor is examining a library or group of libraries falling substantially below the minimum, and is recommending that a state or regional system be established in order to make satisfactory collections available to communities too small to support libraries of the minimum size, he may well rest his case on statistics and standards.[28]

Above the minimal sizes, standards normally specify a given number of additional volumes per capita. The surveyor can also compare the library or libraries he is examining with those of other communities or institutions that seem to have similar needs. He can use, both for checking against standards and for comparison with other libraries, such additional quantitative statistical data as the number of volumes acquired per year, the annual expenditures for books, and the number of periodicals currently received. Per capita calculations and comparisons are normally made for these items as well as for the size of the collection.

While surveys of collections cite quantitative statistics more frequently than any other facts, they normally and quite properly warn that these figures may be misleading and that quality is more important than quantity. They may well admit also that uniformity has not been achieved in methods of counting library holdings,[29] and that many a library has discovered errors in the figures it has been reporting.

Obviously, then, it may be rash to base conclusions on quantitative statistics alone, uncorroborated and unmodified by findings based on any of the survey methods yet to be considered. A cynic might assert that statistics are almost universally used because they are easy to obtain, appear to be clear and unambiguous, and may impress the innocent reader. Nevertheless they are usually significant; "size," as Tauber has said, "does tell something." [30] There is normally a high correlation between the size of a library, its usefulness, and (if it is an academic library) the quality of the institution it serves.[31]

Statistics can also be used in checking the balance of a collection; for school libraries, in particular, there are recommended percentages for each major subject.[32] No one would advocate blind acceptance, but such standards are useful to the surveyor, who ought to examine any substantial departures from the norm and judge whether they seem to be justified by particular local needs. In addition, it may be useful to analyze the collection or portions of it by date of publication.[33]

Though surveys of use are to be considered at a later session, it may be noted here that an ambitious effort was once made at Hamilton College to use circulation statistics as a basis for evaluation of the book collection. There, twenty-five years ago, it was found that three fourths of the titles borrowed during one academic year were borrowed only once, and this was regarded as strong evidence that the collection was reasonably adequate.[34] This might be more convincing if comparisons with other college libraries were possible. As computer-based operations become more common, the alert surveyor may find it relatively easy to obtain statistics of this kind.

List-checking has been widely used by surveyors as a check on statistical data and as a means of assessing the quality of collections. More than 400 lists and bibliographies were used in the University of Chicago survey alone,[35] so enumeration is out of the question here, but something should be said of the types of lists most commonly employed.

Accrediting bodies have prepared or designated lists in some cases, and specific lists are suggested by some library standards.[36] State authorities have issued approved lists for school libraries. Then, of course, there are numerous lists originally prepared to assist libraries in book selection—many of them for children and for schools, the *ALA Catalog*,[37] the *Standard Catalog*,[38] the *Booklist*,[39] and *Booklist Books*,[40] the Mohrhardt [41] and Shaw [42] lists, and now *Choice*.[43] Both Mohrhardt and Shaw, it might be added, have often been used in public as well as in college library surveys. A wide variety of lists of best books, prizewinning titles, and annual selections of all kinds have been used.[44] In at least one public-library survey the catalogue of the Columbia University Press was checked.[45] Specialized bibliographies of all kinds have been used by surveyors of research libraries. Special attention has been given to reference works, and the standard bibliographies—particularly Winchell[46] or selected titles from Winchell—have often been checked. Sometimes, because it was believed that a high correlation can be assumed between general holdings and holdings of reference works,[47] only the latter have been checked; in other surveys, for similar reasons, only lists of periodicals have been used. Periodicals are especially important in research collections, and surveys have used various periodical lists prepared for special types of libraries, lists of titles covered by some of the indexing and abstracting services, Ulrich,[48] and, particularly popular with surveyors, Charles Harvey Brown's lists of most frequently cited journals in certain scientific subjects.[49]

Surveyors of individual libraries have normally depended on ready-made lists of the kinds suggested above, but lists have been specially prepared for use in a number of the multilibrary studies. The Public Library Inquiry attempted, in both fiction and nonfiction, to distinguish between best sellers, and notable and important books; comparing acquisitions of these with acquisitions of periodicals, documents, films, and music, it found evidence that popularity had influenced public library collections of books much more than their collections of other materials, for which quality had been the major criterion.[50] A special list of "expensive books" was checked in Chicago and Westchester surveys.[51] Other *ad hoc* lists include Eaton's[52] for current political science, Martin's[53] for social problems, and Waples'[54] for social science. Strunk, surveying musicological resources, used a list of only forty-five periodicals, historical works, and critical reprints,[55] while Ruggles and Mostecky, for their survey of Russian and East European publications in American libraries, prepared a list of 2,400 titles based on bibliographies compiled outside the United States—a procedure designed to make sure that the adequacy of American resources would not be measured against a standard reflecting the deficiencies of these resources.[56] For the Canadian survey, a handpicked list of only 240 periodicals was used in comparing the strength of libraries relative to one another,[57] but the University of Chicago, assessing its holdings against the total that might be desirable, produced a list of 32,000 serial titles.[58]

Desiderata have not been listed on this scale by any other survey. Yet, unless the examination is as thorough as this, it is evident that any lists used by the surveyor must be regarded as samples. There are many books that would be desirable in a college library in addition to those on a Shaw list; if one checks the list, one assumes that there is a correlation between the precentage of listed books held by the library and the percentage of other desirable works that are in its collection.[59] Such an assumption is obviously unsound if the list in question has been used as a buying guide; hence Shaw lists can be expected to lose their value for surveying purposes even before they go out of date in other respects, and one cannot use the same accreditation list year after year any more than one can use the same examination questions. Moreover, unless a library is very small or weak, a desiderata list based on any ready-made selection will not go far toward filling in the gaps.

While list-checking is commonly a means of qualitative evaluation, it has sometimes been used in multilibrary surveys to obtain quantitative data, for example, to determine the total number of different titles represented in a group of libraries or to discover the extent of duplication between their collections.[60]

Some surveys, it has been noted, have dealt with library collections merely by calling attention to the fact that their size falls far short of minimum standards. This, it was suggested, may be enough to make a case for regional organization; perhaps it can also be justified in the general survey of a public library on the ground that, if a sound acquisition program can be instituted, the library will soon contain the recent books that ought to be in it, and these, after all, are of first importance. Research collections are a different matter, but fortunately there are faculty members whom the surveyor of college and university libraries can consult by means of questionnaires or interviews or both. Ideally, he can hope to base his findings on the expert opinion of men who know their subject, have a broad knowledge of its literature, have intensively used both the library he is surveying and many others, and have also kept themselves well informed of the degree to which the library is meeting the needs of their students, undergraduate and graduate. In practice, of course, the surveyor does not find such men in every subject, and the individuals he consults do not always agree. Even in the largest university there will be some important segments of the collection in which, temporarily, no one is particularly interested. If one man in a department has been depended upon to build up the relevant collections, he will probably know more about the library's holdings in his area than anyone else, but may well be unconscious of deficiencies or indifferent to them; indeed, they will be deficiencies that have developed because of his lack of interest in certain subdivisions of the subject.[61]

If time were available it might be desirable to have each professor fill out a questionnaire and then to interview him in order to provide an opportunity for amplification of his written comments and clarification of questions they might have suggested to the surveyor. In practice, something less than this is normally the best that can be managed. An interview may seem particularly desirable when the professor's reply to a questionnaire seems to be contradicted by his colleagues or by other evidence.

Perhaps little need be said of questionnaires except that brevity and clarity are virtues. Members of the faculty have sometimes been asked to estimate the cost of filling gaps in collections of books, current subscriptions, back files, documents, and other materials.[62] While this may produce specific figures for which the surveyor need not assume personal responsibility, it is not clear that professors are particularly well qualified to estimate such costs. On one recent occasion at least, when a professor thought he was proposing expenditure of "a few thousand dollars" for newspaper microfilms, he turned out to be asking for at least two hundred thousand dollars.

Though the professor may be no more infallible as a prophet than as an estimator of costs, there seems to be no better oracle whom the surveyor can consult regarding trends in research and potential future needs. A survey in progress at Harvard is emphasizing these questions in the hope that, just as it built up strong Russian resources long before Slavic studies became fashionable, the Harvard Library can succeed in anticipating some major demands of research in the twenty-first century.

Students also have been questioned in large numbers by some surveyors.[63] When questions deal with their failures to obtain what is wanted, it may be doubtful whether one is measuring legitimate demands or those resulting from poor choices of thesis topics. It must also be recognized that a faculty and student body of the highest quality may ask for much more than even a very strong library can supply, while a mediocre community may be relatively well satisfied with poor collections.[64]

There is one other thing that many surveyors do, though it is so manifestly unscientific that little has been written of it. This is to go into the stacks and look over the shelves. While there, the surveyor may judge the physical condition of the collection, estimate roughly the size of its various parts, and perhaps form some opinion of how well recent publications are represented in it.[65] Anything more depends entirely upon the experience of the surveyor and the acuity of his perceptions.

RESULTS

Attempts to appraise what has resulted from surveys of collections must be almost as impressionistic as estimates based on looking over the shelves. Erickson's study [66] supports my own impression that the hard facts are few. This is one good reason for brevity; another is that almost anything that could be said about the results of surveying collections might encroach on territory assigned to later sessions, which will consider book selection and acquisition policy, cooperation and regional use, finance, and the value, effectiveness, and use of surveys in general.

It has been said that one purpose of many surveys of collections—a purpose shared with descriptions, guides, and handbooks—is to assist in the location of materials. No studies of the use of survey reports for this purpose appear to have been made, and it would obviously be difficult indeed to make them. One can assume that union catalogues and union lists are more satisfactory tools for many purposes than any survey or guide can be. Yet there are collections of manuscripts, ephemera, and other materials that the ordinary catalogue does not list, and surveys may be useful in locating these even after the National Union Catalog has been printed and after technology has provided quick access to centralized stores of bibliographical information.

The results of surveying are equally hard to determine in the area of specialization and cooperation. The Farmington Plan may be regarded as this country's most ambitious venture in specialization; it was launched, as has been noted, without any careful preliminary survey of library collections, and the results of such a survey probably would not have significantly affected its allocations of responsibility.[67] What will happen in Australia remains to be seen; Professor Tauber has provided the information,[68] but this is no assurance that it will be used wisely.

Even when it seems clear that salutary improvements in acquisition policy or in book-selection procedures have been made in accordance with a surveyor's recommendations, one sometimes wonders if he could not have made these recommendations without having surveyed the collections. The recommendations that stem directly from his appraisal of the collections are those relating to the correction of imbalance and the elimination of deficiencies. As has been suggested, surveys almost invariably propose that the remedy be to channel additional financial aid to the depressed areas rather than to cut back in those that are already relatively well supported.

It has also been suggested that recommendations of this kind are addressed to university administrators, legislators, and all a library's friends or potential friends, rather than to the librarian and his associates on the staff, who normally do not need to be persuaded that additional funds would be desirable. It would seem to follow that the major result at which a survey of collections usually aims is to demonstrate convincingly to nonlibrarians the need for increased support.

The financial results are fully as difficult to assess as any others. If a survey were followed by no increase in the book budget, one might suppose that it had failed; but it might, after all, have prevented a reduction in the budget. Moreover, a negative result would not prove that the surveyor or his survey had been at fault; the best coach or manager is not expected to win every game. When budgets go up, as most of them have been doing, one cannot prove that the increase or some specific percentage of it resulted from a survey as distinct from other factors.

If money is usually the major objective, and if it cannot be determined how much money should be credited to any survey's account, does anything remain to be said? There are, perhaps, a few concluding observations on the nature of the survey of collections, and particularly on the nature of the survey report, that can be deduced from this very inconclusive consideration of results.

What is implied if librarians are not the primary audience to whom the report is addressed? It will be read by a number of persons who do not often read books or articles about librarianship, and it provides an opportunity to bring significant facts about libraries to their attention. This is not to say that the survey report ought to be a campaign speech or an advertisement; it ought not to make extravagant promises. It is not a novel; it ought to be factual. But neither should it resemble a research paper suitable for publication in a specialized scientific journal. Rather, like a good biography, it ought to appeal to the intelligent general reader.

This point may appropriately be made now, rather than at a later session, because the collections are of more general interest than other aspects of the library. Librarians are well aware that all parts and functions of the library are interrelated—that the machine will collapse without good administration and personnel of high quality, that books cannot be found and used without a satisfactory catalogue, and so on. The nonlibrarian is less likely to be attracted by these topics; he can be expected to think first of books when libraries are mentioned. The logical approach, then, is to convince him that the collections can be improved and ought to be. This is where his interest and support can most readily be enlisted.

It ought to be admitted that this conception of the survey of collections as essentially a literary work may seem attractive to me because it has sometimes been a comfortable rationalization. For example, the committee that engaged me to survey Canadian library resources was interested in a specialization plan, and I was instructed to indicate the relative strength of collections in each of the subjects surveyed. A major portion of the report, consequently, was devoted to appraisals of relative strength; yet, when recommendations had to be made, I concluded that it would be unwise for Canadian libraries to establish a Farmington Plan. It was disconcerting to reflect that most of the report consisted of details that could never serve as a basis for action if its recommendations were accepted. As part of a literary work, however, these details were still valuable. People want to know how their university's library collections compare with others; legislators, university presidents, professors, and others were interested in the comparisons. Readers were attracted, and healthy competition in building collections may have been stimulated.

Again, while reading in preparation for this conference, I was sometimes discouraged by the complexities of surveying and the questions it raises. Recalling the hitherto competent centipede who became helplessly entangled when asked how he managed to coordinate so many legs, I wondered if I were becoming so conscious of the complexities that I should never be able to do any more surveying. It was reassuring to reflect that, if surveying collections is more of an art than a science, it cannot expect to deal with neatly controlled experiments and cannot expect to answer definitively many of the questions that recur in survey after survey. This view may also simplify his task by encouraging the surveyor to borrow freely from his predecessors; the result may bore those librarians who have read the other surveys, but librarians are not the audience that counts.

Thus a comfortable conclusion is possible: If the survey of library collections is a literary work, then writing the survey report is probably as easy as most other writing. Of course, if one prefers to end on a less reassuring note, one may conclude that a good survey is probably as difficult to produce and as rare as good writing of any other kind.

REFERENCES

1. Two particularly useful items are Rudolf Hirsch, "Evaluation of Book Collections," in Wayne S. Yenawine (ed.). *Library Evaluation*, Syracuse, Syracuse University Press, 1959—*Frontiers of Librarianship*, II, pp. 7–20; Louis Round Wilson and Maurice F. Tauber, *The University Library*, second ed., New York, Columbia University Press, 1956—*Columbia University Studies in Library Service*, VIII, particularly the table on pp. 576–79.

2. Raney, M. Llewellyn. *The University Libraries*. Chicago, University of Chicago Press, 1933—*The University of Chicago Survey*, VII.

3. American Library Association. *A Survey of Libraries in the United States*. 4 vols. Chicago, American Library Association, 1926–27.

4. American Association of School Librarians. *Standards for School Library Programs*, Chicago, American Library Association, 1960, pp. 73–86; Cooperative Study of Secondary-School Standards. *Evaluative Criteria*. Washington, Cooperative Study of Secondary-School Standards, 1950, pp. 213–16; Lucile F. Fargo. *The Library in the School*. Fourth ed., Chicago, American Library Association, 1947, pp. 149–201; Mary Virginia Gaver and Marian Scott. *Evaluating Library Resources for Elementary School Libraries*, New Brunswick, SSH Press, 1962—*Elementary School Library Series*, I; and Frances Henne, Ruth Ersted, and Alice Lohrer. *A Planning Guide for the High School Library Program*. Chicago, American Library Association, 1951, pp. 56–85.

5. A major exception (a self-survey) is Baltimore: Enoch Pratt

Free Library. *The Reorganization of a Large Public Library*. Baltimore, Enoch Pratt Free Library, 1937.
6. Mount Holyoke and Washington and Lee provide exceptions— Flora B. Ludington. "Evaluating the Adequacy of the Book Collection," *College and Research Libraries*, 1: 305–13 (1939/40); and Blanche Prichard McCrum, "A College Library Makes Its Omn Survey Plan," *ALA Bulletin* 31: 947–52 (1937).
7. The following may be cited: Ralph M. Dunbar, "Surveying Library Needs of the Office of Education," *College and Research Libraries*, 16: 379–82 (1955); Keyes D. Metcalf and others, *The National Medical Library*, Chicago, American Library Association, 1944; and William R. Roalfe. *The Libraries of the Legal Profession*. St. Paul, West, 1953.
8. Two recent medical library surveys are particularly important: Ralph T. Esterquest, *Strengthening Medical Library Resources in New York State*, Albany, The University of the State of New York, the State Education Department, the New York State Library, 1963; and Beatrice V. Simon, *Library Support of Medical Education and Research in Canada*, Ottawa, Association of Canadian Medical Colleges, 1964.
9. Planx, Marjorie. *The Supply of Foreign Books and Periodicals to the Libraries of the United Kingdom*. London: Library Association, 1949.
10. Williams, Edwin E. "Research Library Acquisitions from Eight Countries," *Library Quarterly*, 15: 313–23 (1945); and Edwin E. Williams, "Research Library Acquisitions from Great Britain," *Library Quarterly*, 10: 187–94 (1950).
11. David, Charles W., and Hirsch, Rudolf. "Importations of Foreign Monographs Under the Early Influence of the Farmington Plan," *College and Research Libraries*, 11: 101–5 (1950); also Robert Vosper and Robert L. Talmadge. *Farmington Plan Survey . . . Final Report* (1959). In addition, there have been several unpublished theses.
12. Stone, Elizabeth O. "A University Library Reappraises Its Holdings." *Wilson Library Bulletin*, 29: 712–14, 734 (1954/55).
13. Fussler, Herman H., and Simon, Julian L. *Patterns in the Use of Books in Large Research Libraries*. Chicago, University of Chicago Library, 1961.
14. Ash, Lee. *Yale's Selective Book Retirement Program*. Hamden, Archon Books, 1963.

15. Obsolescence of books in a public library was given particular attention in Margaret E. Egan and others. *Survey of the Saginaw Library System: Final Report* (1948), pp. 80–96.
16. Downs, Robert B. *American Library Resources, A Bibliographical Guide*, Chicago, American Library Association, 1951; and *Supplement 1950–1961*. Chicago, American Library Association, 1962.
17. New Jersey Library Association: Junior Members' Round Table, Union Catalog Committee, *Survey of Special Collections in New Jersey Libraries*. New York, The H. W. Wilson Company, 1940.
18. Gilder, Rosamond, and Freedley, George. *Theatre Collections in Libraries and Museums, An International Handbook*, New York: Theatre Arts, Inc., 1936.
19. *American Library Directory*. Twenty-fourth ed., New York, R. R. Bowker Company, 1964.
20. Tauber, Maurice F. *Resources of Australian Libraries*. Canberra, Australian Advisory Council on Bibliographical Services, 1963, pp. 7–8.
21. Brown, Karl. *Guide to the Reference Collection of the New York Public Library*. New York Public Library. New York, 1941.
22. Downs, Robert B. *Resources of New York City Libraries, A Survey of Facilities for Advanced Study and Research*. Chicago, American Library Association, 1942.
23. Williams, Edwin E. *Resources of Canadian University Libraries for Research in the Humanities and Social Sciences*. Ottawa, National Conference of Canadian Universities and Colleges, 1962, p. 7.
24. Tauber. *Resources of Australian Libraries*.
25. Downs, Robert B. *Resources of Southern Libraries*, Chicago, American Library Association, 1938, p. xii; Andrew D. Osborn, *New Zealand Library Resources*, Wellington, New Zealand Library Association, 1960, pp. 56–61; Tauber, *Resources of Australian Libraries*, pp. 31–33; John Van Male, *Resources of Pacific Northwest Libraries*, Seattle, Pacific Northwest Library Association, 1943, p. 19; Williams (see reference 10). For a follow-up survey of specialization, see Robert B. Downs. *Report on a Survey of the Libraries of the Arkansas Foundation of Associated Colleges*. Little Rock, Arkansas Foundation of Associated Colleges, 1963.

26. Merritt, LeRoy C. "Resources of American Libraries: A Quantitative Picture." In Robert B. Downs (ed.). *Union Catalogs in the United States*. Chicago, American Library Association, 1942, pp. 58–96.
27. It may be noted, however, that too many fine-arts books and too many periodicals were found at Fort Worth—John Adams Lowe. *Report of a Survey of the Public Library of Fort Worth*. Chicago, American Library Association, 1937, pp. 17–26.
28. An excellent recent example is John A. Humphry, *Library Cooperation, The Brown University Study of University-School-Community Library Coordination in the State of Rhode Island*. Providence, Brown University Press, 1963.
29. Downs, Robert B. "Uniform Statistics for Library Holdings," *Library Quarterly*, 16: 63–69 (1946); A. F. Kuhlman, "Two ARL Approaches to Counting Holdings of Research Libraries," *College and Research Libraries*, 21: 207–11 (1960); Eli M. Oboler, "The Accuracy of Federal Academic Library Statistics," *College and Research Libraries*, 25: 494–96 (1964).
30. Tauber, M. F. "The Importance of Developing Australian Library Resources." *Australian Library Journal*, 10: 115–21 (1961).
31. Jordan, Robert T. "Library Characteristics of Colleges Ranking High in Academic Excellence," *College and Research Libraries*, 24: 369–76 (1963). George Piternick. "Library Growth and Academic Quality." *College and Research Libraries*, 24: 223–29 (1963).
32. Fargo. *The Library in the School*. Henne, Ersted, and Lohrer. *A Planning Guide for the High School Library Program*.
33. Fargo. *The Library in the School;* George Walter Rosenlof. *Library Facilities of Teacher-Training Institutions*, New York, Teachers College, 1929—*Contributions to Education*, 347; Elizabeth Opal Stone. "Measuring the College Book Collection." *Library Journal*, 66: 941–43 (1941).
34. Stieg, Lewis. "A Technique for Evaluating the College Library Boon Collection." *Library Quarterly*, 13: 34–44 (1943).
35. Raney. *The University Libraries*.
36. Association of College and Research Libraries. Committee on Standards. "Standards for College Libraries," *College and Research Libraries*, 20: 274–80 (1959); also the same Committee's "Standards for Junior College Libraries." *College and Research Libraries*, 21: 200–6 (1960). The Southern Association's list was used by Mark M. Gormley and Ralph H. Hopp. *The Sioux*

*Falls College Library: A Survey.* Chicago: American Library Association, 1961.

37. *ALA Catalog, 1926.* Chicago, American Library Association, 1926, and Supplements.
38. *Standard Catalog for Public Libraries.* 1934 and later eds. New York, H. W. Wilson Company.
39. *The Booklist.* Chicago, American Library Association 1905–.
40. American Library Association. *Booklist Books.* 1919–1940.
41. Carnegie Corporation of New York. Advisory Group on College Libraries. *A List of Books for Junior College Libraries.* Comp. by Foster E. Mohrhardt. Chicago, American Library Association, 1937.
42. Carnegie Corporation of New York. Advisory Group on College Libraries. *A List of Books for College Libraries.* Prepared by Charles B. Shaw, Chicago, American Library Association, 1931; and also Charles B. Shaw, *A List of Books for College Libraries, 1931–38,* Chicago, American Library Association, 1940.
43. *Choice.* Middletown, 1964–. An issue was checked by Leon Carnovsky; also his *The Racine Public Library, An Evaluation and a Consideration of Selected Problems* (1965).
44. For an interesting group of lists, see Frederick Wezeman and Robert H. Rohlf. *Hopkins Public Library, Hopkins, Minnesota, A Survey and Recommendations for Future Development and Planning* (1962).
45. Baltimore: Enoch Pratt Free Library. *The Reorganization of a Large Public Library.*
46. Winchell, Constance M. *Guide to Reference Books.* Seventh ed. Chicago, American Library Association, 1951, and Supplements.
47. McEwen, Robert W. "The North Central Association's 1943 Survey of College and University Libraries." *College and Research Libraries,* 4: 253–56 (1942/43).
48. Graves, Eileen C. *Ulrich's Periodicals Directory.* Tenth ed., New York, R. R. Bowker Company, 1963.
49. Brown, Charles Harvey. *Scientific Serials.* Chicago, Association of College and Research Libraries, 1956—*ACRL Monographs,* 16.
50. Carnovsky, Leon. "Measurement of Public Library Book Collections." *Library Trends* 1: 462–70; (1952/53); Robert D. Leigh. "The Public Library Inquiry's Sampling of Library Holdings of Books and Periodicals," *Library Quarterly,* 21: 157–72

(1951); Robert D. Leigh. *The Public Library in the United States.* New York, Columbia University Press, 1950, pp. 76–91.

51. Carnovsky, Leon. "The Evaluation of Public-Library Facilities." In Louis R. Wilson (ed.). *Library Trends,* Chicago, University of Chicago Press, 1937, pp. 286–309; Carleton B. Joeckel and Leon Carnovsky. *A Metropolitan Library in Action, A Survey of the Chicago Public Library.* Chicago, University of Chicago Press, 1940, pp. 311–13, 425–26.

52. Eaton, Andrew J. "Current Political Science Publications in Five Chicago Libraries: A Study of Coverage, Duplication, and Omission." *Library Quarterly,* 15: 187–212 (1945).

53. Martin, Lowell. "Public Library Provision of Books About Social Problems." *Library Quarterly,* 9: 249–72 (1939).

54. Waples, Douglas, and Lasswell, Harold D. *National Libraries and Foreign Scholarship, Notes on Recent Selections in Social Science.* Chicago, University of Chicago Press, 1936.

55. Strunk, W. Oliver. *State and Resources of Musicology in the United States.* Washington, American Council of Learned Societies, 1932—*A.C.L.S. Bulletin,* 19.

56. Ruggles, Melville J., and Mostecky, Vaclav. *Russian and East European Publications in the Libraries of the United States.* New York, Columbia University Press, 1960—*Columbia University Studies in Library Service,* 11: 228–49.

57. Williams. *Resources of Canadian University Libraries.* pp. 10, 74–80.

58. Raney. *The University Libraries.* p. 4; Robert B. Downs. *Guide for the Description and Evaluation of Research Materials.* Chicago, American Library Association, 1939. This book contains extensive lists; it was originally prepared for use in the survey of resources of southern libraries (See Note 25), and has been checked in several later surveys, including Richard Harwell, *Research Resources in the Georgia-Florida Libraries of SIRF.* Atlanta, Southern Regional Education Board, 1955; and Louis R. Wilson and Marion A. Milczewski. *Libraries of the Southeast.* Chapel Hill, University of North Carolina Press, 1949; Eugene Hilton. *Junior College Book List.* Berkeley, University of California Press, 1930—*University of California Publications in Education,* VI: 1. This book was also useful in several surveys, *cf.,* Douglas Waples, "The North Central Association's Study of College Libraries," *College and Reference Library Yearbook,* 2:

85–89 (1930), and Douglas Waples and E. W. McDiarmid, Jr., "Comparison of Book Selections in Libraries of Teachers Colleges with Those of Liberal Arts Colleges," in United States Office of Education, *National Survey of the Education of Teachers*, Washington, Superintendent of Documents, 1935— Office of Education *Bulletin*, 1933:10, 5: 233–40. Many public-library surveys have used lists of material particularly relevant to the community in question, *cf.*, William Chait and Ruth Warncke, *A Survey of the Public Libraries of Asheville and Buncombe County, North Carolina*, Chicago, American Library Association, 1965; and Ralph R. Shaw, *Libraries of Metropolitan Toronto* (1960).

59. Stieg. "A Technique for Evaluating."
60. Carnovsky, Leon. *The St. Paul Public Library and the James Jerome Hill Reference Library, A Study of Co-operative Possibilities* (1960). A. F. Kuhlman. *The North Texas Regional Libraries*. Nashville, Peabody Press, 1943; Merritt. (See Note 26.)
61. This may be a weakness of the Bibliographical Planning Committee of Philadelphia. *A Faculty Survey of the University of Pennsylvania Libraries*. Philadelphia, University of Pennsylvania Press, 1940—*Philadelphia Library Resources*, I.
62. Among surveys for which this was done are A. F. Kuhlman and Icko Iben, *Report of a Survey of the University of Mississippi Library*, University, Miss., 1940; Maurice F. Tauber and William H. Jesse, *Report of a Survey of the Libraries of the Virginia Polytechnic Institute*, Blacksburg, Virginia Polytechnic Institute, 1949; Maurice F. Tauber and Eugene H. Wilson, *Report of a Survey of the Library of Montana State University*, Chicago, American Library Association, 1951; Louis R. Wilson, Robert B. Downs, and Maurice F. Tauber, *Report of a Survey of the Libraries of Cornell University*, Ithaca, Cornell University, 1948; Louis R. Wilson and Raynard C. Swank, *Report of a Survey of the Library of Stanford University*, Chicago, American Library Association, 1947; and Louis R. Wilson and Maurice F. Tauber, *Report of a Survey of the University of South Carolina Library*, Columbia, University of South Carolina, 1946.
63. Examples are Donald Coney, Herman H. Henkle, and G. Flint Purdy, *Report of a Survey of the Indiana University Library*, Chicago, American Library Association, 1940; and the Tauber-

Cook-Logsdon survey—Columbia University, President's Committee on the Educational Future of the University: Subcommittee on the University Libraries. *The Columbia University Libraries, A Report on Present and Future Needs.* New York, Columbia University Press, 1958—*Columbia University Studies in Library Service,* IX. There is an account of this survey, Maurice F. Tauber. "The Columbia University Libraries Self-Study." *College and Research Libraries,* 19: 277–82 (1958).

64. *Cf.* G. Flint Purdy. "The Evaluation of University Library Service." *Library Quarterly,* 12: 638–44 (1942), in which an attempt at evaluation on the basis of use is made. Interlibrary loan requests have also been studied—Donald E. Thompson. "A Self-Survey of the University of Alabama Libraries." *College and Research Libraries,* 8: 147–50 (1947).

65. Sample shelves have been checked in detail—*cf.,* Frederick Wezeman. *Public Library Service, Ramsey County, Minnesota, A Survey and a Plan.* St. Paul, Ramsey County Public Library, 1958, pp. 17–25.

66. Erickson, E. Walfred. *College and University Library Surveys 1938–1952.* Chicago, American Library Association, 1961—*ACRL Monographs,* 25, pp. 70–75.

67. For an account of the steps taken in negotiating allocations, see Edwin E. Williams. *Farmington Plan Handbook.* Bloomington, Association of Research Libraries, 1953, pp. 19–28.

68. The printed summary (Tauber, see Note 20) is a highly condensed version of the full report, which runs to some 890 pages as duplicated by the Australian Advisory Council on Bibliographical Services in 1962. Many statewide surveys have been made during the past few years, among the most interesting of which are Robert B. Downs, *Resources of North Carolina Libraries,* Raleigh, Governor's Commission on Library Resources, 1965; Humphry (See Note 28). Lowell A. Martin, *Library Service in Pennsylvania, Present and Proposed,* Harrisburg, State Library, 1958; and Mary E. Phillips and Catherine Lauris, *Public Libraries in Oregon,* Eugene, University of Oregon Bureau of Business Research, 1962.

# 3 Surveys of Technical Services in Libraries

MAURICE F. TAUBER and

IRLENE ROEMER STEPHENS

THE ultimate aim of any library is effective service. Books are selected, acquired, cataloged, and classified, and collections are maintained to provide the best possible service to the particular clientele. The quality of library service is dependent, to a considerable extent, on the policies and procedures of acquisition, and on the character and operations of the cataloging and classification of materials. These activities of the library, commonly grouped under the heading of technical services, should be considered in relation to the general objectives, functions, and standards of the particular library or library system.

Today emphasis is placed on productivity; time and motion studies and evaluations of personnel performance are conducted to provide guidelines for increasing the efficiency of operations. The library, regardless of type, is viewed not only as an educational institution but as a business operation as well. There has been a growing emphasis on development of more efficient library operations and procedures within the framework of an organization providing direct line communication between administrators and well-trained, experienced line officers.

Since technical services are regarded as the backbone of li-

* The authors are very grateful to Robert E. Kingery for his help with this paper and the entire conference.

brary service, the technical services functions are often designated for review when problems develop in the extension of library service programs. Library surveys in this area are frequently requested today; studies of technical services were infrequently conducted prior to 1955. The current trends are apparent. Historically, the organization of library materials revolved around the judgment of individuals charged with responsibility for the library. It was not until 1861 that the Library of Congress adopted an arrangement scheme with numbers designating classes and subclasses, as well as physical location.[1] Nathaniel B. Shurtleff at the Boston Public Library,[2] Jacob Schwartz at the Brooklyn Public Library,[3] William F. Poole at the Chicago Public Library,[4] Justin Winsor at the Harvard University Library,[5] and Melvil Dewey at the Library of Amherst College [6] introduced arrangement schemes for books in the respective libraries indicated, not long thereafter.

The organization of materials was refined through the years; efficient practices were developed and standards were instituted. It was not until the 1890s that the American Library Association adopted the three-by-five inch card, strongly advocated by Dewey, who recognized the importance of uniformity in cataloging practices and in catalog card supplies.[7]

In general, the improvements in operations which were developed through the years resulted from the exchange of ideas among librarians and constant self-evaluation. Unquestionably, the development of processing centers emphasized the importance of systematic operations and procedures and probably brought to the fore the advantages of retaining consultants to review objectively the administration and operation of these technical services activities.

It was probably in 1956 that present-day concepts of processing centers began to emerge. It was in that year that the Library Services Act was passed and the American Library Association issued *Public Library Service; A Guide to Evaluation with Minimum Standards*.[8] The impetus provided for cooperative and centralized processing by the Library Services Act is obvious; nevertheless, it is apparent that the concept of the advantages of efficient coordination within a single technical services unit, as well as the potentialities for cooperative arrangements, were envisioned well before 1956.

It was in 1956, too, that the Resources and Technical Services Division of the American Library Association established a special Committee on Regional Processing. The stated function of the Committee was to make case studies of existing regional processing centers available and to develop a manual of procedures for establishing and operating such centers. The Committee was inactive until January of 1959, at which time it was agreed that the activities of the Committee should be limited to investigations of processing centers serving groups of autonomous libraries.

The experiences of librarians and administrators in the large number of centralized processing centers, as described in the literature, would seem to emphasize the advantages of cooperative arrangements. The accumulation of information on the operation of these processing centers has served another purpose. The attention directed toward the establishment and maintenance of technical processing centers has further emphasized the importance of systematic procedures, consistent practices, well-trained personnel, up-to-date equipment, periodic review of procedures, and a general awareness of developments in technical processing. Administrators and librarians are recognizing, to an increasing extent, that constant attention must be given to promoting the efficiency of technical services operations, if the function and the purpose of this unit of the library are to be effectively fulfilled. Consequently, the trend toward centralized processing has promoted more efficient operation within the technical services unit of the individual library, as well as in the technical processing center.

Perhaps, then, it is reasonable to presume that the establishment of processing centers over the past decade is in part responsible for the increase in the number of processing surveys which are requested by the executives, administrators, and librarians of all kinds of organizations maintaining libraries, even though the great majority of the processing centers in operation involve public libraries.

This brief comment on processing centers is designed to provide a background for the further discussion of surveys of technical services. In order to indicate the nature of the problems in these surveys, attention will be given to (1) the library consultant in this area, (2) the literature, or sources of information on such surveys, (3) reasons for surveys of the technical services, (4) the conduct of processing surveys, and, (5) some typical processing surveys.

### THE LIBRARY CONSULTANT

The measurement and evaluation of library services in terms of the performance of functions, the fulfillment of responsibilities, the accomplishment of purposes and far-reaching objectives should be a constant process in libraries. Through self-evaluation and awareness of the changing needs of the communities served, many libraries have continued to meet the growing demand for library materials. However, the advantages of the perspective view of library operations by a well-oriented and experienced, critical authority are apparent. To an increasing extent, the services of library consultants have been sought and the library survey has had pervasive influence. The merits of objectivity are perspicuous, but "the librarian away from home" can no longer qualify as a library consultant on that basis alone. Even in the small library situation, the advantages of obtaining the assessment and judgment of the experienced individual are real.

A review of library surveys that have been conducted during the past decade indicates that many involved two or more consultants, although studies are frequently made by one consultant. There is no question but that certain types of surveys should involve a team of two or more consultants, particularly in the general survey or the study of a large library or library system. To expect that one individual will be able to evaluate adequately the resources, policies, administration, operations, procedures, and services of a large library or library system, even though well oriented in each area, is probably unreasonable, especially if the study must be conducted on a time schedule. Similarly, the assignment of a study of the technical services division of a library to a team of consultants may also have advantages. In many cases, a consultant is retained only after problems have compounded, and solutions are urgently sought. Two or more consultants can survey designated aspects of technical services activities independently, thereby saving time, and then discuss and integrate findings before projecting recommendations in a final report.

In recent years, the costs of technical services have increased annually as have costs for library services in general. While the role of the library survey in enhancing library service is primary, it is obvious that improved organization and greater efficiency may result in reduced costs, releasing funds for other purposes. The processing survey which includes recommendations that result in greater efficiency of operations at reduced costs may release funds for further development of the library resources and extension of services.

### THE LITERATURE ON PROCESSING SURVEYS

Although the literature in surveys of processing is relatively meager, there are enough studies on the status of technical services in libraries to indicate the nature of such surveys and to provide a basis for discussion. Indeed, processing problems are considered in practically all general library surveys, even though the discussion of technical services may be submerged in the total description of the library's organization and administration. In his book, *The Library Survey*, McDiarmid devotes four pages to "The Administration of the Technical Services." [9] Among the topics which he treats are book selection methods and sources, unit cost studies, and studies of services. The character of the cataloging and classification, deviations from standard systems (in relation to the needs of a specific clientele), speed and efficiency of work, the smoothness of work or actual steps in processing, catalogers' reference collection and equipment, and the use of the card catalog are among the areas which Mc-Diarmid considers to be worthy of analysis in a survey.

In her chapter on "Organization and Control of Materials," in *Local Public Library Administration*, Piercy [10] summarized the areas of processing which should be examined and includes administration of the work, centralization and cooperation between libraries, regional or centralized processing, efficient planning, impediments to efficient planning, statistics, acquisitions operations, cataloging and classification procedures (including variations from standard systems), and binding and conservation.

A third relevant source of information on processing surveys is Erickson's chapter on "Technical Services" in his *College and University Library Surveys*.[11] Erickson directs attention to 147 recommendations made in the twelve surveys which he analyzed. These recommendations are made in reference to technical services activities involved in cataloging and classification, order work, gifts and exchanges, central recording of materials, binding operations, and consolidation of operations within technical services.

In essence, then, discussions of surveys of technical services relate to the areas which have been designated as acquisitions, cataloging and classification, processing, binding, and conservation. Circulation and photographic reproduction may also be considered, since with respect to records, techniques, and equipment, these library operations involve some of the same problems found in the cited areas of technical services. A paper prepared for the Conference on Research Methods in Librarianship, held at Allerton House, September 8–11, 1963, entitled "Survey Method in Approaching Library Problems" is of interest since the survey method as applied to library situations is considered in broad perspective. Types of surveys, the nature of the survey method, sources of information needed by surveyors, limitations, and results of surveys are discussed.[12]

There are several studies and recent developments which have had an impact on technical services and should be reflected in processing surveys. Included among these are the projects of the Council on Library Resources, Inc.; the work of the Library Technology Program of the American Library Association; the Library of Congress studies; Catalog Code Revision; the programs of the Association of College and Research Libraries for shared cataloging and expansion of cooperative relationships; the growth of regional centers and regional processing; the activities of the United States of America Standards Institute Sectional Committee, Z39; the publication of the seventeenth edition of the Dewey Decimal Classification; the acceptance of the Library of Congress classification by new academic libraries and the shift to this system by a large number of established academic libraries; the advent of information storage and retrieval and the technological advances in the design of systems; and various institutional programs, such as those of the National Library of Medicine, the National Agricultural Library, the New York Public Library (including the Matta study on *The Card Catalog in the Large Research Library* [13]), and the Columbia-Harvard-Yale cataloging project. Harvard has since dropped out of the project.

### REASONS FOR SURVEYS OF TECHNICAL SERVICES

Though there are, perhaps, as many specific reasons for the initiation of surveys of technical services as there are studies in this area, the motivations for the initiation of surveys can be discussed under several general headings. Not infrequently, there is a complex of reasons involved in the decision to retain a consultant; sometimes only the obvious problems are apparent, though other problems are later identified.

Consultants are often retained by library administrators in response to user dissatisfaction. Readers may complain about not being able to find the materials which they require, which may suggest either that the resources development program has not adequately reflected the needs of the particular library community, or that the patterns of use of the collection by readers have not been sufficiently considered in the establishment of procedures for the organization of materials. In some cases, the bibliographic control of materials provided by the card catalog, and the arrangement of materials through the use of a particular classification scheme are adequate to provide convenient access to library holdings; in other instances, many revisions and drastic changes are in order. In one library after another, the criticism is made that the acquisitional program is spotty or that it takes too long to acquire materials, that cataloging is in arrears, and that the collections are not being kept in a state of proper care and repair. Reader services' personnel quite routinely suggest that these criticisms relate to technical services operations and, consequently, such complaints have often been the bases for the introduction of a survey of technical processing. At Cornell University, the readers were so handicapped by the faulty catalogs and operations that one of the reasons for the survey was to develop directions for cataloging of materials that would remove the impasse which had arisen in the library's services. Furthermore, it was requested that the surveyors study the administration of the institution, the support for which was divided between public and private funds. The problems arising in connection with the classification system used for the arrangement of materials at the time of the survey have been discussed in great detail by Reichmann.[14]

*Ineffective Operations and Procedures:* It is apparent that in processing units of libraries there have been signal failures on the part of administrators to develop procedures which lead to efficient operation and to what might simply be referred to as adequate production. McDiarmid, Erickson, and Piercy, among others, have called attention to the need for measuring speed and accuracy, eliminating duplication of effort, determining the reasons for rising arrears, and reviewing the achievement of the staff. Following standard rules and practices and dividing work appropriately among professional and clerical staff members may also result in the improvement of production in processing departments.

The number of instances in which administrators of technical

services have failed to develop effective operations and procedures suggests that brief discussion be directed toward the administrative personnel in technical services work. Among indi--
viduals assigned to administer technical services programs, there
are those who are knowledgeable in the organization of materials, industrious, and anxious to prepare materials and provide
bibliographical control expertly and promptly. Too often, however, technical services operations are not administered well
enough to achieve desirable goals. In too many cases, head librarians and directors of libraries have not been able to assess the
technical services operations and procedures and institute effective practices. Supervisory personnel are allowed to continue
procedures which are inefficient, even though minor alterations
might eliminate problems. Knowledgeable, well-oriented, industrious, and imaginative managers, who have insight and understanding of practical as well as theoretical problems in the organization of materials, and are able to administer technical services programs with limited staffs and less-than-ideal equipment
and facilities, are needed. The library profession has not provided
a sufficient number of decisive administrators in the technical
services area, at least in recent years.

A recurring reason for the technical services survey has been
the failure of administrators to identify problems and make
major decisions in organization and/or procedures to provide
efficient operations. Outside advisors are retained to review policies and operations in an effort to eliminate problems which have
existed for long periods of time. Sometimes the problems have
been identified, and the consultant is brought in to recommend
changes which are designed to resolve the problems; in other
cases, the consultant is called upon to assess the overall situation.

Often library administrators, boards, or committees, acutely
aware of the rising costs of processing of materials, consider that
these costs might be reduced if procedures were modified. A
consultant is retained to assess operations and procedures and to
provide an objective judgment. Sometimes the consultant is
brought in to provide another point of view; in other cases the

consultant is retained because the head of technical services has not had time to evaluate the operations and procedures, even though administrative review of activities should be considered a constant responsibility.

In some instances, library administrators are aware both of the problems and the actions which should be taken to improve the effectiveness of library operation. The consultant, then, is retained to administer decisions made before his arrival. Not infrequently, a public library board, university president, library committee, administration, library director, or a librarian is aware of the problems existent within the library structure and attributes the cause to inadequacies of one or more library supervisors. In some such instances, a consultant is retained to "straighten out the situation," by objectively reviewing the administrative organization, policies, operations and procedures, but with the proviso that the recommendations include a means by which the individual head of a unit, who has not been able to keep abreast of developments and effectively administer the activities of the unit, can be assigned to other responsibilities. Probably, it is ethical for boards or committees to retain consultants to work out the specifics of such situations and provide a basis for decisions to discharge personnel; it appears that this purpose may provide an increasingly frequent motive for surveys. It is important, however, that the consultant be apprised of personnel problems before acceptance of the consultation. Too often, the assignment becomes one which might aptly be called an "iceberg survey." To prevent or minimize this development, it is necessary for the consultant to restate, at the outset, what he understands to be the objectives of the survey. As a rule, decisions with respect to personnel who are inadequate, or who have outlived their usefulness in particular positions, should be administered without the crutch of a survey report. It is possible, of course, that during or after a survey it may become evident that the head of a unit will not be able to implement the recommendations. This circumstance constitutes an honest situation in which the consultant participates in evaluating personnel in relation to the functional responsibilities in present and future programs. Most frequently, if the consultant is involved in transferring or discharging of personnel, these actions are taken with due deliberation and not discussed in the survey report.

Often, librarians or library directors, with the approval of their boards or committees, have asked consultants to review technical problems, particularly within the framework of possible mechanization and automation, so that the processing operations of the library could be improved. This motive provides a reasonable basis for the evaluation of a library's services and is a sound preparation for library planning.

*Reasons for Specific Surveys of Technical Services:* Several studies may be cited to illustrate the variation in the purpose for which surveys have been initiated. In the surveys of the University of New Mexico Library [15] and the Nassau County Library System,[16] it was indicated that the consultant should give attention to the whole range of technical services, including administrative organization, personnel, records, equipment, and quarters. Thus, these surveys represented general examinations of the entire fabric of processing, and were similar, even though the libraries differed markedly in purpose and objectives.

In the survey of the Cataloging Department of the Queens Borough Public Library,[17] specific questions related to administrative patterns. The survey involved minute examination of the responsibilities of individual staff members in the department, an examination of the catalogs, investigation of the coordination of the responsibilities and activities of the catalog department with related or similar activities in other departments, consideration of the level of production, and the presentation of an array of staff positions required for a reorganized department. Again, this survey was concerned with manpower, operations, facilities, and costs.

In recent surveys in which we have participated, especially those involving academic libraries such as Pace College, Dartmouth College, Beaver College, Bowdoin College, St. John's University, and the University of Delaware, the single question of whether the library should shift to the Library of Congress

Classification from their present system of classification was asked.[18] In other surveys, the consultants have been requested to evaluate only the acquisitions work, the serials activity, the binding organization and procedures, or the circulation records and equipment.

## THE CONDUCT OF PROCESSING SURVEYS

Processing surveys are no different from other types of surveys since they are concerned with people, operations, facilities, and costs. However, processing surveys, because they are directed at areas of work which are subject to more exact measurement than some of the other areas of library service, require statistical records for the explanation of operations and the assessment of activities. Few libraries keep adequate statistical records for the evaluation of technical services operations. For example, until recently it has been difficult to determine how many titles are added to a library collection annually (the number of volumes is usually recorded), or how the collection is broken down by subject on a quantitative basis. Unit costs for the various operations are seldom calculated, and few libraries have up-to-date procedure manuals.

In the conduct of the survey, the consultant uses such data as may be available to him and his colleague or colleagues. When the existing records are inadequate for a systematic evaluation of operations or production, a period of record-keeping is normally necessary.

The technical services survey involves an analysis of the historical efforts of the library to organize and control the bibliographic records of the library holdings. In both acquisitions and cataloging, for example, the nature of the records, developed over the years, is a crucial matter. Reference might again be made to what was revealed by the survey of the Cornell University Library records. The acquisitions records in this library were quite haphazardly organized and in a state of deterioration, and the detailed description of these records in the survey report indicated the need for drastic innovations. In addition, the problem of the classification system was described within its historical framework.

*Study of the Background of the Library Situation:* While it is not the purpose of the processing survey to study in great detail the history and background of the particular library or library system and the community which the library serves, the first step in a processing survey involves some attention to the background of the particular situation. Despite the basic similarities of processing surveys in various types of libraries, there are aspects of such a survey which differ depending on the type of library, the history of the library, the standards, functions, and objectives, the relationship of the library to the institution, board, and/or governing body, the growth pattern of the institution or community, and the present problems of growth.

A library of an academic institution is regarded as one of the most important instruments of instruction and research. Dr. Paul Buck, recently retired as Director of the Harvard University Library, has stated that the library is basic to learning and the "exploitation of our intellectual resources." He has further volunteered that it is impossible to have "a quality faculty without a quality library." It is equally apparent that students cannot perform at their highest level without proper library collections, facilities, and services. Standards for college libraries were set forth in 1959, and those for junior college libraries and school libraries in 1960. Through the efforts of the Standards Committee of the Association of College and Research Libraries and of the Standards and Criteria Committee of ACRL Junior College Libraries Section, the Standards for Junior College Libraries were revised in 1967.

As a measure of the efficiency of service, the standards of the particular kind of library provide a base line for the orientation of the survey. The objectives and functions of the library, as interpreted and developed through the years, contribute to a perspective view of the library situation of which technical processing is an integral part. The academic library processing survey, of necessity, includes a consideration of projected needs of the academic community and requirements of the library serving the particular academic institution. In this regard, attention is directed toward an assessment of the probable configuration of the academic institution then, and sometimes twenty years in the future in terms of long-range policies and programs, projected trends in student and faculty numbers and interests based on planned or anticipated changes in the curricula, and the roles and purposes of the institution and the relationship of it to the area and other colleges and universities. Not the least of the aspects included in a determination of the orientation of the processing survey is the present and anticipated financial support of the library.

*Public Library Service; A Guide to Evaluation with Minimum Standards* provided standards for public library service and included the essential ingredients of effective public library service. The standards for state libraries, published in 1963, are basic to the measurement of the efficiency of service at the state level. The development of regional service over the past several years provides examples of trends which are useful in determining the multiplicity of requirements for regional library service and the role of technical processes in meeting these requirements. The standards offer a means of measuring the performance of a library or library system in terms of criteria, and may be used as a guide for the extension of services. While there are variations from one library or library system to the next, insofar as details are concerned, broad objectives and functions are comparable. The necessity for considering demography, population trends, community and regional planning, and the interrelation of industrial and educational development as a background for projecting the requirements for future library service, is obvious. The technical processing operations, for example, are an integral part of public library service; public library service is extended within the framework provided by the community and is influenced by all of the aspects of that community. A projection of the requirements for public library service in the future, therefore, includes an assessment of the potential development of the community.

Regardless of the type of library in which the technical processing unit to be studied is located, a collection of background information for the survey should include a view of the present problems of growth, as well as the problems of the past and the means by which these problems were resolved.

*Review of the General Organization of the Library:* The essential functions of any library may be considered to be the provision of materials and services. The basic functions of book selection, acquisitions, cataloging and classification, binding, and photographic reproduction, which are parts of the technical services operation, are similar for all types of libraries. Technical services must be considered in relation to the operation of the library as a whole, since the processing and public service functions of a library are interrelated and mutually interdependent. Effective library administration depends on the efficiency of both service units within the structure provided by the standards and objectives of the type of library and the policies of the individual library or library system. Accordingly, the processing survey is approached first from the standpoint of the overall organizational patterns of the library. The organizational chart is studied to clarify present administrative relationships and lines of responsibility. In many instances, the consultant is faced with a situation in which an organizational chart does not exist and in which lines of responsibilities have been loosely conceived without attention to a customary hierarchical administrative arrangement. In such cases, it becomes necessary for the consultant to construct a chart of the administrative organization of the present library, with the cooperation of the total staff of the library, in order to determine interrelationships and coordinate the various units of operation. Once the consultant has an understanding of the relationships of the technical processing unit to the top administration and to the other units of the library, it is possible for him to review the activities of the technical processing group, evaluate critically the present practices and procedures in light of the policies of the library, suggest systematic revision of procedures for greater efficiency and better coordination, and recommend changes for most effective operation of the technical services unit in the future.

Not infrequently, the organizational structure of the library as a whole restricts the potentiality for most effective operation of the technical services unit and coordination with other library operations. In these circumstances, preliminary attention to the general organization and administration of the library is essential to the conduct of a survey of processing, the results of which can provide a basis for the recommendation of more efficient procedures and practices for assembling, preserving, and making available the printed and other materials required by the particular community.

The extent to which a library serves the needs of a particular community is limited by the financial support provided to the library. For this reason, the consultant retained to conduct a processing survey must be aware of the budget of the total library operation, as well as the amount available for the operation of the technical services unit. Library expenditures for a specific function must take into account the total service program of the particular library. Though several types of budgets are currently in use in libraries and the consultant must be prepared to make recommendations for the future operation of technical services based on the budget breakdowns provided to him, it should be mentioned that the performance budget has decided advantages with respect to the evaluation of the operation of technical services in terms of work units and work load. The use of work measurement in planning and budgeting increases efficiency in the management of the library. It is apparent that it is almost impossible to establish standardized work units in the aspects of library service which directly reach the public; in general, reader services can be defined as work units in terms of hours of service only, except in circulation where the item loaned could be designated the work unit. However, in technical services the work load can be predicted numerically with consistent accuracy in terms of *items* for acquisitions, *books* for cataloging and classification, and similar tangible units. The consultant retained to conduct a processing survey in a library or library system in which the financial appropriation is determined by the amount of unit costs will be able to analyze operations more readily by virtue of the statement of programs representing the objectives of the technical services.

*Evaluation of the Effectiveness of Technical Services:* An evaluation of technical services involves an estimation of the extent to which the departments of technical services provide services at the lowest possible cost and a determination of the value of these services to the user of the library. This latter aspect is examined in some cases by studies of the use of catalogs and classification systems. Usually, an evaluation of technical services is restricted to a consideration of the problems of reducing the costs of particular operations and ascertaining potential savings in manpower and the increase in output to be gained from reconstructing priorities, developing and modifying procedures, and coordinating the services of the technical services unit.

The often-quoted cliché, "Nothing ventured, nothing gained" might well be modified, in light of experience in technical processing, by the recognition that for every gain in the efficiency of operation resulting from modifications and changes in procedures, some price must be paid. In every case, the consultant should make recommendations for changes in procedures only after weighing the gain which should result against the price which must be paid for that gain.

*Evaluation of Technical Services Operations, Procedures and Personnel:* While it is apparent that the various units of technical services must operate in concert, the processing function of the library includes all of the activities and technical operations involved in:

1. acquiring materials of every kind which have been selected for incorporation into the library collection;
2. recording, listing, indexing, and cataloging these materials in sufficient detail to assure their identification, isolation, and retrieval for the provision of library service;
3. organizing these materials by some comprehensible system to facilitate their use and to insure placing together those

items which are common in subject content, form, or some other meaningful characteristic;

4. marking items with a designation for proper location within the collection and with ownership identification;
5. repairing, protecting, or binding materials;
6. providing each item with book cards (if necessary), book pockets, date slips, or other means necessary to permit circulation and control lending of materials to the public; and
7. maintaining each item in the collection to insure its continued availability and use.

The activities included in the above listing of technical services begin after the materials are selected. Even so, it is apparent that there must be close coordination between the selection of materials and the ordering of these materials. The list does not include the discarding of materials from the collection. However, there is also some activity in technical services after the decision has been made to eliminate materials from the collection, and the thoroughgoing survey of technical services will review these activities, including withdrawal of cards, which relate to maintaining the integrity of the catalog.

The following objectives for technical services apply to all types of libraries and should be basic considerations in the analysis of processing operations:

1. prompt acquisition of materials selected for addition to the collection;
2. prompt recording and listing of items acquired, to insure their identification, and to provide adequate bibliographic control;
3. organization and arrangement of the collection by systems appropriate to the requirements for maintaining the holdings and for the use of the resources by the public;
4. adequate marking and identification of the materials with call numbers and ownership marks;
5. adequate preservation, maintenance, and repair of items in the collection, to insure their continued availability;
6. prompt withdrawal and correction of records for those items which are no longer considered useful, based on their content and/or physical condition.

In the evaluation of technical services, the consultant should systematically review the technical operations and procedures, directing attention toward the appropriateness of rules followed and tools used; observe the division of work among professional and clerical staff members, giving attention to the speed and accuracy with which operations are performed and the level of productivity; inspect the files and records of the various departments, noting records which should be maintained in the future, and discuss the activities of the technical services operations with individual staff members and with groups, inviting comments, criticisms, and suggestions, thereby providing a basis for determining the level of morale, and the extent to which communication within the division or within the various departments has been effective. Attention should be directed toward an assessment of the extent of coordination of related activities, noting any revisions in operations which will eliminate duplication of records or personnel activities.

With full cognizance of the vast range of equipment presently available for the automation of operations in acquisitions, cataloging, serials, and binding, the consultant should consider the need for the installation of specialized mechanical equipment to increase productivity, within the limits of the budget. Often equipment which will increase the efficiency of operations in technical services can also be used for other purposes, and the purchase cost can, thereby, be justified.

The consultant should utilize whatever records are available, view them objectively, and make judgments as to their validity and reliability. Attention should be given to the existence and use of procedure manuals. In some libraries new personnel have been employed, and the consultant should realize that they must be closely supervised until they learn the various operations and procedures. In those cases where procedures have not been recorded, the consultant must depend on discussions with staff members to determine operations and procedures, as well as assignment of responsibilities. The consultant may use checklists, questionnaires, and/or interviews, but should devote considerable time to observation of operations, procedures, and the use of equipment.

Operations and procedures are examined in such areas as searching, accessioning, cataloging, classification, card preparation, catalogs, revision of catalogs, book preparation, withdrawals, and transfers. Working files and lists are analyzed as to function, scope, effectiveness, and limitations.

The survey of technical processing extends to an examination of the facilities provided for the technical services activities. The study of the facilities includes consideration of space, lighting, ventilation, temperature and humidity, safety and occupational hazards, equipment, and the proximity of technical services facilities to other parts of the library.

The recommendations made by the consultant retained to survey technical services in a specific library situation should be based on a review of the many aspects included in the study. Often, the recommendations will be direct responses to specific questions posed at the initiation of the survey. In many other cases, the recommendations will relate to areas not initially identified as problems. In all cases, the recommendations should reflect the judgment and insight of the consultant into the broad aspects of technical services and their functions, objectives, and relationship to other services of the library.

More often than not, the consultant is requested to prepare a report on the study. The survey report should be as detailed as seems essential to provide background for the recommendations. Usually the report includes a review of all areas involved in the conduct of the survey, supplemented with discussions of changes in practices designed to increase the efficiency of operation. Figures and tables should be included whenever it is considered that a graphic presentation will serve to emphasize the reasons for certain recommendations. Suggestions for expediting recommendations should be made. For the convenience of the administration, a summary of recommendations is usually included in the report.

SOME TYPICAL PROCESSING SURVEYS

In order to discuss factors considered in surveys of technical services in relation to actual studies, three surveys will be reviewed briefly: a survey of a university library [19] (McGill University), a survey of a public library [20] (Dallas Public Library), and a survey of a library service center (Nassau County Library System).

*Acquisitions:* MC GILL UNIVERSITY LIBRARY. "Discussions with and responses from members of the faculty, heads of departments, directors, and deans stressed the problems of library acquisitions." This is the lead sentence in a chapter on "Acquisition of Library Materials" in the McGill survey. In their report, Logsdon and McCarthy show quite clearly the lack of an acquisitional policy, and the need for one, even if informal, if the collections were to be developed systematically. Parenthetically, the issue of whether a library should have an acquisitional policy has never been really settled, but it appears that more and more libraries are attempting to plan their collecting programs.

At McGill, it was deemed desirable to set forth the bases for an acquisitional policy and a library program related to the educational policy of the University itself. Despite the fact that there were differences of opinion as to what the acquisitional policy of McGill "is or should be," the consultants "recommended that a statement of acquisitional policy be drafted by the library and its academic departments."

In general, little is known about the effects of an acquisitional policy on a library's program of collecting, since there have been no systematic studies over long periods of time. The relationships between budgetary support for acquisitions in several institutions should be evaluated in light of other variables, such as exchange programs, publication programs, gifts, cooperative involvements, and special conditions, such as deposit arrangements. Such factors were considered by the surveyors at McGill.

DALLAS PUBLIC LIBRARY. In the Dallas Public Library Survey, Frarey did not undertake to assess the acquisitional policy or program of collecting. In his definition of the assignment, he stated that "Processing services as defined above do not include those activities which relate to the *selection* for use nor to the *rejection and elimination* of materials whose usefulness has ended, although some processing activity is involved after the decision to reject or eliminate has been made."

NASSAU LIBRARY SYSTEM. Similar to the approach in the Dallas Public Library survey, Tauber and Kingery gave little attention to the problem of acquisitional policy in the Nassau survey. In the background portion of the study, however, and in comments in the report, discussion of the ordering of titles for the central reference collection, and the acquisition of pamphlets, documents, and various nonbook materials was provided. In a system of libraries involved in a cooperative enterprise, the acquisitional policies of libraries may be interwoven in some ways, through *synchronized purchasing,* but on the whole, selection may well be quite different from library to library.

*Cataloging and Classification:* The evaluation of the status of the cataloging and classification in a particular library or a library system is among the more important assignments made to surveyors of technical services, since the issues are more complex than those found in some areas. However, evaluation of operations in cataloging and classification involves the same broad considerations, including functions and responsibilities, policies, organization and management, personnel, quarters and equipment, operations, production, and special problems. Again, for the purpose of discussion, reference is made to the methodology used in the McGill, Dallas, and Nassau studies.

MC GILL UNIVERSITY LIBRARY. In the McGill study, the surveyors called attention to the fact that the major catalog was not a union catalog of all the holdings in the library collections. It was recommended that steps be taken to make the catalog a complete union catalog. Major attention, however, was given to the backlog of work resulting from the failure of the Cutter Classification to provide a means by which the materials could be efficiently classified. The Cutter Classification had been used during the major years of the Library's history. The major recommendation that the McGill University Library shift to the Library of Congress Classification was made after a detailed examination of present practices and production. It was considered that the problems which had developed in the use of the Cutter Classification would worsen in the future.

In addition to this major recommendation, which included adherence to Library of Congress descriptive and subject cataloging, suggestions for improvement of analytic cataloging were provided. The potential use of data processing equipment was described. There were no specific recommendations for automation, but installation was discussed; there has been considerable discussion, but application of new equipment has been slow.

DALLAS PUBLIC LIBRARY. Frarey has given much attention to cataloging and classification in his survey report, primarily because the survey was restricted to technical services. In the section dealing with "The Catalog Department," Frarey examines the background and history of the department, states functions, responsibilities, and areas of coverage, and analyzes the breakdown of the staff. The work assignments of the personnel are examined, and conclusions concerning these assignments are drawn. The inadequacy of the staff, in terms of size, is pointed out, and the need for flexibility among the personnel is emphasized. Yet, the consultant seeks to redistribute responsibilities among personnel assigned to certain grades, to make more concise the distinction between professional and nonprofessional staff.

NASSAU LIBRARY SYSTEM. Since the Nassau study differed from both the McGill and Dallas studies in terms of the assigned responsibility and scope of the study, the portions of the report dealing with cataloging are directed at the problems of centralization, various operations designed to speed up the processing, and the relationship of the work to the union catalog. Questionnaires were sent to the member libraries, and the answers served to provide the surveyors with some data necessary to make recommendations. Synchronized ordering, for example, appeared as a major issue, since this activity was essential for the efficiency of the centralized cataloging and processing. Discussions with librarians of several libraries supported the impression that other libraries would join the cooperative enterprise if the bottlenecks in the Center could be removed. As in many surveys of this type, much attention was given to organizational charts and tabular material. No effort was made to draw up flow charts, although these are normally useful to show up impediments in smooth operation (as in the Queens Borough Public Library Survey). Data processing equipment has been introduced since the survey for the handling of technical processing operations.

## REFERENCES

1. Dewey, Melvil (ed.). *The World's Library Congress.* American Library Association Congress held at the Columbian Exposition. Washington, D.C., U.S. Government Printing Office, 1896, p. 869.
2. *Ibid.,* pp. 869–70.
3. *Ibid.,* pp. 872–73.
4. U.S. Office of Education. *Public Libraries in the United States of America; Their History, Condition and Management.* Special Report. Washington, D.C., U.S. Government Printing Office, 1876, pp. 493–94.
5. *Ibid.,* pp. 467–68.
6. *Ibid.,* pp. 623–48.
7. Sawyer, H. P. (ed.). *The Library and Its Contents.* New York, H. W. Wilson Co., 1925, p. 334.
8. American Library Association. Coordinating Committee on Revision of Public Library Standards. *Public Library Service; A Guide to Evaluation with Minimum Standards.* Chicago, American Library Association, 1956.
9. McDiarmid, Errett W. *The Library Survey.* Chicago, American Library Association, 1940.
10. Bowler, Roberta (ed.). *Local Public Library Administration.* Chicago, International City Managers' Association, 1964, Chap. 10, pp. 195–240.
11. Erickson, E. W. *College and University Library Surveys, 1938–1952.* Chicago, American Library Association, 1961.
12. Tauber, M. F. "Survey Method in Approaching Library Problems," *Library Trends,* 13:15–30 (July 1964).

13. Matta, Seoud M. *The Card Catalog in the Large Research Library: Present Conditions and Future Possibilities in the New York Public Library.* DLS Dissertation, School of Library Service, Columbia University, 1965.

14. Reichmann, Felix. "Cornell's Reclassification Program." *College and Research Libraries* 23:269–74 (September 1962). Also, Wilson, L. R., Downs, R. B., and Tauber, M. F. *Report of a Survey of the Libraries of Cornell University.* Ithaca, Cornell University, 1948.

15. Tauber, M. F. *Technical Services in the Libraries of the University of New Mexico.* Albuquerque, University of New Mexico, 1964.

16. Tauber, M. F., and Kingery, R. E. *The Central Technical Processing of the Nassau Library System.* Hempstead, N.Y., The Nassau Library System, 1962.

17. Tauber, M. F. *The Queens Borough Public Library Cataloguing Department.* New York, School of Library Service, Columbia University, 1956.

18. Tauber, M. F., and Stephens, Irlene R. *Report on Classification System of Beaver College Library.* Glenside, Pennsylvania, 1965.

19. McCarthy, S. A., and Logsdon, R. H. *Survey of the McGill University Libraries.* Montreal, McGill University Library, 1963.

20. Frarey, Carlyle J. *The Processing Services of the Dallas Public Library.* Dallas, Dallas Public Library, 1959.

# 4 Survey of the Use of
# Library Resources and Facilities

LEON CARNOVSKY

No aspect of library surveys is at once so superficially easy and so extraordinarily difficult to measure as library use. Virtually any library can produce figures on registration (however inaccurate), circulation, and circulation per capita; some can tell how many books in each of the Dewey classes were loaned; most can divide their circulation into adult and children's —based on the books and their classification, not on the readers. No library knows very much about what these many figures mean, and sometimes, when the surveyor attempts to read meanings into them, he may be far off the mark.

Though this paper will devote attention to weaknesses in measures of library use, let me say at once that all library surveys use such measures as are available and as time and funds permit; and until we can improve our measures we shall continue to use those we have. To indicate their weaknesses is not to deprecate their use, but only to underscore the caution that must be exercised in interpreting the results.

The difficulty of finding meaning in registration and circulation figures is aggravated when we examine other areas of library activity, such as reference work and reader guidance. Some libraries keep a meticulous count of reference questions— including those involving looking up a telephone number or word pronunciation and definition, each counted as one question, along with, say, the assembly of material on the background of the Crimean War or the exasperating search for the solution to some esoteric puzzle or for a scientific formula, also counted as one each. Again, what do these figures mean? Is a library that receives many questions necessarily better than one that fielded only a few? Maybe the latter library received few questions because its collections were so beautifully organized and so plentiful that the patron could find the answers himself, and therefore there was no way of recording his inquiry at all. Also, there must be hundreds of inquiries that never get answered because the patron, after suffering frustration in a personal search, was too timid to ask for help. If significant figures of library reference use are difficult for the library to assemble, they are virtually impossible for the library surveyor, and he contents himself usually with a simple tabulation based on an examination of such library statistical information as may be available.

Since libraries vary so sharply in so many ways, one cannot generalize about the interpretation of their statistics. How has library use been considered in surveys of different types of libraries? *A Metropolitan Library in Action*,[1] the survey of the Chicago Public Library, devoted one chapter to "Major Trends in the Development of Library Service," another to branches and the use made of them, another to the library as an agency of adult education, and still another to an analysis of library registration and public opinion about the library. Though few surveys can or need deal with all these matters, it may be useful for a beginning to review the procedures employed in the Chicago survey. The trends were described for book stock, circulation, and registration.

Circulation and other trends may be presented simply as a record of what happened, or as a basis for explaining why they happened that way, or as a prelude to prescribing what they may be in future—that is to say, why or how certain causes or influences may be changed to bring about a change in future trends.

First, then, what happened? The simplest way to show this is to select a year, or the average for three or more years, as the base and then translate the gross circulation figure into index numbers based on the year or years selected. This clearly shows percentage increases and decreases for preceding and succeeding years. Thus, with 1927 as the base year (index 100), circulation in Chicago increased 23 percent (index 123) in 1931, then dropped to 81 in 1937 and 95 in 1938.

Second, why did it happen? Several explanations are possible; or rather one might suggest possible causes and look for such evidence as can be found to test their applicability. Among such causes might be changes in total population, up or down; changes in the character of the population—more literate or less; changes in the social background, e.g., larger school enrollments; or changes in library structure and operation, and these may be the most obvious if we would only look for them. Among such changes are addition (or elimination) of branches, multiplication of circulation outlets like deposit stations, community centers, bookmobiles; change in location of the main library; changes in book selection policy, emphasizing more popular books or books needed for school assignments, or, on the other hand, deemphasizing them in the interest of reference books and significant titles in less demand; changes in the overall amount of money available as well as in amounts spent for books; and by no means least, changes in overall policy or practice, such as adding or discontinuing responsibility for school libraries. Once, in two successive years, the gross circulation of the Chicago Public Library dropped from thirteen to eight million, simply because school libraries were shifted to Board of Education responsibility in the second year. Clearly, unless these and countless other factors are taken into consideration in explaining trends, we are left with all sorts of speculation that are more likely to be wrong than right.

Third, as to whether changes within the library can lead to greater circulation in the future, this is a matter of judgment based not only on certain values but perhaps even more on what is possible in a given situation. If one values circulation for its own sake, it may be increased by emphasizing popularity in book provision possibly at the expense of other types of books; or by adding more books that the school population is clamoring for, again perhaps at the expense of books in less demand. These value decisions are basically those of the librarian and library board. As to what is possible, it is pointless to say that the library should spend more money if more is not available, or if the city finds it must spend more money for police protection or whatever rather than for its library. This too is a value decision, but one beyond the control of either library or library surveyor. Then there are other matters of a social type which are beyond them. If a library's circulation falls because of a drop in reading interest or ability of the citizenry, there may be precious little that anyone can do about it—at least as far as library use in the conventional sense of book circulation is concerned. At one time, a branch library in Chicago was surrounded by a highly literate population eager for books; year after year the branch ranked among the first five in circulation. Then the population moved away, to be replaced by an altogether different one, poorly educated and strange to city ways; it was not long before circulation plummeted, and today the branch ranks near the bottom, all this in spite of the fact that the library's location, book stock, hours of operation, and character of personnel remained the same. This is not to imply that branch policy remained unchanged; quite the contrary, but the changes are not of a kind that are reflected in the maintenance of high circulation figures. Library use may depend to a far greater extent on population characteristics than on anything the library itself can do about it.

To return now to description of circulation trends, it is frequently desirable, for clarification, to go beyond gross figures, and here I shall suggest other approaches. An obvious one is circulation per capita. Like all per capita measures, this has the virtue of holding population constant if we wish to compare one library's showing with another's, or with a per capita standard. But population figures on which per capitas are based are reasonably accurate only once every ten years in most cities, and trends from year to year in per capita circulation are therefore suspect. To divide 1965 circulation by 1960 population may suggest an increase altogether spurious. It would be more accurate to present trends by five-year intervals, taking census figures for, say, 1930–60, then assigning half the increase between decades to 1935, 1945, 1955, and 1965, and using the resultant figures as the basis for per capita computation. This is admittedly rough, but at least it is better than basing 1965 circulation per capita on 1960 figures.

The circulation pattern may be clarified by various types of breakdown. The following were used in the Chicago survey, or have been suggested by it:

### CIRCULATION TRENDS BY TYPE OF AGENCY

Total circulation annually was presented for the main library, the branches, the high schools, elementary school deposits, and all other agencies, again by index numbers. Through this presentation it was possible to show the relative growth in circulation from each major type, and it helped to answer the question whether losses in main library circulation were compensated by gains in other agencies. (Generally the answer was no, but the question is an interesting one and may be important in planning the development of the library system.) Another way of showing the relative importance of the various types of distributing outlets is to compute the *proportion* of total circulation for each type, holding the year constant. One can then see how the proportions varied from year to year.

### CIRCULATION TRENDS BY CLASSES OF MATERIAL

The obvious division here is between fiction and nonfiction, but, as suggested earlier, if the library has maintained circulation records by Dewey classes it may be of some interest to examine trends in subject matter circulated. Are more books in science being borrowed today than ten years ago? What about the reading of fiction, has it been displaced by the paperback or by television? One would like to pursue fiction reading by breaking it down into types—by date of the book, literary quality, major themes (historical, science-fiction, light romances, westerns, mysteries, etc.), but since such data are elusive the surveyor can do nothing about them.

It may be objected that all such analyses constitute pleasant busy work, perhaps of some interest to the social historian or cultural anthropologist but not to the librarian. This may be so; in any event they rarely figure in surveys of library use. Still, it is not beyond possibility that armed with such findings the librarian might gain clearer insight into matters about which he does not hesitate to speculate in his annual reviews. I make no claims for the relevance of such information to practical administrative matters, such as distribution of the book budget or decisions on book purchase; the chances are that such decisions are affected by certain insights based on publication output, conscious and articulate demand, book reviews, and the usual listings or recommendations in bibliographical media. For whatever revelations they may provide, the least that can be done is the presentation of trends in the circulation of fiction and nonfiction. Several years ago, in a survey of a public library in Ohio, I did this using index numbers, and I found that in 1950 total adult circulation suddenly dropped sharply, though nothing that the library did could have precipitated the loss. It was still keeping up its purchases of current books, maintained the same service program, etc. The loss was particularly sharp in fiction circulation, about 37 percent from the base year of 1944. In nonfiction the loss was 8 percent. It turned out that a television booster from Cleveland had been constructed early that year, and in the competition reading lost out. But it was interesting, if nothing else, to note that the loss was mostly experienced by fiction; the need for nonfiction, undoubtedly strongly influenced by school requirements, could not be satisfied by television.

CIRCULATION TRENDS BY READER

Whatever analyses of this type have been made have usually consisted of special investigations or surveys of the Public Library Inquiry type; they are not typical of the ordinary library survey. Libraries do not keep statistics that readily permit identification of readers by age, sex, occupation, or otherwise. The closest they come to this is the division of book circulation into adult and children's—a book, not a reader classification, but it may reasonably be assumed that children ordinarily do not read adult books and vice versa. Once more it is easy to plot trends in the circulation of both types, and there may be administrative implications in the findings particularly if they are related in some way to the work of the local school libraries. It would be interesting to compare the use of children's books in a branch serving a neighborhood where it was the only source, with one where an elementary school library also flourished. Does the presence of two libraries stimulate increased reading? Does the public library compensate for the absence of a school library? Or does it make any difference at all? These are not idle questions, but the surveyor with limited time available is in no position to answer them.

The temptation to relate circulation figures to other factors on the basis of statistical correlates is attractive, but it may lead to unwarranted conclusions. It is easy to show, for example, that a library with below-standard circulation may also be one with a below-standard book collection. (I use the word "standard" in its numerical, not qualitative, connotation, for numbers are tangible and are therefore cited.) One might conclude that if the collection were enlarged to meet the standard, circulation would show a concomitant growth until it too met the standard. This line of reasoning has a superficial attractiveness because of its simplicity; unfortunately, it is too simple. For circulation is a function of many factors, of which size of book collection is not nearly the most important. If I presently read, say, fifty books a year, I am not likely to read more than this simply because the number available to me was suddenly increased five- or tenfold. (This of course is not to argue against a larger book collection, but simply to indicate that it is not the only factor that affects the amount of reading, either by an individual or by a community.) The simple matter of library location may have a far greater effect on circulation than anything else. Before the Vancouver Public Library moved into its present spacious building in the heart of the downtown district it was housed in a deteriorating neighborhood which presented both physical and psychological barriers to potential patrons. This was enough to account for substandard use; needless to say, once in its new quarters, the library attracted more people and circulated more books than ever before.

In view of the foregoing, it is doubtful whether anyone can say how large circulation should be; it would be as well to ask how many books *ought* to be read. This, however, has not prevented us from attempting it. Typically, the two approaches have been the use of ALA standards as a backstop, and a comparison with other libraries. As far as the ALA standard is concerned, in *Public Library Service*,[2] there is no quantitative prescription; as the introduction to the volume points out:

> Quantitative standards having such a wide range that they do not measure requirements in the qualitative sense have been avoided. An example of such a rejected standard is that the per capita circulation of adult books should be from 3 to 10 per capita, and of children's books from 10 to 30 per child.*

Instead, we have a number of principles and standards to which no one can possibly object; and which, taken as a whole, are designed to encourage and facilitate library use. Any librarian could use them to advantage, interpreting them in the light of his conception of community needs and possibilities. The surveyor, however, has tended to pass them up in favor of the quantitative approach. This has led him to the sometimes illogical but widely practiced device of comparison with libraries in the same geographic area or with those responsible for similar population totals. The implication, whether expressed or not, is that there is something seriously wrong if a library ranks near

---

* The quantitative standard for circulation was adopted by the Canadian Library Association and was used as a backstop by R. R. Shaw in his *Libraries of Metropolitan Toronto* (1960). But Shaw himself observes that standards developed to raise quality of service "cannot be applied blindly to a metropolitan area like Toronto in which high levels of service are available to all the people at certain points together with exceedingly low levels of service at most others." (p. 24)

the bottom in circulation, and something ought to be done about it—more money, more books, more help. The comparative approach, whatever its faults, does have the virtue of suggesting the question of why a given library varies from its contemporaries, and conceivably may lead to changes that may in turn affect library use. (It might be noted in passing that the comparative approach is of no help to libraries ranking at the top, unless it stimulates them to renewed efforts to hold their position. I have no evidence on this point.)

Many other uses of circulation data are suggested by Berelson [3] in his *Library's Public*, prepared for the Public Library Inquiry. Berelson brought together the methods and results of numerous studies, those using methods already described and others relating library use to certain social indices. He has a good deal to say about such matters as library use in relation to general reading behavior; users classed by educational achievement; the sex, age, and occupational distribution of library patrons; the relative importance of the library as a reading source; economic status of library users; their marital status; political sophistication to some extent; seasonal variations in use; relation of book borrower to book reader (he reported that "recorded circulation undervalued actual circulation by from one-fifth to one-fourth"). Most of these studies were made independently of conventional library surveys and they throw considerable light on the general reading pattern as of fifteen or twenty years ago. While many of the results reported would still apply today, others would not, especially in view of the paperback and television; and up-to-date studies of the type Berelson reported would be welcome. However, since use is only one of the many areas to which the library surveyor must address himself, it is unlikely to receive the intensive attention it has received in independent researches.

Though strictly speaking the Deiches study [4] of student library use is not a survey, it demonstrates how use studies may be seminal in pointing directions for change. Based on a questionnaire to high school students, Lowell Martin shed light on the amount of reading they do, the readers vs. nonreaders among them, their sources of reading, the amount of time spent in

public and school libraries, and the reasons for their preferences
as between public and school libraries. Martin's study reveals
conditions in one city as a realistic basis for indicating a necessary and desirable future and how it may be effected through
action by city, school board, and public library.

Second only to use as a measure of library impact is registration. It is possible to determine what proportion of the reported
population are cardholders; but as with circulation it is impossible to say what the proportion *should* be. The conventional
figure of 30 to 35 percent is frequently exceeded in small and
mediumsized communities, and it is rarely reached in the larger
cities. It is extremely difficult to say much about the relationship
between registration and use; one study made twenty years ago
and reported by Berelson showed that three fourths of the adult
circulation was charged out to only 10 to 12 percent of the adult
registrants; even more revealing of the selective character of
library patronage was the finding that half the circulation went
to 5 percent of the registration, and only 2 percent of the population. Berelson concludes: "In quantitative terms the public library spends a major part of its resources and effort in the service of a relatively small segment of its potential clientele."

One can only guess as to how accurate this generalization
would be today. I should be willing to accept it, without considering it either an indictment or a criticism of the library. The
library has always been a minority service, just as book reading
is a minority activity. But more to the point, we may ask of
what importance are registration figures anyway. As with circulation statistics, they may be compared with the showing of
other, presumably comparable, cities, and if they are badly out
of line we may ask the reasons, and then determine what, if anything, can or need be done about it.

Registration figures may be related to population by age
groups. Thus we may ask what proportion of the five-to-
fourteen age group is registered, on the assumption that the library issues special cards to this group, and what proportion of
the fifteen-and-over group? One additional piece of information
that seems worth collecting is the number of nonresident regis-

trants, especially in these days when we are concerned with out-of-town use. (Statistics on out-of-town use would be even more important, but difficult to get without a special study.)

Another refinement of registration measurement, unfortunately requiring a special study, undertaken in Chicago was aimed at learning the proportion of adults of voting age who were library card holders. This study was designed to eliminate the high school students who make up a large segment of the registration, and to focus specifically on the population twenty-one years of age and over. What proportion held cards? A sample of nearly 10,000 names was carefully drawn from the voters' registration list, representing every ward and precinct of the city, and these names were checked against the library's registration file. It was found that 4.6 percent of the men and 6.9 percent of the women were library registrants, or 5.7 percent combined. One can only speculate what the results would be if a similar study were conducted today. With many more branches and subbranches in Chicago (fifty-eight contrasted with forty-five in 1939), the chances are that a *larger* proportion would be registered; on the other hand, with the increasing competition for the attention of the potential library user, the proportion might be lower. It is an interesting question, though again I am not sure how helpful the library would find the answer to be. Nor do we know whether Chicago's showing would be better or worse than that of other cities in the over one-million population category. Wight and Merritt, as part of their survey of the Hayward, California, Public Library in 1955, made a similar but more limited check of voters in four precincts; of 901 names, 19.5 percent were library registrants: 21.7 percent of the women, 17.1 percent of the men. Hayward's population at the time was 34,500; for many reasons one would expect the small and mediumsized communities to enroll a larger proportion of their population than the large metropolitan centers. In any event, as Lowell Martin stated in the *Library Journal* for May 1965, "The public library will not be measured by the number of customers it gets, but by whether it keeps the door of opportunity open to all."

The survey of library reference work is particularly difficult to report in any quantitative way to give it meaning. If the surveyor devotes any attention to this at all, he contents himself with a check of reference collections, periodical subscriptions and bound files, government documents, vertical files, etc., on the assumption that a strong showing suggests at least the possibility of good reference service, but the actual reference inquiries and their disposition are too diversified, vague, and generally intangible to give a quantitative report any significance, even as an index to what a library does to say nothing of how it might use the information if it had it. As noted in the Chicago survey: "There can be no doubt that reference work looms large in every library worthy of the name; yet it is so complex, so varied, that practically all attempts to measure its quantity or significance have met with but little success."

The two ways suggested for measuring reference work are, first, simply recording the number of questions asked, perhaps arranged by type or complexity, and second, classifying them by the length of time required to answer them. (Query: What should be done about questions when the answer is *not* discovered?) Altogether aside from the busywork and exasperation either procedure entails, I see no point in them, any more than I see in the outmoded (and happily discarded) standard of "one-half to one reference question per capita." (But Wheeler and Goldhor seem interested in restoring it, raising the figure to three-fourths to one reference and advisory question per capita.) Instead of reviewing the familiar reasons for doubting the quality of these measures, I raise the question of what use are they? We surely do not need them to "prove" that high school students frequently overwhelm the staff, and that more assistance or more books are needed. In a couple of sentences Wheeler and Goldhor [5] build up and demolish the case for keeping statistics of reference work:

If a library is compelled to report output, the reference department may record some of the following: attendance, directional questions, reference questions, unanswered questions, bibliographies prepared, reference volumes used, telephone questions, and questions by mail. Some of these almost defy definition, and to record them is so time-consuming that it seems inconsistent with the efforts which libraries are making to cut out all possible records and paperwork elsewhere.

In his monograph "A Statistical Reporting System for Local Public Libraries" Professor Kenneth E. Beasley [6] observes that reference work is a function of professional personnel and size of collection. He states: "A large library in both respects will have a good reference service and indeed will generate a demand for the service in excess of almost any budgetary allocation made for it." Beasley suggests that the only precise way to measure reference work is "in terms of the number of employees who devote their time primarily or exclusively" to it. What we have, then, is not a measure of reference use at all, but rather of certain "means" to the end of providing reference service. Of course it bristles with assumptions, but no more so than other measures we commonly use.

Related somewhat to reference work is reader guidance. Here, too, as in reference work, so much depends on personnel competence, on sympathetic insights, on the establishment of rapport between patron and librarian, that the surveyor can do little beyond describing the administrative setup. If the figures are available he may report the number of persons requesting assistance, the number of reading lists prepared, the number of referrals to other, more formal, educational institutions. But all these matters are highly elusive; for one thing, few libraries today still maintain a readers' advisory bureau and it is difficult to know how many people receive assistance, much less how many want it. In a real sense, all of the personnel who come in contact with the public may be asked for reading guidance, and how well the function is performed cannot even be guessed at.

Beyond individual guidance there is the broad area of adult education, and numerous surveys centered on this topic have been conducted. Sometimes they are part of the general library survey, as in Chicago, where a separate chapter was devoted to the library as an agency of adult education. This chapter described the work of the Readers' Bureau and activities in the branches, such as forums, book review meetings, cooperation with adult education activities outside the library, and preparation of reading lists. As I reread the recommendations today, advocating maintenance of records of high school graduates and adult education classes for follow-up library campaigns, and provision of books in quantity for adult education courses, they seem almost quaint—not that they fail to make sense, but in the current race to keep up with simple demand for books of whatever description, most libraries are hardly in a position to carry on campaigns to enroll high school graduates or to maintain contacts with students in adult education classes. And yet, with society's present concern over dropouts and the war on poverty, it may well be that libraries can ill afford to plead indifference because of staff shortages or the articulate demand for other types of library activity. The surveyor, if he is convinced that the library should take part in such campaigns as the war on poverty, may be helpful in indicating what such participation would require in the provision of personnel, books, and a specific program.

As we know, adult education has received attention from the very beginnings of the public library, though the phrase itself was not emphasized until the 1920s, and since then the library profession has always been aware of it. The literature is vast, and includes a number of surveys devoted specifically to adult education and the library. One of the most comprehensive in recent years (1954) is Helen Lyman Smith's *Adult Education Activities in Public Libraries*. Based on a questionnaire, it spelled out a host of activities in which libraries were engaged in the name of adult education, ranging from posters on bulletin boards to personal guidance. The vast territory between these extremes suggests the ambiguous character of the phrase "adult education" and should serve as a warning to any future surveyor that he had best start with a definition.

Somewhat related to library use is public reaction to the institution, for satisfaction and frustration in using the library will be reflected in attitudes toward it. One of the earliest systematic attempts to get at this was Haygood's study of New York Public Library patrons, in 1938; similar investigations were carried out, either independently or as part of larger surveys, in Baltimore, Chicago, Cleveland, Los Angeles, and other cities. The basic problems in such a study are the construction of the questionnaire and the selection of a sample to give a reliable cross section of the population. The questionnaires used in these studies have usually asked frequency and purpose of library use, reasons for limited use, and likes and dislikes.

It is difficult to say how to use these surveys of public opinion. All too often the results are predictable, and the fact that the library has done little about the complaints is due not to indifference but to inability to combat them. How can New York or Chicago possibly provide enough copies of *Herzog* or any other bestseller to keep people from complaining that they cannot find it when they want it? Even more, how can it interpret the chronic complaint that the library does not have the books (unspecified) the patron wants? What shall it do about the demand for subliterary materials? Even when the demands are specific and legitimate, the library may be hampered by limited funds. This, however, is not to deprecate the value of opinion or attitude surveys; if well conducted so that the responses are reliable, they may indicate a favorable climate of opinion, which strengthens the library's position in the community; or they may suggest so much dissatisfaction that the library should seriously consider its shortcomings. Complaints may stem not from deficiencies in book resources but from rudeness or bad manners on the part of the staff; or they may suggest that lack of use may be corrected by more branches or by placing them in more convenient locations. An intelligent and alert librarian may be aware of these deficiencies without a survey, and he may not be altogether to blame if financial limitations or board apathy or antagonism prevent their correction.

Thus far I have concentrated exclusively on studies of public library use; I next consider the approach in academic and school library surveys. In general surveys of college and university libraries, where the surveyors have devoted attention to use, they have focused on rules and regulations, physical convenience of the facilities, and stimulation of reading through publicity, browsing rooms, open stacks, and similar matters. They have not been concerned with circulation statistics, and, in fact, the statistics for college and university libraries issued by the Library Services Branch do not include them at all. This is tacit recognition of the fact that circulation is largely a function of curriculum and teaching method, and perhaps also of the realization that the sheer number of books a library circulates is no measure at all of its true contribution to the educational process. In spite of the fact that Wilson and Tauber advocate the maintenance of circulation records, Wilson and Swank, in their survey of Stanford University, reported:

> Because statistics of use are kept for only a few of the University libraries and those that are kept are not consolidated and consistently reported, it is impossible for the surveyors to present any meaningful discussion or evaluation of this significant aspect of the Library program.

Since the surveyor can make but limited use of circulation data as an index of library performance, what can he tell the university about its service program? This obviously must depend on the individual situation, but it might be helpful to list the kinds of recommendation identified by Erickson, under Readers Services, in his dissertation on "College and University Library Surveys, 1938–52." These included suggestions for improving circulation procedures, centralizing loan services, maintaining uniform records of use, checking up on faculty long-term withdrawals, providing assistance at the card catalog, liberalizing loan privileges for certain kinds of materials like government documents. Since so many of the surveys were made by the same individuals—the names of Wilson, Coney, Downs, Tauber frequently appear—it is not surprising that the same recommendations appear over and over again. One suspects that with the coming of automation a new group of recommendations will emerge.

Finally, a word about school library surveys. It is significant that the *Standards for School Library Programs*, though geared at all points to the concept of efficient service to pupils and teachers, has nothing to say about measurement of service. Instead, there is a great deal of attention to factors that are assumed, on logical grounds, to make for efficient service; the assumption throughout is that given these factors, efficient service, which certainly implies library use, has a better chance of realization. This means that the surveyor must devote his attention to a number of aspects, some severely quantitative, others not, and forego consideration of use altogether, except inferentially. The quantitative aspects include library location in the school, annual expenditures, size of collection, and personnel; the *Standards* volume, however, has a lot more to say about quality, and here the judgment of the surveyor must be invoked to supplement the measurable factors.

The *School Library and Audio-Visual Survey* conducted in the state of Washington (published May, 1964), and for which Eleanor Ahlers was largely responsible, provides an illustration of a survey keyed to the school library standards. Following an introductory section of "General Information," chapters are devoted to "Personnel," "Materials Collection," "Quarters and Equipment," "Organization and Administration," and "Program of Services." Each section lists criteria and standards, then measures performance against them based to a considerable extent on the testimony given in questionnaires. The services provided included assistance in developing reading, viewing, and listening taste, developing skills in library use, and providing guidance in book selection. None of these is a measure of use, but all may be regarded as desirable steps in contributing to use. Since we do not know precisely how these activities were carried on, to say nothing of their effectiveness, we can only assume that they have some value, and short of extended viewing and intensive analysis, which no surveyor can possibly undertake, the surveyor cannot go much farther than report what is done and suggest additional procedures if he knows of any.

The work of all social institutions may be considered as means to an end. A symphony orchestra plays music as a means to personal pleasure and the cultivation of taste; the same may be said of the ends of the art museum. One can record the pieces an orchestra plays, or the works of art a museum puts on display—their number, perhaps an indication of their quality, the felicity of their arrangement, etc., but one can only assume that they lead to instruction and pleasure, without the slightest knowledge of how well these ends have been achieved. We assume a connection between means and ends, but this is an act of faith, bulwarked in part by the experience of the race. So, too, with the library. Book collections, personnel, finance, administration, all are means to the end of library use; in the school and college accurate measures of use have been all but given up as an index to achievement; in the public library, though we still faithfully maintain records of use, we know the story they tell must always be incomplete. In this connection it is pertinent to observe that Professor Beasley advocates that the number of registered borrowers, number of reference questions, and number of books circulated be omitted from the state statistical reporting system. He suggests that "circulation data are among the least significant now commonly reported to a central agency." On the other hand, he does approve maintaining circulation statistics for whatever suggestions or implications they may have for internal administration.

The job of the surveyor, then, is to concentrate on means, evaluating them as best he can in the faith that superior personnel, book collections, organization, and administration cannot fail to effect the largely intangible end of reading satisfaction through library use.

REFERENCES

1. Joeckel, Carleton B., and Carnovsky, Leon. *A Metropolitan Library in Action*. Chicago, University of Chicago Press, 1940.
2. American Library Association. Co-ordinating Committee on

Divisional Library Standards. *Public Library Service; a Guide to Evaluation, with Minimum Standards.* Chicago, American Library Association, 1956.

3. Berelson, Bernard. *The Library's Public.* New York, Columbia University Press, 1949.

4. Martin, Lowell A. *Students and the Pratt Free Library: Challenge and Opportunity* (Deiches Fund Study). Baltimore, Enoch Pratt Free Library, 1963.

5. Wheeler, Joseph L., and Goldhor, Herbert. *Practical Administration of Public Libraries.* New York, Harper and Row, 1962.

6. Beasley, Kenneth E. *A Statistical Reporting System for Local Public Libraries.* University Park, Pa., Institute of Public Administration, Pennsylvania State University, 1964.

7. Wilson, Louis R., and Swank, R. C. *Report of a Survey of the Library of Stanford University for Stanford University.* Chicago, American Library Association, 1947.

# 5 Survey of Library Buildings and Facilities

DONALD E. BEAN

## SOME HANDICAPS TO CONSULTATION WORK

DESPITE the well-known fact that there is rapidly increasing demand for consultants in library building projects, there are many projects which are erected with little, if any, consultation service. For this there may be several possible causes. One is the unwillingness of the librarian to make a forthright declaration in favor of the engagement of consultants. This unwillingness may stem from the naïve and incorrect belief that the librarian is quite capable of writing an adequate statement of program and checking the architect's plans without outside assistance except from published information and perhaps a few conferences; or it may be the result of the librarian's equally unfounded belief that a request for consulting assistance may be construed by his employers as an admission of weakness; or it may be caused by pure ego.

All of these reasons for the librarian's hesitancy to recommend consultants are sometimes supplemented by an architect who may not like the idea of engaging consultants unless he can control them. Again, the need for paid building consultants is sometimes minimized in the minds of the clients by well-meaning but overzealous representatives of some state library extension departments who do not realize the harm they do a library when they say "Why pay for consultants? We'll give you the service free of charge."

These attitudes may have been reinforced by the fact that until comparatively recently much library literature has treated in a rather casual manner the question of engaging building consultants. Fortunately, these attitudes are changing rapidly. There is more than ample evidence that no one librarian's, indeed no one consultant's, opinions can safely be accepted as solutions to library building problems. At least one large state now requires the engaging of a library building consultant before an application for financial assistance for a library building is considered.

## THE ANALYSIS OF BUILDING NEEDS

There is a wide difference of opinion among consultants as well as among clients as to the nature and the amount of consultation service which a library building project requires; all are agreed that there should be a written library building program of some sort. However, some believe that the statement of program can be limited to very general statements covering, for instance, the number of total volumes and a few general categories, the number of periodicals, the total quantity of seating and a few general areas, and a few other suggestions about various aspects of the building. The librarian of a very large library once told me that a written library program need require no more than four and a half pages.

Some believe that consultation service regarding a statement of program is sufficient if it consists of advice, verbal or written, given to the librarian, who then proceeds to write his own program, no matter whether he has had sufficient experience in this or not. Others, and I believe their number is increasing, believe that the analysis of building needs is a problem so important and so complex that a solution requires a thorough, comprehensive, written, detailed statement of program which may occupy 75 to 150 doublespaced typewritten pages.

Let us recount some of the things which a good statement of program for a library building should attempt to describe:

1. The service which the library may be required to render in

future years—say twenty years hence—both in extent and in nature.

2. The quantities of library materials that may be needed in order to render that service. This point includes not only books and periodicals but also all other library materials including such items as audiovisual materials, documents, maps, ephemeral materials, etc.

3. The future departmental organization of those library materials.

4. The future library staff required to render the needed service, in detail, department by department.

5. A detailed list of furniture and equipment that will be needed to carry out the future service.

6. The estimated square footage, department by department, complete and in detail, that will be required to house the materials and equipment.

7. The relationship of each area in respect to other areas, both horizontally and vertically.

8. Other aspects of the building design and structure which are likely to affect the cost of operation of the library or the effectiveness of its service or both.

What are some of the characteristics of a good statement of program, one or more of which are likely to be missing from many of these reports? There are several.

The statement of program should be a statement of *future need*, not merely of current need. It should be entirely unrelated to the amount of money available for the building. Any standard formulas which are used should be adjusted to the future. Furthermore, the statement of program should recommend that the site to be selected and the earliest architectural sketches to be prepared should be based upon this described future need, again without any reference to funds for current building. The statement of program should be based upon the library needs of the particular community or the particular college being studied, not based on average formulas. The statement of program should avoid the indiscriminate application of favorite preference in building design. The reports should be written in complete detail. The statement of program should contain no attempt to draw outline sketches for the architect. Finally, the statement of program should include a complete equipment list geared to the future insofar as possible. Some of these remarks require further development.

*Future Needs:* It has been said that the statement of program should be a statement of future need. In its basic recommendations it should ignore entirely the amount of money which may be currently available for building. Yet much of the effort of some consultants has been concerned with the problem of specifying a building which is limited to the size and design for which funds are available. Indeed some library literature of twenty years ago gave this as a laudable objective.

Yet the first objective of the statement of program should be to estimate the nature and extent of the service that will be required of that library in future years; only when that need is assessed can planning go forward logically. It is difficult to overemphasize this practical point.

Another common error in statements of program prepared by some consultants, or nonconsultants, is the use, without adjustment, of average standards. The published standards for both public and college libraries—splendid guides though they are —are current guides. Yet a public library building is supposedly planned for at least twenty years in the future and a college or university building for at least ten to fifteen years in the future and in almost all cases the buildings will have to serve for fifty years or more.

Furthermore, as we all know, we are only at the beginning of an educational revolution in which the library is at the very center, and which presages greatly increased per capita use of the public library and of the college library. In ten years, with a much better educated generation growing up, the current standards will be as far out of date as the standards of 1930 are now. It is the job of the consultant to assess future trends, yet in case after case future trends are given no more than casual reference and the statement of program is based upon current standards.

It may be worth emphasizing that we are not talking about the erecting of a library building; we are not even talking about the final planning of the library. In respect to this point we refer only to the written statement of program and the earliest preliminary sketches of the architect.

Furthermore, as has been said before, the statement of program should insist that the site to be selected and also the earliest architectural sketches to be prepared should be based upon this described future need. Only after those earliest sketches for the ultimate building have been reviewed and approved should the attempt be made to cut down the size of the building to fit the present funds or present needs.

The reason, of course, is that there are certain features of most library buildings which may be very difficult and expensive to change once the structure has been erected. These are fixed features such as stairways, booklifts, elevators, entrance details, and circulation areas.

The ultimate size and shape of the building may affect the original size and location that should be given these features. In college libraries, for instance, the location of the technical processes area may be affected. Frequently it is difficult to enlarge these areas or change their locations at a later date. The original planning should be done with the ultimate building in mind so that these adjustments can be made in the future.

Seldom is this point stressed sufficiently in statements of program. In many it is not even mentioned. A further handicap is that the architect may not relish the extra cost of designing, even in preliminary sketches, a larger building than he may be paid for designing.

*Individual Studies:* The statement of program should be based on the library needs of the particular community or the particular college being studied. For example, it is well known that the educational status of the community is perhaps the most important factor in the amount of use that is made of a public library.

Yet program after program is based on average standards, without adjustments for variation in the educational status of the community. The work and the insight which went into the establishment of these various published standards are truly magnificent. However they *are* averages and should be considered as such. A library building designed on those standards in a community in which the educational average is one third or more above the national average is likely to prove inadequate very shortly after it is erected. We have seen that unfortunate situation occur many times.

*Favorite Designs:* It is a habit of some who prepare statements of program to attempt to apply, in almost all cases, one's own favorite preference in building design. Some are wedded to extreme versions of the modular design in the mistaken belief that this is the answer to all problems of flexibility.

Some planners are tied to the core arrangement in which a main stairway, an elevator, and a bookstack arrangement of two levels or more are grouped in one area of the building. However, in some cases these very features are obstructions to flexibility and future expansion.

Some who emphasize, as we all do, the necessity of a grade level entrance, are fond of mezzanines in reading rooms in spite of several facts: that mezzanines are usually a handicap to flexibility, that older public library users will find it difficult to climb the stairs, that the percentage of these older public library users (who are also taxpayers) is rapidly increasing, and finally, that the high area not covered by the mezzanine constitutes a cubic footage which will have to be heated in winter and cooled in summer yet is not used.

*Written Reports:* To some it may seem axiomatic and therefore superfluous to say that all consultants' reports should be in writing. Yet there are librarians, active as consultants, who avoid written reports as much as possible. One told me quite frankly that he did not wish to undertake any consulting work which involved written reports. He would contract for a day's service, visit the community and the library in the morning, discuss the problem with the librarian and/or the board in the afternoon and perhaps evening, and then go home and send a bill. This practice is wrong; this practice is very wrong, but this practice is not at all unusual in college libraries as well as in public libraries. It is not uncommon for a college administration, faced with an urgent library expansion problem, to call in half a dozen individual consultants on different days. Each goes over the same problem with the library staff and the architect in the morning, meets with various committees in the early afternoon, and about 4:00 P.M. gives his views verbally to a full meeting of the building committee, the architect's representative, and university officials.

Now I suppose that this procedure might be dignified by the term "consultation service" for lack of any other label. However, it cannot be called library building consultation service in the sense in which I am attempting to discuss the term. This is not to say that in such a case the consultant's advice is not good; it is probably excellent. It is simply that there is not enough of it. When a library is spending hundreds of thousands and often millions of dollars on a library building the project needs and deserves more than the casual haphazard consultation service furnished by a few verbal discussions.

Furthermore, sometimes it is difficult for us to remember that reports should be written, not for librarians, but for library laymen, who may be board members or other local leaders or architects, or college officials, and who often have a high intelligence sharpened by skepticism, and are not likely to accept as "manna from Heaven" a bald statement unsupported by reason.

*Sketches for Architects:* Some consultants like to draw outline plans for architects. This practice is of such questionable advantage that it may not be too extreme an admonition to say: *Never* attempt to draw a sketch for a client in order to illustrate an idea. It can be expressed clearly enough in writing, if sufficient care is taken.

Designing a plan is an architect's responsibility and prerogative. Often an architect, trained as he is, can come up with a solution to a problem that is quite different from the sketch a consultant or a client might draw, and yet is a better solution, provided the requirements and possible alternatives have been accurately and fully set forth in writing.

Within these limits the architect's imagination should be allowed free rein, unconstricted by those unacquainted with problems of architectural design and structure. On the other hand, it
is important that the client and the librarian should retain their
dominant positions and their freedom of choice as critics and
judges.

One of the most practical aids to an architect is a full discussion of the projected arrangement of facilities. Too many statements of program do not go into sufficient detail in this respect.
For instance, in a public library project for an average-sized library, the survey may stop with a few general remarks such as:

It is advantageous if all public service departments can be
kept on one floor. If this is impossible, the Children's Room
of X number of square feet may be moved to another level.

Beyond this, if adult public services must be split, the
first and, hopefully, the only department to be moved to
another floor should be Arts and Music.

It would be of much more assistance to the architect if, for
instance, Arts and Music, in the case cited, were specifically expressed in square feet, shelving needs, and seating. In most public
libraries it is helpful if the entire departmental organization is
discussed in its relationship, department to department.

In the college field, the situation is a little more difficult. The
typical academic library will frequently have more stories or
floors devoted to public services than the average public library.
The architect needs information as to the future needs of major
book classifications and related seating, expressed in square feet.
If land is limited, or if the new building must be an addition, the
architect may be very much in need of this information.

Consultants are often loathe to make such detailed guesses.

This is understandable, for nobody can foretell the future with accuracy. As Stephen McCarthy says: "It is almost impossible to keep books and readers in phase as the years pass." Yet somebody should try to make these future estimates for the guidance of the architect. For example, in the case of one undergraduate college library, the report divided the books into three main classes by related subject, and an estimate was made that Group A subjects might constitute approximately 42 percent of the future book stock, Group B subjects, 41 percent, Group C subjects, 17 percent. After explaining the advantages of the intermixing of books and readers, it was estimated on the basis of comparative amount of use, that Group A might require 50 percent of the seats, Group B, 35 percent, and Group C, 15 percent.

Translating these percentages into books and reader seats, and then into square feet, the report recommended 31,000 square feet for Group A, 26,000 square feet for Group B, and 11,000 square feet for Group C.

Following this were a few paragraphs explaining how, in a small floor area, subject classes of books become divided more frequently and, because of lack of space, related material must be shelved on different floor levels, constituting an obstruction to the effective use of the resources, and explaining further that librarians have found that these obstructions inhibit the use of the materials.

*Equipment Lists:* Very few statements of program contain equipment lists based on future needs. Yet an equipment list, provided it is complete, is a very effective check against the calculations for square footage of the various rooms and areas, and also of the entire building.

It is interesting to note that in a great percentage of cases the total building measurements for a public library need to be 10 to 25 percent more than one would expect from the formulas expressed in library literature in various sizes of communities. This points up the remark made earlier that these formulas, splendid helps that they are, nevertheless suffer because they are averages, and because they are based on the past.

These formulas would prove to be even more inadequate were it not for the fact that many of the buildings on which the statistics are based were constructed during the time when library architecture was characterized by rotundas, grand staircases, and other waste space, part of which modern architecture has been able to eliminate.

As has been stated, the equipment list is not effective unless it is complete. *Every* piece of equipment which requires floor space should be included. It is sometimes surprising how much extra space is found to be needed beyond the usual requirements for shelving and seats. It may be well to follow the principle, that if there is any question regarding the need for an item, the question should be answered in the affirmative. This stage of the planning is not the time for compromises.

It may be objected that it is impossible to estimate accurately the amount of equipment that will be needed in the building twenty years hence. This may be the case. Nevertheless, the attempt should be made; otherwise, why try to plan at all?

Admittedly, preparing an equipment list is a very slow and painstaking process. It means more costly consulting work. It also means the consulting work will be that much more valuable to the client.

REVIEWS OF PLANS

It is frequently assumed, by those inexperienced in dealing with architects (and by "inexperienced" I mean those who have worked on fewer than five or six library buildings) that, given a reasonably adequate statement of program, the architect can proceed to devise a good library plan, and the client will need very little further assistance from the consultant. On the contrary, experience indicates that at least one third of the total consultant time on the project, and sometimes as much as one half, should be devoted to reviews of plans. The reviews, like the statement of program, should be in writing and in detail.

One such review can best take place immediately after the architect prepares his earliest sketches. This is the time in which the architect can make changes in his sketches with comparative ease. Sometimes the review may cause him to change his entire concept of his design. It is not fair to the architect to allow the designing to proceed too far without making a thorough review of the plan. The architect's drafting room is his factory, and in most cases he receives no more compensation for having to do a job over again.

Here is where the first compromises may need to be made, where the consultant needs a true sense of perspective, to know when and on what items to agree to a compromise, and where many mistakes can be made by failing to be sufficiently stubborn and insistent about important points.

Perhaps it will be worthwhile at this point to consider the approach which most architects take toward their assignments and the attitude which the consultant should have. The architect must be an artist but also a businessman. After he obtains the client's initials in the lower righthand corner of his drawings it becomes increasingly difficult and sometimes expensive for the client to have changes made. This is as it should be. However, consider that fact in the perspective of the architect's training; that training is largely in aesthetics. It is true that the architectural schools and colleges spend a great deal of time and effort in teaching the budding architect the theory of the functional approach. Perhaps they do every bit as well with it as can be expected. The fact remains that in any conflict between the aesthetic and the functional, most architects are by inclination and training likely to lean toward the aesthetic.

There is nothing wrong with this. On the contrary, I would not have it any other way; for we all want beauty in our architecture and who is to supply it if not the architect.

What is needed in any conflict between the aesthetic and the functional, and there are always several such conflicts, is a person who is trained and knowledgeable in the functional aspects of library buildings and who knows how to interpret plans, to uphold the functional interest just as capably as the architect will look out for the aesthetic. That person must be the consultant. It is naïve to think that the college administration or the public library board can do it; it is also usually futile to hope that the client librarian can do it.

This job requires much training and it requires experience on many library projects. It requires an ability to read and understand the drawings with facility. More important, it requires an ability to put into proper perspective the problem at issue, to know when to compromise, when to give up the functional in favor of aesthetic considerations, and, on the other hand, when to stand firmly for the functional and insist that the architect should find some other aesthetic solution than the one he is advocating. This is one reason why the consultant should be engaged by and work for the owner, not the architect. Otherwise, the architect will be free to accept or ignore the consultant's recommendations, as he sees fit; whereas it is the owner who should reserve the right to make these decisions. This is why those consultants who are content to spend a day here and a day there examining sketches with clients are doing a most unfortunately superficial job and may do their clients more harm than good.

Before passing on to the next phase of this discussion it may be pertinent to consider also the reviews of plans offered by the various Building Institutes held in connection with ALA Conventions. No doubt everybody will agree that those reviews of plans have done a tremendous amount of good, not only for the institution whose plans are discussed, but also for the several hundred librarians, faculty, and trustees who listen to and sometimes participate in the discussions.

It would be advantageous, however, if some way could be found to emphasize sufficiently, and officially, to all concerned that no more than a very superficial analysis can be offered in this manner; that bad advice as well as good advice may be given, because any one is privileged to speak; and that those who offer plans for analysis should not assume, therefore, that they are getting authoritative consulting service gratis. It is surprising how many librarians think this casual advice is all they need. Consultants who had furnished the Statement of Program for a large library received a letter which said in part: "I had not planned on a review of our plans prior to presenting them at

[ALA] since the content of that program is in the nature of a review and criticism. . . . I will discuss with [the Board] whether we feel further general consultation is desirable in view of the costs involved."

## CONSULTANTS' QUALIFICATIONS AND CHARACTERISTICS

Keyes Metcalf, in a paper delivered at a Building Institute a few years ago, gave an excellent outline of the qualifications a consultant should have, and no repetition is needed here. It may be worth mentioning, however, that a person can be an excellent library administrator and yet be a poor library building planner —and that a person can be a good library planner and yet be a poor consultant. Sometimes this is because, as Metcalf says, the consultant is not articulate; often it is because of other personal characteristics.

A good consultant must be able to see the other side of the question, willing to have his views questioned critically without being offended, and willing to admit error and yet stand firmly for his opinions if the issue is important enough. In short, he must be objective.

The dominant need of many consultants today, though some obviously do not realize it, is training and experience. There are some who are ambitious for consulting work, including some on the so-called ALA list of consultants, who are definitely lacking in the necessary experience.

It is unfortunate that with many millions of dollars being spent on library buildings throughout the country, this important matter should be treated in such haphazard fashion. Admittedly, ALA should not set itself up as a judge of the qualifications of building consultants. However, the inference, if not an actual statement, is that all those on the ALA list of building consultants are qualified. It is unfortunate if this list is sent to inquirers without an accompanying statement that no attempt has been made to judge the experience or the capability of those on the list. A few examples may serve to illustrate this.

There is, for instance, a statement of program, prepared by a consultant who is on the ALA's list. The statement attempts to describe the public library needed by a certain city with an estimated future population of 55,000 people. For this population, the statement recommends a library with a total area of only 20,000 square feet. Even the twenty-five-year-old Wheeler and Githens formula recommends about 50 percent more space than that.

Furthermore, there is, in this particular statement of program, no attempted substantiation of the recommended size. Then again, no detail whatsoever is given to break down this recommended square footage into its component parts.

As another example, there is a statement of program for a certain college library, which specifies a number of doublefaced book stack units, for each of which is allocated an area of 13½ square feet. Now this is adequate for the average book stack unit and its lengthwise aisle. However, the total square footage needed for book stacks as recommended in this statement of program was obtained merely by multiplying the recommended number of book stack units by this average of 13½ square feet. No consideration was given to any cross-aisles. The omission was, in fact, recognized, but it was avoided by stating that the end aisles would probably be shared by table aisles. No consideration was given to the possibility that, in some areas, the length of book stack ranges might have to be quite short, depending upon the arrangement of the area, thus requiring considerable space for cross-aisles. No consideration was given to the possibility that it might be desirable or even necessary to utilize wider aisles in some arrangements; no consideration was given to the possibility that it might be desirable or even necessary to utilize, in some arrangements, book shelving less than seven shelves high.

In the same statement, there was a recommendation of 25 square feet per reader for all reading areas and this was supposed to be sufficient to cover, in addition to tables and chairs, all other reference equipment such as atlas cases, dictionary stands, map cases, microfilm readers, attendants' desks, and a host of similar items.

As a third example, there is a statement of program, also written by a consultant on the ALA suggested list—and, I may add, one who has had many assignments—which specifies approximately 30,000 total square feet for a new public library building. There is neither an indication of the future population estimate upon which this recommendation was based, nor an indication of the educational or financial level of the community. In fact, there is no background information whatsoever.

A recommendation is offered regarding the location of the future building, but no evidence is offered to support the recommendation. For architectural requirements, items such as stairways, elevators, corridors, heating and ventilation, wall thicknesses, custodial requirements, and rest rooms, the statement allows less than 10 percent of the total building area.

In general, it may be said that among the many statements of program examined in the preparation of this paper, it was quite common to find recommendations for a quantity of book housing or seating without square footage recommendations; or to find square footage recommendations without any substantiating detail. Then there are recommendations like these: "Shelf space for six sets of encyclopedias should be available," with no information given the architect about the space required. Again, "Three or four tables are needed in this immediate area," but there is no indication of how large the tables should be, how many seats there should be, or how many square feet are required.

There are naïve assumptions that it is sufficient to indicate the floor size of a piece of equipment without considering the space needed around it. One obtains the impression from some of these statements that the architect is expected to be a magician and thus be able to fill in the gaps between the general guidelines offered.

THE COST OF CONSULTING WORK

Some qualified consultants charge very little; in fact, some consultants have been known to give consulting service on library buildings to neighboring libraries free of charge. This laudable generosity may be unwittingly misleading, if the client thinks he is getting complete and adequate consulting service. On the other hand, at least two consulting organizations exist whose total fees average three-fourths of 1 percent of the total project cost.

Some qualified consultants may make trips away from their home bases, spending a day or so with the client and then another very few days writing a report, and this practice too, may result in a very superficial piece of work and one that can cause positive harm. I am sure most, if not all, of these men are genuinely interested in doing a thorough job, but have different ideas than do some others as to what constitutes thorough consulting work.

This situation is well illustrated by statements which appear in Ellsworth's book, *Planning the College and University Library Building:*

> One hundred and fifty dollars a day plus expenses is a normal nominal fee for an experienced consultant. . . .
> The amount of time a consultant spends . . . would be somewhat as follows: A preliminary meeting of three to five days—studying the local problem and getting a first draft of the program written . . . a second meeting of one or two days on the site problem and another two days on the final draft of the program. After the architect has developed preliminary plans there will usually be a series of short meetings to discuss the plans. From this point on, careful studies of the plans should be made with the librarian and other local officials not just for layout but for all aspects of lighting, heating and ventilation, location of control, etc. A college planning a million and one half dollar building should budget $1,500.00 for this kind of consultation service [pp. 24–25].

In other words, ignoring consideration of travel expenses for the moment, we are to assume that consultant service for a total of ten days would be sufficient to write the program, analyze the preliminary plans, and study the later plans in detail. How are we to reconcile this thinking with that of others, which would indicate that something like ten times the Ellsworth estimate is needed for a thorough job?

Ralph Ellsworth does not mind having his views questioned, and so I wrote him, and after a couple of exchanges of correspondence I received this letter: "I think the answer to the question about the time required for a consultation is that we are talking about different kinds of problems. I am talking about the kind of situation when there is a competent and experienced architect and a librarian who has ideas and knows how to get the job done."

Ah, but Ellsworth made no such qualification in his book, and who is to judge whether the librarian "knows how to get the job done" when he has had little or no building experience? Furthermore, the reference was quoted without any qualification whatsoever in a paper delivered by Metcalf at a Building Institute and printed in the *ALA Bulletin* of December 1963. Perhaps a great many librarians, both college and public, may have included in their budgets an allowance for building consultation service which is grossly inadequate.

It is certain that the depth of consulting service which has been discussed in this paper simply cannot be rendered for any such paltry sum as one tenth of 1 percent of the building budget. As Charles Mohrhardt has said, ten times that percentage is more accurate for a mediumsized building.

There may be valid objections to the theory that the statement of program should be written by the local librarian with some help from the consultant. The program, to be truly and certainly objective, should be written by an outside consultant. For best results, the consultant should serve the owner, the institution, not the librarian. The librarian, as a representative of the owner, should remain in a position to recommend acceptance or rejection of any recommendation in the statement, and he should be a part of the consulting team; but he should desire, for best results, that the original recommendations come from the outside.

SOME SUGGESTIONS FOR IMPROVING
CONSULTING STANDARDS

Two suggestions come to mind for the improvement of consulting service for library buildings.

One is to have the consulting service performed by groups of three or four consultants who can check each others' work. Without exception, there is no one person in the country who is knowledgeable enough and experienced enough to be entrusted with the preparation of a complete statement of program for a library, and to review its architectural sketches, without considerable experienced assistance. One may be splendid at setting up a future departmental organization; another may be expert at technical processes; a third may excel at estimating detailed space requirements; and a fourth may be better at interpreting plans and suggesting improvements. One of the four may be adept at writing. A group operation takes advantage of the strong points of each consultant and will avoid errors of judgment which almost inevitably occur in a one-person consultantship.

The other suggestion is prompted by this question: How can the conflicts of opinion of which we have previously spoken, and which are confusing to a librarian who is seeking assistance, be clarified and brought into reasonable control for the benefit of both clients and consultants? I realize that I may be treading on thin ice when I suggest adding yet another set of initials to the many which now cover various aspects of librarians' activities. However, might it not be feasible to have an Association of Library Consultants which could do the sort of thing that the AIA (American Institute of Architects) does so well for the architectural profession?

What could such an association do? A few objectives may be listed for library consultation work alone; there may be others for other types of library consultation. Such an association might:

1. Define the extent of good consultation work.
2. Set standards for qualification of individuals as members of the Association of Library Consultants.

3. Provide means whereby those who are interested in consultation work can achieve much needed training and experience, to replace the hit-or-miss methods of today.
4. Clarify the percentage of the building budget which should be allocated to consultation work if a qualified consultant is to participate.
5. Provide a clearing house of building information for the benefit of its members.

It seems to me that library consulting work, and in particular that part of it which has to do with library buildings, needs some sort of organized effort to establish and maintain high standards.

# 6 Survey of Library Administration: Budget and Finance

JOHN A. HUMPHRY

LIBRARIES have made real gains with respect to support during the past several years, along with hard-won rceognition and general acceptance of the services they provide. A study of the finances of a library and of its services necessarily requires an evaluation of virtually every other factor that relates to its operation. While it does not always follow that an effective library program is the result of adequate support, the two factors are, of course, related. Before discussing a surveyor's investigation of a library's finances, it may be helpful to take note of the changing patterns in sources of library support.

## PUBLIC LIBRARIES AND LIBRARY SYSTEMS

Many public libraries can trace their origins to the philanthropies of the eighteenth and early nineteenth centuries when association, subscription, apprentice, athenaeum, or some other form of private library was established. In New England, especially, public libraries were established and financed by entrepreneurs who also controlled the economy of the villages that grew up around their mills or other business or industrial establishments.

By the middle of the nineteenth century states began the enactment of legislation which permitted communities to establish public libraries and support them through appropriations from public funds. A retrospective view of the financial history of the public library movement in this country shows this to be more significant than the more recent trend toward state and federal financial participation in providing public library service. The financial participation by other than local units of government is a natural result of the changing tax structure.

During the last thirty years, the federal government has outdistanced by a large margin the tax collecting roles of either state or local governments, despite the fact that the state and local governments are each collecting more money. For example, in 1932 local governments collected 53.6 percent of all taxes paid; in 1961 they collected 16.9 percent. In 1932 the federal government collected 22.7 percent of all tax receipts, but by 1961 this figure had risen to 66.7 percent. The change in percent of tax receipts by states was much less dramatic and significant—only a 7 percent drop in receipts took place during this thirty year period. It follows, of course, that with the increase in tax collections at the federal level, there has been a corresponding increase in expenditures by the federal government.

An analysis of these trends and figures shows that local governments are receiving an ever-increasing proportion of their revenue from federal and state grants, and state governments are receiving increased sums from federal grants. The system works both ways; one fifth of state revenues in the early 1960s came from local governments and the federal government. Furthermore, analysis and study of these expenditures and trends reveals the fact that all levels of government are becoming increasingly concerned with education, including library service.

While it has been a long-standing tradition that local governments have given public libraries and institutions of higher education property-tax exemptions, and state governments and the federal government have not collected taxes on the incomes of publicly-supported, charitable, and educational institutions, there is now concerted action to encourage direct subsidies for education and libraries through grants by the state and federal governments. In addition, incentive for giving to libraries has been increased recently; taxpayers may include gifts to public libraries in computing the maximum deduction of 30 percent to charitable and educational agencies on their federal income-tax returns.

Twenty-five to thirty years ago the measure of adequacy of a library's financial support, and thereby its effectiveness, was thought to be the application of a per capita figure to its level of expenditure.

During the intervening years, however, the Public Library Division of the American Library Association, prepared a study entitled *Public Library Service* which treats the subject from a qualitative point of view. In the process of change of emphasis from quantitative evaluations, it was clearly apparent that the per capita figure was virtually meaningless in evaluating public library service. This fact is even more true in view of the development of systems of public libraries and the interdependence of all kinds of libraries. If one wishes a per capita cost figure, one need only divide the number of people in a service area into the cost of providing an *acceptable* level of service. A base figure of financial adequacy, therefore, must be built by determining the personnel, resources, building, and service program requirements after having formulated a statement of objectives and goals. This per capita figure will be in inverse proportion to the size of the population served; the smaller the number of people served the higher the per capita cost.

In view of the foregoing, the library surveyor cannot be content merely to identify and tally sources of support, and amounts spent for various components of library service; he must also analyze and probe deeply into the statement of goals and objectives of the library as they relate to methods of operation, management, and statistics of library use. Percentages of support from local, state, federal, and private funds must be determined as well as budgeted allocations made to personnel, books and other materials, building maintenance, and other operating costs, including capital improvements and public relations. If the surveyor learns that a sum which is indefensible is being received from state and federal sources, does this mean that local initiative and pride are being stifled instead of encouraged or does this

mean that the library is serving a much larger role? What kind
of proportion can be justified insofar as participation by the
three levels of government is concerned? Should there be a one
third contribution from each or should such support depend on
whether the library is a member, a central, or headquarters library in a system of libraries, or a resource center for a larger
geographical region? To what extent has local support increased
since state and/or federal funds have been a source of inspiration
to local communities in providing more interest and support? Answers to such questions will not have much meaning unless figures are assembled, maintained, and evaluated over a span of several years; then meaningful trends can be observed and valid
recommendations made.

Support for libraries which are part of a system is not always
supplied in money. The surveyor must determine if payments in
books or other library materials are provided as incentives to
join and retain membership in a system. Professional direction
and consultant services are other payments to a library, especially for smaller units that previously have not had the advantage of such direction. In many instances libraries serving as administrative headquarters or central libraries receive, in addition
to money grants, such benefits as supplemental book collections,
educational and documentary films, additional staff members,
and larger physical facilities for assuming additional responsibilities. It is essential, however, to carefully analyze such remunera-
tion, whether in money or kind, to determine the extent to
which reimbursement is fair. The foregoing will, I believe, serve
to point out the need for careful study of a library's financial
support—regardless of source—as we move toward greater cooperation among various kinds of libraries.

The interdependence of libraries, long under discussion and
now becoming a reality, is the next step in general library development following the formulation and acceptance of standards
by library leaders for the various types of libraries. An example
of this interdependence, cooperative effort, joint responsibility,
and financial participation by many agencies can be described
from my own experience.

In 1960, Massachusetts enacted legislation establishing regional library service and providing grants-in-aid to local public libraries that met certain standards of service. The Western Region includes cities in which several strong libraries are located, namely Springfield, Northampton, Pittsfield, Greenfield, and North Adams. The Springfield Library was named headquarters library to direct the administration of the system and the other four shared in the direction. All five serve as resource centers. For this service Massachusetts provides about $186,000 annually to these five libraries. In addition to assistance in administration, credits for books, films, and other resources are made available.

One of the interesting features of the plan for the Western Region is its financial structure. The appropriation from the state includes a sum of money to pay a membership fee for the Forbes Library of Northampton in the Hampshire Inter-Library Center, a cooperative venture including Smith, Mt. Holyoke, and Amherst College libraries, and the University of Massachusetts Library. Thus, in addition to already existing resources, the Western Massachusetts Regional Public Library System has immediate access to a collection of books of considerable depth, and numbering more than a million volumes. The state pays the membership fee authorized and approved by its division of library extension; the public libraries receive service for their more serious readers from college and university library collections, and there is more adequate financial support for the four-college cooperative library system. The system is a happy interdependence among libraries, avoiding unnecessary duplication of effort and expense and involving support from local, state, federal, and private endowment funds.

In addition to the growing interdependence of libraries, caused by state and other large units of service bringing total library resources into efficient relationships, contract service is developing making it possible for smaller communities to purchase library service from a larger library instead of setting up additional expensive independent service organizations. The savings in overhead expenses, such as administration and book processing, are worthy of mention. Interstate compacts are also being implemented whereby state library extension agencies can legally support service programs that are not completely contained within the boundaries of a single state.

A study of the standards for public, school, college, university, state, and special libraries shows the necessity for building a system based on adequate and inviting physical facilities, qualified personnel, good resources, and the other special requirements for quality service. These standards do not propose an arbitrary figure per person upon which a budget is prepared. Budgets for public libraries can be divided into three principal categories: salaries, collections or resources, and all other operating expenses.

Salaries should be further divided into professional and nonprofessional categories, including subprofessional, trainee or college graduates, plus costs of benefits for personnel. Resources include books, periodicals, newspapers, films, recordings, microfilm, miscellaneous materials, and binding. Other operating expenses include custodial costs, maintenance of buildings and equipment, supplies, travel, and fixed costs such as dues, rent, and insurance. Salary costs should comprise approximately 70 percent of total expenditures, resources about 15 percent, and all other expenses 15 percent. Variations in these percentages will depend upon the section of the country and the degree of independence with which the library operates or to the extent that it serves as a link in a system of libraries.

SCHOOL LIBRARIES

School library service should be developed in the same way as any other kind of library program. Standards have been carefully devised to guide the educator, administrator, librarian, and teacher in placing this important educational function in proper perspective with respect to the complete educational program for youth. The school library takes its direction from the philosophy of the school itself, but there are specific and attainable goals outlined in the standards, from which cost figures can be computed. A surveyor will wish to become acquainted with the attitudes and convictions of all concerned with the school library and its service, from the policy maker and chief school officers to teachers and students.

After the surveyor has become acquainted with the educational program, philosophy, and convictions of the state board of education, the administrative officers, and the supervisor of school library development in the state department of education, as well as with the corresponding program and personnel at the local level, the following specific questions should be answered and recommendations and direction for the future based on the answers:

1. Are funds for regular library books being provided in schools with 200 to 249 students, at least in the range of between $1000.00 and $1500.00 annually? In schools with enrollments of 250 or more students, are funds provided to purchase books at the rate of between $4.00 and $6.00 per student?

     These figures are not compiled for establishment grants nor are they to include systematic purchase and replacement for such reference materials as dictionaries, encyclopedias, magazines, and pamphlets. Funds for binding, rebinding, supplies, and equipment are also to be considered additional. The school library book collection to which these quantitative standards apply involves books used by students in the completion of assignments and in their personal enrichment.

2. Are books also purchased to support a collection of professional materials for the administration and faculty? Dependent upon the needs and size of the faculty, between $200 and $800 will be required annually for such a collection, plus supplies and equipment.

3. Is the provision of audiovisual materials the responsibility of the school library personnel? If so, the school library budget should include $2.00 to $6.00 per pupil for such materials in addition to money required for the general and professional collections just described.

The surveyor will also check the adequacy of physical facilities, the personnel program, and staffing patterns to determine to what extent the necessary service is being provided and also to learn if sufficient staff is provided to do all the tasks that must be performed. It should also be determined if the library is being used as a study hall, for lectures, and other nonlibrary functions since this dissipation of library use will be reflected in its financial picture. It should be emphasized that a materials instruction center, a district materials center, and an audiovisual center will require greater financial support because of space, personnel, and resource needs.

Under the newly enacted federal Elementary and Secondary Education Act of 1965, substantial sums of money will be available for school library development through direction from the state departments of education. Surveyors will need to become familiar with the terms of all legislation, state and federal, in evaluating a library's finances and to make certain that the school is receiving all the support to which it may be legally entitled.

## COLLEGE AND UNIVERSITY LIBRARIES

College and university libraries have undergone an equally dramatic change in their development since the turn of the century. Service patterns have been revised to meet such challenges as revolutionary revisions and expansion in the curriculum, the emphasis on independent study and research, the startling increase in knowledge, book, and periodical production in all fields and the numbers of students entering institutions of higher learning. Perhaps the most heartening and significant impetus for college and university library growth, however, has been the financial interest and support by foundations, individuals, corporations, and alumni. This kind of activity has had the salutary effect of giving the library increased status and recognition by college trustees and administrators. The Carnegie Corporation deserves special mention in this instance for pointing out the need of adequately financed college libraries to support educational programs. The Ford and Rockefeller Foundations have also been instrumental in focusing attention on the need for substantial support of higher education, including college and university libraries. The Council on Library Resources has made possible many significant library studies which have provided benefits, some indirectly, to libraries of every kind. Accreditation standards have also had profound and beneficial effects on college and university libraries since an adequate library with a defined statement of purpose is a requirement for accreditation.

While, as a general rule, a college library should receive a budget of no less than 5 percent of the total operating budget of the college, the librarian should build a budget request based on need. The surveyor must acquaint himself with the general academic program of the college and its courses of instruction before he can intelligently analyze the adequacy of the budget. As is the case with the public and school librarian, the college librarian will present to his superiors, usually the college president, financial officer, who is often a vice-president, and sometimes the academic dean, a budget request based on providing a collection of books and other communication media serviced by a qualified staff in a functional building with a service program based on supporting the curriculum and stimulating students to use and love books on their own.

Principal sources of support for the college library are:

1. The general income which supports the college.
2. Endowment income—usually restricted to books in particular fields or to special collections.
3. Foundation grants, individual, and corporate gifts, including funds raised by friends or alumni groups.
4. Public funds.

Examples of miscellaneous sources include income from fines, telephones, and sale of duplicates.

Another method used in checking the adequacy of the library budget is the student formula, that is, an adequate college library program requires expenditures of between $50.00 and $80.00 per student. As in public library per capita support figures, these costs per student vary inversely to the size of the student population. A surveyor should use such a rule of thumb with caution, since it is no better as a guide for college and university library finances than a per capita cost figure is for the public library. More important, however, a financial evaluation of the college library should provide answers to such questions as:

1. Does the college library receive the *additional* funds needed when a curriculum revision is approved? Is the book collection and book budget sufficiently generous to provide adequate numbers of copies for undergraduate level courses and for broad coverage in all disciplines and all schools in the college or university?

2. Are the programs of instruction and the college library's service program parallel?

3. Do faculty interests and requirements distort the library budget or are allowances made for these factors?

4. Are specific and approved working and cooperative relationships established with other academic libraries?

5. Are allocations of funds included in the budget divided properly? The usual distribution is 60–70 percent for salaries, the remainder divided equally between collections and all other operating costs.

SPECIAL LIBRARIES

The finances of libraries which are part of a business, industry, or private cultural agency are linked with the organizations the libraries serve. Little has been written about the financial structure and support of the special library. The general pattern of organization, however, parallels the school, college, or university library in that a study of the functions and finances of the parent organization will determine the functions and finances of the library.

The administrator of the special library should work with his immediate superior in determining the scope and extent of library services desired. From this decision can come a financial plan for producing such a service. Personnel will usually be subject specialists in their particular fields in addition to having library education or experience. Thus, salary costs may exceed the standard of 65 to 70 percent generally used in proportioning budgets of public and college libraries. It may be that costs of supplies, materials, and services will not be charged to a library budget. Support will usually depend on the ability of the librarian to convince the administrative officer to whom he is responsible of the value of the service, the extent the library is used, and how well the library staff serves the personnel in the organization. In every kind of library or information center, support is directly related to acceptance and respect for service rendered.

In summary, a surveyor should study the finances of a library with the following principles in mind:

1. The library serves an educational function, and its budget and personnel program should support the philosophy.

2. The annual operating budget reflects the program of service for the ensuing year, and serves as a tool in long range as well as immediate planning. Budget requests should be prepared from cost accounting figures, and where possible, unit costs included to show actual prices paid for books, supplies, equipment, and other materials. Salaries to be paid for all classes of positions should also be included in the budget request. It is difficult and in some instances impossible to reduce library service to a dollar figure, but where possible it should be done.

3. The budget message should stress the need for larger libraries to assume roles of leadership and permit smaller libraries to participate in cooperative ventures. This message should be part of a statement of goals and objectives.

4. The responsible staff will assist in the preparation and justification of the budget to assure their knowledge of the library's program. Very often, the library's budget will carry requests for expenditures that appear in no other municipal, college, industrial, school, or state budget. It is therefore necessary to explain these requests to appropriating authorities in clear concise terms, intelligible to the layman. In particular, the school librarian should be permitted to recommend a budget, be included on a curriculum study committee and other academic committees, and

be told the budget under which he is expected to operate during the ensuing year.

5. The budget should be flexible enough to permit some degree of judgment on the part of the administrator but not foster irresponsible actions.

6. Efficiency and economy are vital factors in financial administration. Specific spot checking should be done by a surveyor to determine if:

   a. Professional personnel are assigned professional tasks.

   b. Periodic review and study of work processes and procedures are made.

   c. New services are instituted only after present services are made qualitative, and when new funds are provided.

7. Performance or program budgeting should be considered for adoption. This type of budget involves the preparation, analysis, and interpretation of the financial plan in terms of services and activity programs rather than outlining and preparing in detail a list of anticipated disbursements. Performance budgeting requires the establishment of cost accounting methods if it is to be executed properly. It is usually difficult for libraries to determine units of measurement and to find a common set of standards to measure results. Its advantages, however, include the fact that a library can tell at a glance what its various kinds of services cost in terms of personnel, books, supplies, and maintenance as well as administration and book processing. Librarians should become acquainted with this type of budgetary procedure, in view of its rapid and widespread acceptance by fiscal authorities.

8. Each annual budget should be prepared as if it were the first. Use last year's figures but don't neglect to examine carefully the library program and prepare the budget so that it will permit a sound and dynamic service. The budget should be timetabled to permit recruitment of qualified personnel for authorized positions. It should take account of inflationary trends, changes in the library's constituency

such as the type and number of people served, technological developments and improvements, and necessary salary revisions.

It must be remembered that budget work and financial administration are never-ending processes. The successful administrator is one who is very well informed in fiscal matters so that he commands respect from those with whom he works as well as from his superiors.

### REFERENCES

American Association of School Librarians. *Standards for School Library Programs.* Chicago, American Library Association, 1960.

American Association of State Libraries. Survey and Standards Committee. *Standards for Library Functions at the State Level.* Chicago, American Library Association, 1963.

American Library Association. Co-Ordinating Committee on Revision of Public Library Standards. *Public Library Service; a Guide to Evaluation, with Minimum Standards.* Chicago, American Library Association, 1956.

—— Supplement. *Costs of Public Library Service, 1963.* Chicago, American Library Association, 1964.

Association of College and Research Libraries. Committee on Standards. "Standards for College Libraries." *College and Research Libraries,* 20: 274–80 (July 1959).

Bowler, Robert. *Local Public Library Administration.* Chicago, International City Managers' Association, 1964.

Council of Chief State School Officers. *Responsibilities of State Departments of Education for School Library Services.* Washington, Council of Chief State School Officers, 1961.

Frodin, Reuben. "Finance and the College Library." *Library Quarterly* 24: 374–81 (October 1954).

Lyle, Guy R. *The Administration of the College Library.* Third Edition. New York, H. W. Wilson Company, 1961.

Municipal Finance Officers' Association. *Performance Budgeting for Libraries.* Chicago, The Association, 1954.

Special Libraries Association. Professional Standards Committee.

"Objectives and Standards for Special Libraries." *Special Libraries* 55:672–80 (December 1964).

U.S. Bureau of Census. *Summary of Governmental Finances.* Washington, The Bureau, 1962.

Wheeler, Joseph L., and Goldhor, Herbert. *Practical Administration of Public Libraries.* New York, Harper and Row, 1962.

Wilson, Louis R., and Tauber, Maurice F. *The University Library: the Organization, Administration, and Functions of Academic Libraries.* New York, Columbia University Press, 1958.

# 7 Personnel in Library Surveys

## LOWELL A. MARTIN

LIBRARY surveys come in all sizes, shapes, and colors. Some survey reports are no more than long letters, while others require several volumes. Some are simply an outsider's opinions about current local issues, while others—such as the Joeckel and Carnovsky *A Metropolitan Library in Action* of the 1930s—point the way to the future. There is, by the way, no implication in these remarks that length necessarily equals significance.

Because of the wide variety of reports, I would like first to make some general comments about library surveys. These will serve to reveal some of my predispositions and prejudices on the subject, and should aid in evaluating my later remarks about personnel.

### GENERAL COMMENTS ON LIBRARY SURVEYS

I am constantly astonished at the number of library surveys commissioned in recent years. This no doubt reflects a healthy self-criticism on the part of librarians, and a faith in formal planning. At the same time I confess to a somewhat jaundiced view of the trend, and I find myself asking—is this survey necessary?

Let me put it this way, using the library staff to make my point. Relatively sound standards exist for library personnel in public, school, and college libraries. Many people at this conference could give the recommended figure for the size of the staff for their type of library without even referring to documents. As to the kind and quality of the staff, there is fairly wide agreement as to what constitutes a proper education for librarianship, and the profession has a procedure for accrediting educational programs for librarians. Whatever may be wrong with library education is not going to be corrected by another library survey.

My point is that any competent administrator can count his staff, consult the personnel records, refer to standards, and make his evaluation. In fact most administrators not only have done this, formally or informally, but can go beyond the figures and the formal record of education to valid observations about morale, responsibility, and productivity of the staff. The same idea is applicable to collections, organization, and other aspects of library programs. Why, then, should a survey be made by an outsider?

The usual answer is that the general standards and principles are all right to start, but they need to be adjusted and applied to the local situation. However, knowledge of the local situation is precisely what the outside surveyor lacks. Why call him in to apply general criteria to local realities which are not known to him?

It seems to me worth thinking for a few minutes about the function of the surveyor and the contribution of the survey. Surely these are not to do what the administrator should do for himself and what he in fact does. It would be hard to locate a head librarian who does not evaluate his staff in one way or another. If he cannot accomplish this with any validity, is it better to call in a surveyor or to get a new librarian? No survey can substitute for a manager in the front office and no classification and pay plan can correct lack of fairness, firmness, and judgment in human relations.

There are, of course, several proper roles for the surveyor. He may have specialized knowledge neither possessed nor expected to be possessed by the administering librarian or the local staff. Examples are the building expert, when a new structure is in prospect, or the cataloging expert, when a change in a classification system is under consideration. Or the surveyor may be called in as a friend of the court to help make the case for a line of action that the librarian wants and may already have proposed. Thus, the campaign of the chief librarian for a more competitive salary scale or for faculty status for the professional staff of a university library may need outside support. The surveyor brings his prestige to the cause or his power of convincing, or both. The expert as a witness for the prosecution has his place, so long as this downright function is clearly recognized as such, but I question this type of survey when the so-called expert is used essentially as a rubber stamp.

The survey and the surveyor seem to me most useful when they are called upon to analyze a genuinely complex situation, with disparate factors and hard alternatives ahead. The most challenging of such situations often involve more than one library: the public or university libraries throughout a state, all libraries in a metropolitan region, or the several libraries serving students in a community. Existing problems *among* libraries are not the sole or prime responsibility of any one local librarian. The survey becomes a means to engage in intensive planning not possible to administrators on the job, no matter what their capacity and leadership. In this role the surveyor becomes planner, and in a sense functions as a staff officer for a group of librarians.

What does the surveyor bring to the problem under these circumstances? Not, I hope, a ready-made plan, peddled under the guise of research; nor, I trust, a mere facility for transferring a pattern developed in another situation and trimming it here and there to fit local conditions.

The surveyor must start with a facility for absorbing the new situation, sensing its forces, appreciating its traditions. Yet he must also stay outside the situation, unattached to current movements and pressures, for he has not served his purpose if he merely picks up the prevailing view and builds around it. At the same time he must be attuned to the potentialities of the situation; certainly he cannot fly in the face of all exising forces, because this will result in a report on which no action is taken. There is a delicate question of balance here.

The surveyor must also be quick to isolate and define central problems. He must know how to bring data to bear on the problems, but beware of the surveyor who gathers every statistic within reach and keeps the punchcard operators busy overtime; the machines can give useful answers only after the right questions have been asked. Then he needs that rarest of commodities, creative capacity, held within the limits of practicability. There comes that moment in every study of significance when the data are in, the field work done, the problems neatly outlined, and no fresh, right, viable plan comes to mind. This is the moment when the surveyor wonders why he didn't stay home where he knows what should be done next and can still get in some golf on the weekends. But sometimes the light comes on and the planning process can move ahead full cycle.

Two other preliminary comments on library surveys are in order. The outsider cannot bring a sense of purpose to a library or a group of libraries where it is lacking. I often ask librarians considering a survey what their long-range objectives are, where they hope to be ten years hence. Often the answer, with just a touch of asperity, is that is why the surveyor has been called in: "You tell us what the objectives should be." This strikes me as similar to the librarian's experience when a patron comes in and requests a good book; the librarian asks what type of book he likes to read and the reply is "You tell me, that's why I'm asking." In these circumstances I doubt whether the visitor is likely to become a constant reader, and I doubt whether the librarian looking to a survey to define his basic objectives will become much of a constructive force in library development.

The surveyor should involve local leadership in his planning activity. It is easy to play the knowledgeable and enigmatic expert who reveals none of his views or conclusions until he drops a written report on the desk and promptly catches a plane, or even mails the surprise package from home. Close contact and discussion, whether informally along the way or by means of an advisory committee meeting at stated intervals, can help the visitor to absorb the real situation, stimulate useful reactions to what he believes are the central problems, and ferret out indicative responses to his conclusions while they are still tentative. This does not mean that he will adjust his report to every objection raised, but by means of pretesting the results in discussion he can often catch and eliminate the detail around which opposition may rally. The ideal survey is the one for which there is substantial agreement before the final document is written, and action to start implementing the report before it is delivered.

Also, I wish more consideration were given to the follow-up study, the survey five years after, to evaluate the progress made. Pennsylvania is one of the states that has a follow-up study, and New York is currently engaged in evaluation of the results of its 1957 legislation.

These preliminary remarks have several implications for the personnel sections of library surveys. The surveyor can seldom build up a sense of purpose in library staff members when it is lacking. The surveyor has done little if he only distributes a questionnaire to staff members, tabulates the results, and copies down standards already known to local officials. He must dig deeper not only into present competence of the staff but also into emerging needs that may not be fully apparent from the vantage point of the librarian's office or the reference desk. He may have to prepare new standards to meet the needs which he discerns. I will try to suggest some of the relevant factors as I go through the several headings usually covered in the personnel section of a library survey.

## NUMBER AND DISTRIBUTION OF STAFF MEMBERS

How many staff members should a library have? What standards should a survey use in recommending quantity of personnel? The answer is simply as many as necessary to accomplish the objectives of the library.

This answer seems clear enough, but it is far from easy to apply. Library service, unlike many other educational and communicative enterprises, is open end in character, with more and better staff members leading to greater use, and this, in turn, requiring still more staff members. The same relationship is not true of an editorial office for example, one can determine how many pages must be produced to meet a deadline, build the staff to that point, and stop; when you get full staffing you do not automatically have more pages to produce. Similarly, in staffing classrooms to a certain size, more students do not magically appear when the ratio is met. But library use increases with better service, and I have seen few libraries that have reached the saturation point. Any figure given for size of the staff must be tentative and transitory until we reach the millennium when everybody is reading everything he should.

The effect of this open-end condition can be illustrated in the experience with standards for library personnel. The public-library standards will serve as well as any for the purpose; these call for one employee per 2500 people in the service area. Some libraries have now met this standard, yet the surveyor finds them having as much difficulty meeting demands as before the build-up. Of course the standards may never have been high enough, but equally important is greater use precisely because of the staff being strengthened. It is a rash surveyor who categorically sets down a figure for staff complement necessary to meet demands. This is a little like highway planning, in which arrangements are made to build capacity highways to handle the scientifically-determined traffic count, but are out of date by the time the fa-cilities are completed; we are all familiar with the traffic jam on the brand-new superroad.

Librarians have developed guidelines for division of the staff between professional and nonprofessional positions. At an earlier stage we wanted to increase the number of professional posi-tions, and surveys in the 1930s usually recommended more trained librarians. Then the analysts observed frequent use of trained personnel for routine tasks, and advocated decreasing the professional proportion to one third or less of the total. As automation of some library functions occurs, with records kept and processes performed by fewer clerks, we may well find our-selves going the other way again and advocating a larger profes-sional ratio.

I have the impression that we may be at a turning point in this matter of the ratio of professionals to nonprofessionals. Use of many libraries is increasing in both amount and complexity, put-ting greater pressure on staff members directly in contact with the public. We can clearly see some of the factors at work: for example, greater individualization of instruction from the primary grades through the college years, or the complexity of the informational demands from our technoeconomy.

We see these developments; we tell each other that they will grow, but there are moments when I wonder whether we really believe what we say. The reaction of the profession to what is widely called "the student problem" is a case in point. I recall the critical response of a perceptive friend of mine, a nonlibrarian, to the report of the huge ALA conference on this student question a year ago. He asked me if librarians had failed to note the figures for birth rates ten or fifteen years earlier. I assured him that we had not only noted the figures but had bandied them about in our meetings. Then were we unacquainted with changes in the school curriculum, which call for more individualized work? With some indignation I said that librarians keep up with educational developments. Had we missed the fact that a larger and larger percentage of young people were going to college? Of course not. Then why the surprise at the amount of student reading, as though somebody had slipped something over on us? Why the lack of preparation for the increased student demand which all the factors indicated would occur? I found myself on the defensive, talking lamely about the lack of money to do the job.

What is next? Some unexpected and unforeseen new demand on libraries? On the contrary, what is next is a development as simple as the fact that these many students with us now will grow up, the many college students and graduate specialists will get their degrees, marry, settle down, and take jobs in the community. I make that prediction with some assurance. They will come to our libraries seeking more and better specialized materials, in keeping with their background and activities. If the reading studies have shown anything, they have forcefully established the relation between education and reading.

In five or ten years we will be talking of the "specialized reader problem" as we are talking today of the "student problem." Where will the specialized reader go for his materials? To his public library, which cannot even meet the less advanced demands of younger students? Back to his university library, which is hardpressed to serve those on campus? Some years ago we began urging students to read widely, without providing the books. Now we are preparing specialists who then move into the general community, without having libraries for them. At the moment I am making a study in California, the first state in which I have worked where the average education of adults is above the high school level, and the first state with over one third of its population engaged in formal education. California is well advanced in library development by the usual standards, but where are the resources for the people who are working in the think factories of the Santa Monica area or the specialists in the electronic research centers around the southern end of San Francisco Bay? I know that the organizations for which they work should and often do have the material needed regularly on the job, but I am talking about the whole range of reading of this new kind of community resident. If California had remained about as it was in 1950, the library program today would be approaching adequacy, but in the interval a new society has emerged.

This may seem far afield from my assigned topic of personnel in library surveys, but such underlying factors strike me as more significant than our usual standards. There is emerging a definitely growing demand for bibliographic specialists, information specialists, and subject librarians which has a direct influence on the number and kind of professional staff members needed.

We see automation moving rapidly into other fields, although it has just entered the library doors. My guess is that it will shortly be used on a larger scale in the processing and record-keeping departments. The more fundamental changes will come from basically new methods for providing access both to information and to the printed page, and unless librarians soon get more directly involved these developments are likely to come from outside the library. At any rate, there are existing forces which can be used to reduce the clerical complement of the staff.

I am not making a plea for an increase in the ratio of professionals to nonprofessionals under present organization and methods. This would only make for more librarians engaged in routine tasks. But I am saying that more professional service and more specialized service is needed for the kind of society we are becoming, not just for isolated enclaves but for broad segments of life, and unless librarians find ways to develop their existing agencies to meet these needs, new service centers and facilities will emerge outside the library.

## QUALITY OF THE STAFF

Obviously, the number and distribution of the staff is only part of the picture. Quality of personnel, we would all agree, is close to the heart of the matter. How can a survey get at this central but elusive question?

The usual methods call for a listing of the degrees held by staff members, a roster of specialties, noting of amount of continuing education, and statistics of turnover. All are relevant, but all relate more to preparation for service, the potential, rather than to actual performance. We all know that the person with the paper requirements may, for a variety of reasons, not be the person who performs best at the service desk.

I have often been struck by the fact that practicing librarians have very little built-in evaluation of how well they perform from day to day and year to year. The librarian selects some books and rejects others, but there is no direct check on whether his judgment was good or bad. The librarian answers the questions of a reader, but there is no review as to whether the response was wise, routine, or even downright inaccurate. There are times when one suspects that librarianship might be a nice spot for the mediocre performer to slide through for some years, with little more than a vague feeling on the part of the administrator that the staff member is not really up to standard.

The conditions of library performance differ, for example, from those of editing. An editor also needs broad background, a subject specialty, and experience in his craft. But the judgment of his work is quite concrete: The edited manuscript is there for evaluation as to scope, clarity, and accuracy. Most publishing houses actually have an independent research or fact verification group that double checks what the editor believes is accurate copy. Library service does not result in a tangible product (except in the case of recorded work such as bibliographies) that can be analyzed and independently evaluated. Teaching might well be thought of as comparable to librarianship, and to a degree this is true. But even in teaching there are some built-in controls. Students take standardized tests and the results can be compared. Students go on to more advanced schools or to college, and their later grade records can be checked. But of course no one would say that these objective measures fully evaluate a teacher.

Schools have developed the practice of periodic observation in the classroom by the principal and superintendent and by subject and grade coordinators. Librarians not working in schools may not realize how pervasive this evaluation practice is. It is not unusual for teachers to be observed several times a month, at unscheduled intervals, while carrying forward the regular work of the classroom. Observation, of course, can be overdone, and there are reports of teacher reaction and irritation, but for the most part both teacher and students evidently accept this as a normal relationship. The result is both genuine evaluation of teacher performance by competent supervisors, and a continuing opportunity for advice and guidance toward improved performance.

Classroom observation seldom extends up through college. Here the professor is autonomous in the classroom, and I have the distinct impression that at the college level there is some very uneven teaching, which we are likely to hear about more frequently from our very vocal college students.

I am not necessarily advocating regular observation of the librarian—working, say, at the reference desk—although I am not sure that this need be ruled out. A desk audit of activities is used in some surveys, and could be applied to library practice. My experience with evaluation of professional personnel is that if evaluation is handled carefully and fairly, staff members, who in the abstract resent or fear such control, will in time come to accept and even in some cases welcome it as a means for improving performance and building morale.

But I do believe the surveyor has the responsibility of trying to get an actual performance record of both the professional and clerical staff. It is quite possible to prepare reasonable lists of questions for reference librarians, or use sample inquiries about reading for children's librarians, and to get a degree of insight into what actually happens. I can't say that staff members welcome this—it has been so long since anyone has checked directly on what they are doing—but they usually accept it, and some even take pride in showing what they can do.

Another important consideration concerning quality of personnel which is often overlooked in library surveys is that of identification of the staff with the objectives of their library. Is there an actual decline in a sense of purpose on the part of many librarians? Is there a loss of the educational fervor of the thirties? The informational fervor of the fifties? I encounter community librarians who might as well be in industrial libraries, or research librarians who might as well be in school buildings, for all their dedication to the aims of their particular agencies. No special techniques are needed on the part of the surveyor to get at these qualities; it is surprising how much can be learned across the luncheon table, or better yet over cocktails at the end of a busy day. This is the alcohol test for the quality of library personnel: After the second cocktail, is the discussion about the opportunities of the library or about the frustrations of the job?

## SALARIES AND STATUS

Salaries are not a matter of what should be paid for a given type of work but of what the market provides. Lawyers in their first job get $50 per week, secretaries get $100 per week, and printers $200. Librarians and teachers start somewhere in the middle. Ten years later the lawyer has passed the others, the secretary has gained a little, and the librarian is still caught in the middle.

Library surveys customarily compare salaries among librarians, surveying libraries in the same locality or the same type of library nationally. This may be a useful measure when a library has fallen behind the pack, but it does not prove that salaries are adequate if they are at or above the average for the profession. The salary survey could be better extended to comparable fields of work outside librarianship, fields involving equivalent education, a similar level of judgment, and performance without close supervision. The comparison should extend to private as well as public employment, for we draw from a common and limited supply of human talent.

I would not presume to say what library salaries should be to be competitive, but I find myself hiring in one aspect of what has come to be called the knowledge industry, and I am familiar with library salary scales, so I can offer a few observations. For persons with one year of graduate study, outside of the sciences, one can get enough good candidates to have some selectivity with a basic salary range of $8,000 to $12,000 in today's market, that is $8,000 or more to start, and a chance to move ahead to $12,000 as a professional without management responsibilities. For administrative purposes it may be desirable to have two distinct grades within this range, junior and senior, but the door to advancement should be open to all sound performers. This range refers not to management or administrative assignments, but to progressively responsible professional assignments. It should be possible to move up this scale, if one has no prior experience, in well under ten years. Above this, there must be various management and administrative opportunities for those so inclined.

Actually many libraries now come up to a starting figure of more than $6,000 to $7,000 a year. However, not many double it for purely professional assignments, and salary increment is a critical factor in getting the kind of people to whom I am referring. Certainly libraries will have to do better if they are to compete, because they lack the frequent chance that business offers the exceptional person to go well beyond the $12,000 figure.

There is something of a paradox in relatively low library salaries in the face of the shortage of qualified librarians. Usually those fields in which there is a shortage, whether of good translators or of topflight nightclub entertainers, experience a definite inflation of salaries. How, exactly, does one account for the fact that some libraries have had noncompetitive salaries and vacant professional positions for some time? Wage theory tells us that if salaries are too low to get needed personnel, the rate goes up; thus, if television repairmen will not work for $2 per hour, you will soon find yourself paying double that rate to get the job done. But in libraries we often go along in dead center, with noncompetitive salaries *and* unfilled positions. The only pertinent answer is that those who control the purse strings do not really believe that it is essential to fill the library positions that are vacant.

### STAFF MORALE

Quantity, quality, and morale: there should be enough staff to do the job, quality of individuals to do it well, and morale to sustain and improve both quality and productivity. With these three dimensions, a personnel program is complete.

I am using morale in the broadest sense, ranging from attitude in staff to equity in the classification and pay plan. The various methods of personnel administration contribute to recruitment and kind of staff as well as to morale, but the main purpose of personnel methods is to keep staff performance at a high level.

In a library survey, it does not take long to get an impression of the level of morale. Some staff members want to communicate either from pride or from grievance, and others reveal their attitude in even the most casual contacts. An evening spent by the surveyor in the library, ostensibly looking over the collection or just reading, gives an idea of the attitude of the staff on the job. What is more difficult to ascertain are the factors that account for the state of morale, either good or bad. There may be specific grievances, on salaries, promotions, or working conditions. Individuals are quick to find a lack of fairness in the treatment they have received. The source of difficulty may be vague and general, but none the less potent, in the form of a lack of sense of purpose in the whole organization or a feeling that high standards of performance are neither expected nor rewarded.

The matter of dedication or sense of purpose on the part of staff members presents some special conditions in libraries. On the one side is the fact that many librarians feel called to their profession and believe that it has social value. They are clearly engaged in education, which to them has more intrinsic value than producing bottle caps or lines of advertising copy, but there are pervasive factors working in the other direction. The results of library practice are intangible and remote; it is easy to start with a strong sense of purpose, wonder whether it is being achieved, and in time relax for want of concrete results. Librarianship is practiced in an institutional setting, and it is difficult to sustain a sense of dedication over a campus or through a large city library. The librarian may have a vague sense that the important work is being done elsewhere, in the classroom or the research laboratory, so that he feels like an auxiliary rather than a frontline fighter.

Supervision is often not as close nor as incisive as that prevailing in a profit-making organization. This, of course, can be a positive factor in morale, as long as that supervision is not so lax that it seems as if nobody cares. If I may be permitted another observation from the commercial publishing and communication field, it is clear that competition is stiff among these organizations. Most of them are privately owned and subject to constant scrutiny by stockholders, so that decisions on personnel are often rapid and harsh. Firing of senior staff is common, and few persons in this field have even a one-year contract, much less lifetime tenure. I am not making a case for this kind of ruthless supervision or weeding out of the ranks, but I can report that it keeps many people on their toes, as well as on diets for ulcers.

The librarian depends more on an inner fire, which is the best source of motivation, so long as the fire has not gone out.

The library survey will give attention to a considerable range of conditions and administrative practices that affect morale. Very important is whether the requirements of a career service exist; everyone worth his salt has some kind of ambition, and looks to his vocation to give him some opportunity to achieve his aims. Regular increments in salary, for example, may be as important as the level at which the paychecks start. There should be definite rungs on a ladder of advancement to which the staff member can aspire. It is one function of a classification and pay plan to define these rungs of advancement.

The other function of a classification and pay plan is that of fairness or equity in personnel administration. People should be recruited under the same standards, paid at the same rate, and confident that the other fellow has not unfairly got ahead of them. I must confess that I look on these as negative virtues, and even at times see them as a source of inequity, because real performance is not rewarded. But the pragmatic approach is to use the classification and pay plan at least as a guideline for group personnel decisions, a set of rules known to everyone, which can help to anticipate routine complaints, and which need not get in the way of rewarding the very best people if there is ample opportunity for promotion built into the scheme.

Separate from dollars and titles, but equally important in maintaining morale, is the atmosphere and opportunity for growing and learning on the job and in the profession. Every survey of a library should ask how much the library administration does to keep the staff in touch with new ideas and vital developments in the field, which in part gets down to simple considerations of time and money to engage in organized professional activities. Certainly librarianship is not lacking in such programs in its professional organizations. We all agree that in-service training is very important, but this is one of the administrative activities that often slips below the surface in day-to-day management activity.

Personnel administration is a matter of human relations. At the abstract level most of us know the principles of human relations. Communication should be clear among staff members, we say, and people should be treated as individuals. Differences among human beings should be recognized and even encouraged. We would all score 100 percent on a true-and-false test on such points, but our performance is not at the same level. Take as obvious a point as a simple word of appreciation for a job well done. I can personally testify that more than once in talking to a disgruntled staff member it has suddenly dawned on me that what the person was really saying was that he had the impression that I didn't know or appreciate what he was doing.

There is a fine play in New York, called "The Subject Was Roses," that I hope the members of this conference can see. It turns on an elementary truth; we live and work for bread, and for roses. Staff morale is partly a question of roses in library administration.

RECRUITING THE STAFF

Library surveys usually cover quality, salaries, and training of staff members. The recommendations growing out of such studies may be useful—if one has the staff members to whom they can be applied.

But the hard question that may properly be raised by the practitioner after the survey report is completed is simply: "The recommendations sound fine—but where do I get the staff to carry them out?" Often the question is directed to the library schools, the buck, in a sense, passed to the educational agencies, which cannot spread their limited number of graduates over the large number of vacancies. Many a sound survey has stagnated for lack of human hands to carry out its recommendations.

The question about the availability of staff must be asked, but it should be rephrased. The relevant inquiry on the part of the administering librarians is how are *we* going to get the necessary staff, for recruitment starts in communities and on the college campus, not in the placement office of the library school. If recruitment of the June graduating class is postponed to the spring, and recruitment activity limited to inquiries and visits at that time to professional schools, the pickings will be slim for all libraries.

Library surveys have often been remiss in passing over the topic of getting the staff to do the job. Recruitment is more than an administrative detail that can properly be dismissed along with matters of where to buy typewriters or paper clips. If recruitment is needed, it should be built into the survey recommendations. In a statewide study, for example, the proposals for scholarships and for the program of library education may be as important as any. There is some evidence that statewide recruitment efforts in Pennsylvania have borne enough fruit to help keep the total plan moving forward.

I have seen significant results from library trainee and work-study programs as a means for recruiting potential professionals, and I suspect that even a greater return is possible from this approach. The number of college graduates is increasing rapidly. Some have long had a specific vocational goal and are educated for that calling. But many young people going through college, selecting a literature, history, or sociology major and approaching the beginning of their careers, are uncertain as to what they want to do and are engaged in a somewhat worried search. I can report that a surprising number, somewhere in their last six months of college, decide they want to be editors—without having much idea as to just what an editor does but attracted by a certain assumed glamour. It would be a mistake to dismiss these uncertain graduates just because they have not made an earlier choice; the selection of a career is seldom easy, and some of these young people have just that wide background and genuine sense of service that can be crystallized in librarianship. I also belong to that group that welcomes recruits from among women who have raised families and now seek a career.

This is not the place to go into the details of a trainee or work-study program. It is sufficient to say that the positions must be genuine, not a subterfuge for temporarily holding onto some college graduates on the gamble that they may go to library school. There must be challenging experience on the job; there must be rotation in assignment; there must be convenient work and study schedules; and there must even be special effort to bring the trainee into a sense of identification with the institution. I know full well the difficulties faced in providing such special arrangements for new employees when the library is already hardpressed to meet service demands with the limited number of older employees, but unless both the necessary budget provision and the extra measure of effort can be made, we will find ourselves several years hence no further along than we are today.

Of course, back of any methods of recruiting librarians is the question of the view that young people have of the profession, the image of librarianship, to use the current terminology. I have tried to analyze this question from my own position one step removed from library practice. For example, I find among publishers, editors, and the communication people generally an attitude toward librarians that corresponds with what the general opinion surveys show. There is respect for the profession and admiration for individuals within it, but there is still only limited understanding of the function of the librarian, and when the question is raised as to whether the individual himself might have thought of becoming a librarian, there is a perceptible drawing away. Librarianship, one concludes, is thought of as a nice place to visit but not as an attractive place to live.

But there is no need to throw up our hands in despair. For some years we have read of increasing college enrollments, yet you may, thus far, have been looking in vain for the results. What has sometimes been overlooked is that we are only now coming to the point where graduation as distinct from enrollment will start to reflect the upturn. I have just returned from a state that has over five-hundred thousand young people in college and that spends almost one-fifth of its public budget on higher education, even though it may not always allow these students to express what is on their minds.

I am not saying that recruits will automatically come flocking to librarianship. Many segments of our society compete for trained young people, not the least being other aspects of the educational and cultural establishment. But library service has a chance at its share of the human potential.

I would like to think that sound, wise, and bold surveys will help to get both the recruits and the necessary money, but I know that the most influential factors in the labor market and before the budget committee are what libraries do and how important people consider this to be. Which brings us back to personnel, but not so much to the staff examined in library surveys as to library administrators who commission surveys. It is administrators who determine what the library does, and therefore how it is viewed by the public at large and by young persons choosing a career. In the long run it is not the recruiting leaflet but the significance of the library's program that determines what staff members will be recruited and how they will perform.

# 8 Administrative Organization and Management

STEPHEN A. McCARTHY

THIS paper takes as its point of departure Walfred Erickson's *College and University Library Surveys, 1938-1952*. It is assumed that Erickson has reviewed and analyzed the principal surveys for the period covered and that there is no point in going over again what he has done so thoroughly and capably. The Erickson study reported that approximately 18 percent of the recommendations made in the twelve surveys included in his review dealt with the general area of "Government, Organization, and Administration"—roughly the same topic with which we are concerned today.

If we turn to a consideration of the surveys which have been published in the years since the Erickson review, we find that the majority of them are concerned with the libraries of smaller institutions and that, if we limit ourselves to American and Canadian institutions, only four large libraries have been surveyed in this period; Boston, Columbia, McGill, and North Carolina State. For Boston and McGill, the surveys disclosed conditions not unlike those reported in several of the surveys reviewed by Erickson. Hence these surveys present similar recommendations. The Columbia survey, on the other hand, described a new administrative organization for which one of the surveyors had partial responsibility. Thus, there was no need for the substantial amount of attention to administrative organization and management which the earlier surveys had included.

In surveys of libraries of small colleges in which the organization is relatively simple, the pattern of library government, organization, and administration tends also to be simple and straightforward. This is noticed with approval in a number of the surveys and there is little more to say about it. It is customary for the librarian to be appointed by the president, be responsible directly to him, and have the advisory assistance of a faculty library committee. Unless there is serious incompetence on the part of one of the officers, this type of administrative organization presents relatively few problems. Apparently this was the finding of the surveyors in the studies referred to. Two of the larger institutions surveyed, Boston and McGill, presented many of the usual problems: the lack of an adequate library statute, no definition of the libraries, no provision for a single university officer with authority and responsibility for all libraries, and the lack of clearly understood and appropriate relationships between the central library and branch and department libraries. No followup has been attempted on these two libraries, such as that undertaken by Erickson, to determine to what extent the institutions have attempted to carry out the recommendations of the surveyors.

In the Boston University and North Carolina State College surveys, recommendations for the type of administrative organization considered desirable were outlined in considerable detail after the manner of several of the surveys reviewed by Erickson. In the McGill survey, the areas of responsibility to be assigned to several administrative officers were described, but there was a conscious effort not to prescribe the precise form of organization. The view was that it was important to point out the areas of responsibility which needed attention, but there should be considerable flexibility as to just how those areas of responsibility were to be covered. The assumption was that the new director should be given the opportunity to develop his own preferred type of administrative organization. Some might consider this a shortcoming; another view might be that some earlier surveys may have attempted to be too definite in outlining a proposed form of organization. Experience suggests that there is a case to be made for leaving the precise administrative structure open and flexible enough to adjust to local circumstances and take advantage of opportunities as they arise.

In addition to the surveys of domestic libraries, the reports of surveys of four foreign university libraries were available to me. Three of these were concerned with the libraries of three Egyptian universities; the fourth, by Donald A. Redmond, dealt with the library of the Middle East Technical University, Ankara. Since the libraries under consideration in all of these studies were, although at different stages of development, faced by many and serious problems, the reports attempt to outline in considerable detail what the surveyor considered to be the desirable form of administrative organization. In many respects these documents are not especially relevant to the American university library scene.

It would seem to be useful for us to consider now how one proceeds in a library survey with the investigation of the particular area we are concerned with. There are, obviously, three principal sources of information: interviews and conferences, special questionnaires developed as part of the information gathering process of the survey itself, and regular and special reports and other administrative papers and documents. The usual procedure, as I have experienced and observed it, is an inquiry from an administrative officer of the institution, sometimes from the librarian, as to the proposed surveyor's availability and interest. Assuming that there is agreement on this matter, the first order of business when a surveyor appears on the scene is an interview with the administrative officer who has initiated the study. It is of considerable importance to determine, either in advance or during the initial conference, for whom the surveyor is working, by what authority he has been appointed, and to whom the survey report is to be directed. Sometimes these matters are quite clear; at other times they can be very hazy. Once this point has been determined and the opening conference is under way, the administrative officer may be expected to outline what he considers to be the problem and what, in his judgment, is required to solve it. It is not an unusual experience to find that the initiative has come originally from a faculty group or committee. The administrative officer is responding to complaints and faultfinding. If he is a perceptive man, he is perhaps also hoping to find a way to correct the library's unsatisfactory performance. Frequently, this officer is not able to describe in detail the weaknesses and problems which exist in the area we are concerned with. Unless he has previously been in an institution in which the library organization functioned well and gained a good understanding of it which he carried on to his present position, the chances are that he will merely realize that there are problems, that the library is not providing the resources and services required. He knows it needs something which it does not have, but he is not sure what.

In this conference it is important to discover what the relationships of the librarian to the central administration are, to whom the librarian reports, and with whom he takes up his serious problems. It is generally possible to get fairly definite answers to these questions. It is also desirable in this interview to explore the normal channels through which the library budget passes and the location of budgetary responsibility for branch and department libraries, as a key to the relationships between the central library and other library units. Frequently this administrative officer will not know in detail what the relationships are between branch and department libraries and the central library, but even to discover this is important. Information on the library statute or bylaw, if there is one, may also frequently be obtained at this time. The legislation itself can, of course, be read and analyzed but frequently an administrative officer's view or evaluation of the legislation is as important as the legislation itself.

An example from my own experience is the library legislation at Cornell. When I was asked to consider the position of director at Cornell, I sought out and read this legislation carefully. I believed then, and I still do, that a fair interpretation of this piece of institutional legislation is that it provides for committee administration of the library, with the director serving as the instructed executive officer of the committee. Naturally this concerned me very much, and I discussed it frankly and at length with the president. The president told me there was nothing to worry about. He took the position that even if my interpretation of the legislation was correct, no one expected or wanted the library to be operated by a committee. He assured me that he and the members of the committee were in complete agreement that they wanted a director to administer the library and that there would be no attempt on the part of the committee to enter into administrative, as opposed to policy, matters. I can say now that President Day was right and that, despite the legislation, there has never been any attempt to establish committee administration at Cornell. I am sure there are similar instances in which the institution's interpretation of its legislation may be of greater importance than the legislation itself.

Further areas to be explored with the administrative officer are the designation of those whom he considers to be the key people on the campus to be interviewed, and the special and thorny problems which he sees as being involved in the library situation. In the course of this discussion it may be possible to draw attention to the fact that some of these problems may derive from aspects of the administrative organization and government of the library which, at first thought, might seem to be rather far removed from the problems themselves.

Following the administrative interview there is frequently an arrangement for the surveyor to meet with either the standing library committee or with an *ad hoc* committee of faculty and administrators. In my experience these meetings can be very useful as a means of helping committee members to understand some of the underlying causes of their problems. As in the case of the administrative officer, committee members frequently will not relate problems to the administrative and governmental structure of the library, but will think of them only in the context in which they directly experience them. It is also frequently possible to obtain from a committee of this kind general guidelines on the situation which will prove helpful. In some instances the committee members will quite explicitly bring out their views that there has been inadequate library support, and that the administration has not taken steps to provide for the library with the vigor, energy, and generosity required. At other times, there may be complaints of the lack of suitable or adequate library facilities or of competent library personnel. In some instances all of these factors enter into the picture. The meeting also furnishes opportunity to ascertain the library committee's views of its own role, and there may be an opportunity to suggest what the surveyor considers that role to be. Again, as in the case of the interview with the administrative officer, it may be useful to draw attention to the fact that the governmental and administrative structure may be a factor of critical importance although not recognized as such by members of the committee.

The surveyor will, of course, spend a great deal of time in conference with the librarian and with the library staff. It is desirable to encourage the fullest possible discussion of administrative relationships between the library and the central administration, and between the central library and the department libraries. The budget procedure from the point of view of the librarian is sometimes different from that presented by the central administration. The librarian is also in a position to evaluate the contribution of the library committee. A comparison of the views expressed by members of the committee on the one hand, and the librarian on the other, may show that there are misunderstandings which need clarification. It is obviously important to get the librarian's evaluation of the total situation and his own analysis of the problem areas. It is enlightening to compare the views expressed by the administrative officer, the library committee, and the librarian on the same questions.

At times the librarian may be on the defensive because he feels that he is being attacked. If this is the case, it may be difficult to obtain a candid picture of the situation from him; information normally available from the librarian may be unobtainable or only partially available. This slows the whole operation considerably and makes it more complex. If possible, it is desirable for the surveyor to try to find ways of making clear that he is approaching his job without preconceptions, and that he seeks to learn only in order that he may be of assistance in improving the situation. For this purpose it is of the greatest importance to enlist the sympathy, understanding, and help of the librarian who should be regarded as the person best qualified to assist the surveyor.

As one moves from the librarian to members of the library staff, attention is first given to department heads and librarians in charge of branch and department libraries. Many of the same questions are relevant because they will disclose facts about the administrative organization and management of the libraries. It is, for example, enlightening to know what the views of the librarian of a branch library are regarding his relationship to the chief librarian and to such departments as acquisitions and cataloging in the central library. If there are differences in the evaluation of these relationships, the surveyor has clearly discovered a matter of considerable importance. In all such cases the surveyor must be on guard lest he be taken in by the person who is sure that he is right and all the rest are at fault.

At some point in the survey it will be important to talk with individual faculty members and invite their appraisal of the library and its services with respect to their departmental needs and the needs of their faculty colleagues and students. In most cases, in talking with faculty members, the surveyor encounters complaints of inadequate or unsatisfactory service, limited resources, and lack of funds for the development of resources. The surveyor seldom gets from faculty members the kind of analysis directly applicable to administrative organization and management. Complaints of inadequacy, however, frequently disclose weaknesses and failures in the administrative organization and management of which unsatisfactory service is a natural result. Faculty members generally are in a much better position to give directly useful evaluations of the collections in their fields, and the adequacy or inadequacy of support for the development of these collections. This is seldom the case with respect to administrative structure. Faculty members sometimes take the view that administrative relationships are not important or are not relevant to their problems. It is helpful if the surveyor can point to some examples where changes in administrative organization and management might solve particular problems that concern faculty members.

In these interviews the surveyor is not only seeking information on current conditions, he is also using the opportunity to indicate what, in his judgment, might be a sound pattern of organization and administrative management. On one occasion in meeting with a library committee, I discussed the importance of the government and administrative structure of the library. I referred to the need for a library statute and mentioned some of the elements generally considered appropriate for inclusion in such a statute. After I had finished one of the deans said: "I feel very naked, because we don't have any of these things, and we haven't missed them." While this dean was interested in the overall library service of the university, his particular concern was with the branch library which served his school. Since this was one of the better libraries on the campus because the dean had made it so, he was really not concerned with the administrative structure of the library system at all. This is frequently the case, especially with strong deans who have an interest in good library collections and services for their own divisions. If this occurs in an institution where the central library is weak and inadequately supported, there may be reluctance to consider the kind of library administrative organization which librarians tend to think of as the most satisfactory.

I have stressed interviews because I believe that they are of the very greatest importance in making surveys. Many surveys use questionnaires addressed to faculty members, department heads, members of the library staff, and even to students. They are all useful, but it is very difficult to draw up a questionnaire which will elicit the kind of information which one can obtain in the personal interview. It is also true that in the personal interview or the group conference one can begin the process of suggesting changes that may appear desirable. This cannot be done by a questionnaire. In surveys of large institutions, some use of questionnaires is essential because it is not possible to have personal interviews with as many people as would be desirable. Too, the questionnaire is better suited to deal with other aspects of the library survey than government, administrative structure, and management. For example, evaluations of the book collection and estimates of the sums needed to develop the collections can be obtained by questionnaires; questionnaires can determine the availability of certain services, or the lack of them, and the degree of satisfaction with which these services are received by the university community. On the other hand, since there is frequently far less understanding of the relative importance of government and administrative structure and management, interviews and conferences with committees tend to be far more instructive and helpful in securing information on these matters and in conveying suggestions for changes and improvements.

The third principal source of information, as outlined earlier, consists of reports, manuals, budget documents, and compilations of statistical data. If there is a university staff manual or a book of statutes or bylaws, this will naturally be one of the basic documents to be studied and analyzed. If there is an organization chart of the institution, it also will be illuminating to the surveyor, and the existence of an administrative organization chart for the library will frequently be very helpful. Many times when surveys are requested there is no organization chart, and it may take a good deal of study to construct even a tentative one. Several of the surveys appearing in the period with which we are dealing do include charts of the library organization and a few include additional charts showing recommended organization. In others, this material is presented only in the text.

It is frequently enlightening if the surveyor reviews the agenda and minutes of the library committee before and after he meets with it. These documents sometimes indicate more precisely than do the individuals what the relationship of the committee to the librarian and to the university administration is. If a situation has developed in which the library committee or some members of it have undertaken administrative actions rather than policy and advisory matters, this will be disclosed by the minutes of the meeting.

The surveyor will also wish to review library reports that cover a period of several years. The usefulness of regular departmental and special reports to the librarian may be evidence of the means the librarian has set up to keep informed of what is going on in the library. Such reports also disclose what matters have been of concern to department heads and which ones have or have not had attention from the library administration. The annual reports of the librarian are among the most important basic documents for the use of the surveyor; this is true both for what they include and for what they omit. Omission may mean failure to deal with problems and needs or it may reflect inadequate financing, facilities, or staffing. If possible, it is desirable for the surveyor to study the annual reports, covering a three-to-five-year period, prior to his visit to the campus. This is one of the best ways to get oriented to the problem. I recall an incident several years ago when I was called in to confer with an *ad hoc* committee on the library because there was grave concern on the part of the faculty and the administration at the condition of the library. Prior to my visit I had an opportunity to review the annual reports of the librarian for the preceding five years. At my meeting with the *ad hoc* committee, at which the librarian was not present, I heard faculty members present a series of complaints against the library administration because resources had not been developed and services had not been provided. This was attributed to the incompetence of the librarian. I was able to point out that the librarian had dealt with each of these subjects on several occasions in his annual reports and had made recommendations for their correction. The university administration, however, had failed to take the recommendations seriously and to provide the financial support necessary to carry them out. Here was an instance in which a librarian was being held responsible by a faculty group for failure to perform even though the librarian had done all in his power to meet the needs. He was well aware of them but he had been unable to get the necessary administrative and financial support. The *ad hoc* committee had a complaint against the university administration, not against the librarian.

In addition to the reports from department heads, it is important to ascertain what type of financial records the library keeps and what financial records are provided by the central business office. Normally, the accounting in the library is determined by the central administration in order to coordinate it with the central accounting, but the library administration must have sufficient records and must be able to produce reports on the current status of funds which will serve as the basis for sound administrative decisions. The librarian can only make such decisions if he has up-to-date and accurate records and reports on all library accounts, and is in a position to authorize action within normal administrative channels as to the use of these funds.

It is of more value to the surveyor to review library budget documents than it is to study the accounting procedures. Along with the annual report, the budget submission and the supporting documents are frequently indicative of the quality and nature of the administrative structure and management of the library. It is, for example, revealing to find that there is no strong presentation made in a budget document for book funds, or for new staff positions, or for salary improvements. In most situations the budget presentation is the best opportunity there is to bring the needs of the library to the attention of the proper administrative officers. If this opportunity is not utilized fully and effectively, it is clear that the library administration is not meeting its obligations. It is also instructive to learn through what channels the library budget is submitted and by whom and at what point decisions with respect to recommendations are made. It is, for example, very illuminating to find in the budget material a letter from the president informing the librarian of a special allocation for the purchase of books accompanied by the statement that in the president's judgment it would be desirable to have a planned program of book purchasing rather than a series of emergency appeals for special grants. Clearly, in this situation, the librarian has not presented an appropriate budget document.

In many surveys there is evidence of weakness in the internal administrative structure. This shows up in the form of departments that are exceedingly large and that cover a very broad range of different activities. This can develop naturally as the demands for new services arise. Because of inadequate staff new services are assigned to existing departments. If they are performed satisfactorily they tend to stay there. In many cases this is desirable, but there are also many other situations in which this is not true. The need of creating new departments may not be recognized by the central administration and the faculty, but it should be recognized by the librarian and by members of the library staff.

If we move from the problem of how the library should be departmented and look at the administrative organization and procedures within a department, it is frequently instructive to try to determine how the department functions, how its procedures are established and maintained, and how its policies of operation and service are not only established but are consistently carried out. If there are manuals of procedures or memoranda series which not only record policies, procedures, and decisions but which also are conceived as a means of instructing new staff members, one can frequently conclude that the department is being effectively operated. If this is not the case and if there is no clear evidence of a plan of operation which is understood by all concerned, there is reason to question whether a department has faced up to its problems, reached decisions, and adopted procedures designed to produce the desired services and results.

It is most instructive to attempt to determine to what extent authority has been delegated by the librarian to his associates and department heads and by these officers in turn to those staff members working under their general supervision. This question can be explored from both sides. If the answers do not tally, something is wrong. It is apparent that responsible staff members should be able to take initiative and independent action within established policies. If this is not the case and if there is over-centralization by the chief librarian, the library will be the poorer for it. Competent staff members should have sufficient scope and freedom of decision to enable them to develop their talents to the full. It is a nice point to determine to what extent decentralized decisionmaking is consistent with the maintenance of an overall policy. This is not a matter on which one can give precise answers but it is certainly an area that calls for the greatest skill than can be brought to bear.

Related to the delegation of authority is the question of staff meetings, the agenda for such meetings, and the methods followed in putting decisions into effect. One of the problems in any organization is the difficulty of keeping open and free the lines of communication and being sure that everyone who is involved in a certain action or decision is aware of this action and understands its relationship to his own line of activity. It is for this reason that meetings of department heads, branch librarians, and various supervisory groups with the chief librarian at regular or relatively frequent intervals are of the greatest importance. If this is not done, situations will surely occur in which actions are taken which do not produce the desired results because some of the people who are affected or involved simply do not know about them or do not know about them in time. This purpose can be assisted by regular meetings, and by the issuance of memoranda or a staff bulletin which help to keep all members of the staff informed on matters of library operations and policy. Similarly, means of communication with the faculty are of importance because some of the difficulties which arise to plague librarians result from lack of information and understanding. The easy availability of the chief librarian and his principal associates to talk with and mix with the faculty is one of the best means of carrying on this communication. The library committee can also be of inestimable service in this respect. A wide circulation of the annual report of the library is still another way of affecting this understanding. Bulletins issued directly to the faculty are commonly used, but one hesitates to recommend the increase of mimeographed material going into faculty wastebaskets.

This paper has dealt largely with my own experience and observation in the library survey work that I have done. I have referred to a number of surveys but I have not devoted much attention to them. I have been concerned rather with how one approaches the problems that fall under the general heading of administrative organization and management. My experience and observation suggest that there is no single formula for the administrative organization and management of a university library. There are, I believe, some ways that are better; some other ways that are less good; and still others that are downright poor; but there is no one best way for all institutions under all circumstances. There are, however, some general principles of administration and of administrative organization and management which apply to libraries as well as to other organizations involving a fairly large number of people. There must be a hierarchy; there must be a clear definition of responsibility and authority, and these must be commensurate; there must be good communication; there must be competent people in sufficient numbers to carry the workload; and there must be adequate facilities and reasonably adequate financial resources. Without these principles and without adequate facilities, funding, and staff, no administrative structure will be successful; with them, administrative structures that exhibit a considerable range of variations may be found to function satisfactorily in different institutions at different stages of development.

REFERENCES

1. Erickson, Ernst Walfred. *College and University Library Surveys, 1938–1952.* Chicago, American Library Association, 1961 (ACRL Monograph, no. 25).
2. Gormley, Mark M. *The Sioux Falls College Library; a Survey.* Chicago, ALA, 1961.
3. Harwell, Richard B., and Talmadge, Robert L. *The Alma College Library; a Survey.* Chicago, ALA, 1958.
4. Harwell, Richard B., and Moore, E. T. *Arizona State University Library.* Chicago, ALA, 1959.
5. Jesse, William Herman. *Report of a Survey of the Libraries of the North Carolina State College,* September, 1957–January, 1958. Raleigh, N.C., North Carolina State College. 1958.
6. *Library Program for San Diego College; a Survey of Library Holdings, Needs and Services.* John Paul Stone (ed.). Rev. 1957–58. San Diego, State College, 1958.
7. McCarthy, Stephen A. *Final Report to the Rector, Alexandria*

*University, of a Survey of the Libraries of Alexandria Univer-*
*sity.* Cairo, 1954.
8. McCarthy, Stephen A. *Final Report to the Rector, Cairo Uni-*
   *versity, of a Survey of the Libraries of Cairo University.* Cairo,
   1954.
9. McCarthy, Stephen A. *Final Report to the Rector, Ibrahim*
   *University, of a Survey of the Libraries of Ibrahim University.*
   Cairo, 1954.
10. McCarthy, Stephen A., and Logsdon, R. H. *Survey of McGill*
    *University Libraries.* 1963.
11. Redmond, Donald A. *Report on the Library of the Middle East*
    *Technical University, Ankara, Turkey, July 1959–June 1960.*
    Submitted to UNESCO and Middle East Technical Univer-
    sity. 1960.
12. Tauber, Maurice F. *Barnard College Library; a Report on the*
    *Facilities and Services.* New York, The College, 1954.
13. Tauber, Maurice F. *Hampton Institute Library.* Hampton, Vir-
    ginia, 1958.
14. Tauber, Maurice F. *Libraries of Boston University; a Prelimi-*
    *nary Report on Problems and a Tentative Design for a Future*
    *Program.* New York, 1956.
15. Tauber, Maurice F. *The Processing Operations of the Library*
    *of Hawaii.* Honolulu, 1960.
16. Tauber, Maurice F. *Technical Services in the Libraries of New*
    *Mexico; a Report of a Survey Made; July 2–17, 1964.* Albuquer-
    que, University of New Mexico, 1964.
17. Tauber, Maurice F., Cook, Donald, and Logsdon, Richard C.
    *The Columbia University Libraries.* New York, Columbia Uni-
    versity Press, 1958.
18. White, Carl M. *The National Library of Nigeria: Growth of*
    *An Idea, Problems and Progress.* Lagos, Federal Ministry of
    Information, 1964.

PART TWO

*Special Approaches and Problems*

*of Library Surveys*

# 9  Introduction

MORRIS A. GELFAND

PRECEDING discussions have dealt with the origins and evolution of the library survey and a variety of major problem areas and approaches either from a general viewpoint or from that of a particular type of library. Evaluation of library collections —a most elusive and difficult problem—has been examined and described chiefly from the university library viewpoint. Various aspects of the evaluation of technical services have received comprehensive, general treatment. The dangers and pitfalls inherent in approaches to measuring library use have been presented chiefly in terms of public library applications and to a lesser degree in the context of academic and school libraries. Evaluation of staff size and quality has been discussed in the light of present and emerging social and technological forces and in terms of the personal qualities and viewpoints the surveyor and the chief librarian must possess and apply in studying personnel problems. The viewpoint of the professional building consultant has been applied to the problems of planning new library buildings. Finally, the evaluation of certain major problems of administration, chiefly in public and university libraries, has received thorough treatment.

Despite the fact that some of the contributors have chosen to limit their approaches it is clear that much of what they have said is susceptible of broad applications. Inevitably, there has been some overlapping as major library problems are so closely interrelated, and there have been some omissions. It is against this background that the following papers have been written. The object of the papers will be to bring some of the major problem areas into sharper focus and to identify and describe special approaches and problems which have not been treated previously in detail, and attempt to represent the viewpoints of both the surveyor and the sponsoring agency.

## COMMON PROBLEMS

There are certain fundamental problems which it is appropriate to emphasize, namely: defining the aims of the survey, identifying the problems to be investigated, obtaining approval and financial support, and providing for implementation of recommendations. Without a definition of aims it is difficult to identify and describe the problems which need to be studied.[1] Are the aims the establishment of a regional library system, the evaluation of the library's collections to determine their adequacy for proposed graduate and research programs, the achievement of full academic status for the professional staff, the improvement of cataloging and processing? Whatever the aims may be, it will be necessary at the outset to define them explicitly, to indicate as fully as possible the problems which need to be considered and the possible benefits to be derived from a survey, in order to obtain the approval and financial support that will be required.

The agency sponsoring the survey may require assistance in identifying and defining the problems, but once this has been accomplished it should be possible to design the survey and make plans for carrying it out. In a sense the early stages of survey planning are analogous to those of building planning. The architect is given a statement of the client's requirements—the building program—at the outset. He then submits his ideas for meeting these requirements in the form of preliminary sketches and plans. Only after mutual agreement is reached with respect to design, costs, etc., does the architect proceed to prepare final plans and specifications. Similarly, the library consultant will indicate how he intends to study the problems of the client—the methods and devices he will use, the type of report he will make, and the follow-up procedures he recommends, and, accordingly, he will reach an understanding with the client before proceeding with the survey.

Tauber discusses some additional problems under the heading, "Limitations of Surveys" in a recent paper: unqualified surveyors, inadequate sampling, difficulties in evaluating book collections, inadequate statistics, lack of valid standards, inadequate financial support of the survey, poor timing, and faulty arrangements for dealing with the report after it has been completed.[2]

## SPECIAL PROBLEMS AND APPROACHES

Among factors which affect the nature of a library's problems and the approach to their solution are the following: (1) the type of library and its objectives; (2) its environment; (3) its size, organization, and internal management; and (4) the availability and applicability of standards as measuring devices.

In general, the objectives of a library tend to reflect those of its constituency. College and university libraries aim to serve the instructional and research needs of their respective academic clienteles; these clienteles are relatively homogeneous groups. Public libraries, including local and regional systems, serve a variety of needs of a heterogeneous population. School libraries aim primarily at being resource and teaching centers for their respective schools, and secondarily, in some instances, at serving the outside community. Special libraries, particularly those in commercial and industrial organizations and in private research centers, primarily serve the information and research needs of their own organizations. State libraries may have a variety of objectives: serving state legislative and administrative agencies, providing extension services, serving public and other types of libraries in the state, and, in some cases, performing an archival function. But while these objectives may serve as general guides to the functions of the respective library types they usually need to be defined in more specific, concrete terms to provide a basis for evaluating the library in terms of its mission. Tauber observes in this connection: "In several instances during the past few years, one of the first tasks in the survey was to determine just what the library was supposed to do in respect to the work of the parent institution."[3] The objectives will acquire additional meaning when viewed in the context of the library's environment.

The environment of the library is characterized by a variety of tangible and intangible factors: (1) the size, nature, interests, and needs of the population it serves; (2) the purposes of the institution, organization, political unit, or general constituency to which it is responsible; (3) the nature of the controlling body, public or private, under which it must operate and the relation of the librarian to the chief executive officer of that body; (4) the proximity of other libraries and cultural institutions and their size, character, and willingness to cooperate with each other; (5) the attitudes toward the library of those whom it aims to serve [4, 5] and of the officials and groups with whom it must work; (6) the sources of financial support and the nature of the controls over budget, finances, purchasing, and staffing; and (7) in academic institutions, particularly, certain intangibles such as the nature of the intellectual climate, and the administrative sophistication of high officials.

The size, organization, and internal management of the library are obviously important factors. Differences in these factors within and among the various types of libraries will significantly affect survey design and operation.

The availability and applicability of standards may have a significant bearing on the conduct of the survey. Where they exist they may be useful bench marks for describing as well as evaluating library conditions. Standards now exist for college, school, public, and special libraries, and for library functions at the state level. How objective are these standards? How well have they been received? What cautions should be observed in applying standards? These questions will be treated in the discussions which follow.

*Special Problems:* Colleges and universities are facing increasingly serious problems that arise from the tremendous increase in student enrollments and the vast and rising flow of new library materials. More universities are considering the advisability of organizing separate library facilities for undergraduate students; many university libraries are concerned with fundamental problems of growth and organization not comparable with those of other types of libraries. Clapp says the problems of general research libraries (including university libraries) arise "from the gap that exists between what its users require and what it can supply." [6] He goes on to develop this point by discussing "the gap between production and acquisition of library materials . . . obstacles to sharing resources . . . bibliographic deficiencies . . . [and] inadequacy of techniques for physical maintenance, record-keeping and administration." [7] Even this brief extract from Clapp's remarks is sufficient to suggest certain major problems of academic and research libraries and those of other types of libraries outside the research field. The Council on Library Resources seeks universal solutions to some of these problems; however, library surveyors will continue to deal with them on an individual basis.

Public libraries and public library systems have some apparently unique problems: community analysis, student-use pressures, site selection, systems organization and administration, governmental relationships, and civil service personnel problems, among others.

In school libraries the introduction of the new AASL standards has presented special problems, and relations with school officials, coordination of services in large school systems, and recruiting and training continue to be matters of special concern.

Special libraries in commercial, industrial, and independent private research organizations have a common problem of which they appear to be more acutely aware than other libraries; the problem is how to evaluate the impact of the library on the research and related programs of the parent organization.

One of the problems of state libraries appears to be that they are under-surveyed with respect to administrative performance. Another problem is the place of the state library agency in the rapidly developing regional systems.

*Special Approaches:* Special approaches to the solution of survey problems may involve a variety of research and investigatory methods and techniques. These may be applied by the library staff in self-surveys or by outside consultants—librarians, nonlibrarian management consultants—working as individuals or as groups.

Employed objectively and skillfully the self-survey can be a valuable reporting, planning, and management device. In this category, librarians' annual and special reports may qualify if they meet the criteria for an objective survey. Metcalf's report on the Harvard Library [8] is an admirable example; the Tauber-Cook-Logsdon report on the Columbia libraries is another.[9] The Metcalf report is a comprehensive description and analysis of the major problems of the Harvard University Library, with recommendations for their solution. The main body of the report deals with problem areas common to all types of libraries: "acquisition, cataloging, service to readers, interlibrary cooperation, space, personnel, administrative organization, and finances." [10] Seven supplements provide supporting data and additional recommendations. Based on library records, the report proper is descriptive and analytical. Statistics are used mainly as descriptive devices. Metcalf was assisted by a committee of the library staff and an advisory committee appointed by the president of the university.

Like the Harvard report, the one about Columbia is comprehensive, analytical, objective, and constructive. From the viewpoint of the surveyor it has the added virtue of being so well organized and developed as to make it a helpful survey guide. It is based not only on the library's records and other documents, but also on data collected through the use of a series of carefully designed and tested questionnaires and an equally well-prepared interview schedule. These are reproduced in full in the appendix.

Another type of self-survey is that which is conducted in connection with an institutional evaluation by a regional accrediting association. A helpful example can be found in the practices of the Middle States Association of Colleges and Secondary Schools. About a year before an institution is to be evaluated, it may begin an institution-wide survey following the guides provided by the Association. These guides consist of statements of qualitative standards, memoranda on specific aspects of higher education, including an excellent one on the library,[11] and a battery of questionnaires calling for preparation of specific data. The Association suggests that the college form a representative committee to conduct the self-survey. Where this suggestion is followed and the librarian is a member of the committee, he has an unusual opportunity to relate the library to the institution's program and to assess the attitude toward the library of faculty and administrative colleagues. The librarian is often given the opportunity to make a comprehensive study of the library in preparation for the Association's visit, but some librarians confine themselves to preparing data for the questionnaire.

In the Middle States Association it is the practice to invite one or more librarians, depending on the size and complexity of the institution to be visited, to serve on the evaluation team. In advance of the visit each team member receives a copy of the full report of the institution as well as its catalogs and selected additional documents. The library member thus has an opportunity to study the library in relation to the institution as a whole and to prepare himself accordingly for the visit. During the visit the library evaluator confers daily with other members of the team and uses many of the methods and devices customarily used by library surveyors: conferences with the institution's librarian, key library staff, faculty members, and administrators; documentary study and analysis, physical observations, etc. After the visit the library evaluator sends his report to the chairman of the team, who edits and incorporates it in the team report. After the Association has acted on the evaluation it sends the report to the institution.[12]

A study made in 1960 of library evaluations by the Middle States Association showed that the self-survey, and the visit and report of the library evaluator were found to be distinctly helpful by the libraries of the institutions that were visited.[13] An appraisal of different methods of library evaluation by librarians in higher institutions revealed no significant differences in the ratings of various methods, self-survey, surveys by outside consultants, et al., except for surveys by management consultants, which appeared to be the least desirable method.[14]

A self-survey using scientific management techniques is reported by Dow, who used work measurement in a special library to develop standards by which to evaluate the effectiveness of the library.[15] A series of internal studies at Purdue University library resulted from a weekly seminar in operations research which was conducted by a professor of industrial engineering for a selected group of librarians and graduate students.[16] In 1954, Shaw, writing in Library Trends, reported an increasing trend toward the application of scientific management in libraries.[17] In the same issue, however, Howard criticizes library surveys for neglecting to apply scentific work study.[18]

Scientific work study characterized the approach of the management engineers who surveyed preparation procedures for the New York Public Library Reference Department, in 1951. The viewpoint and methods of the firm which conducted the study are described by Morris.[19] The reaction to the report and its implementation are discussed by Kingery, who reports that the consultants made seventy-five recommendations nearly all of which were approved and carried out after thorough discussion.[20]

Since the organization of the Council on Library Resources and the passage of the Library Services Act we have witnessed the appearance of many consultants from the ranks of engineering, and from business and industrial management specialties. And more will probably appear as grant funds become more plentiful. Librarians should know enough about the capabilities of nonlibrary consultants to be in a position to judge when it is most desirable to employ them. At the same time, it would be wise for us to continue to encourage further use of scientific management techniques in our libraries and further teaching of the subject in our library schools.

CONCLUSION

In addition to the major problem areas which have been discussed earlier in this book all libraries and organizations contemplating a survey have the common problem of stating their survey aims explicitly, defining the problems to be investigated, obtaining approval and support for the survey, appointing a competent surveyor, and implementing the survey. Special problems and approaches develop out of the differences in the nature and objectives of the type of library or library organization that is involved and in the environment of the library. Whether it is a self-survey or one conducted by a qualified library consultant, the survey should be conducted in an objective way in accordance with accepted research practice, and the methods of scientific management should be employed where practicable.

REFERENCES

1. McDiarmid, E. W. *The Library Survey; Problems and Methods.* Chicago, American Library Association, 1940. p. 5.
2. Tauber, M. F. "Survey Method in Approaching Library Problems." *Library Trends*, 13: 22–26 (July 1964).
3. *Ibid.*, pp. 21–22.
4. Purdue University Libraries. Staff Association. Research committee. *Purdue University Libraries Attitude Survey, 1959–1960.* Lafayette, Indiana, Purdue University Staff Ass'n., 1964. 51 p. mimeographed.
5. Bergen, D. P. "The Anthropocentric Needs of Academic Librarianship." *College and Research Libraries*, 24: 277–90; 307–08 (July 1963).
6. Clapp, Verner W. *The Future of the Research Library*, Urbana, University of Illinois Press, 1964.
7. *Ibid.*, pp. 59–61.
8. Metcalf, K. D. *Report on the Harvard University Library: a Study of Present and Prospective Problems.* Cambridge, Harvard University Library, 1955.

9. Tauber, M. F., Cook, C. D., and Logsdon, R. H. *The Columbia University Libraries.* New York, Columbia University Press, 1958.
10. Metcalf, *Report on the Harvard University Library.* p. 7.
11. Middle States Association of Colleges and Secondary Schools. Commission on Institutions of Higher Education. *Evaluating the Library; Suggestions for the Use of Faculties and Evaluation Teams.* Document no. 4.81, Oct. 1957.
12. Gelfand, M. A. "Techniques of Library Evaluators in the Middle States Association." *College and Research Libraries,* 19: 305–20 (July 1958).
13. Gelfand, M. A. *A Historical Study of the Evaluation of Libraries in Higher Institutions by the Middle States Association.* Unpublished Ph.D. dissertation. New York, New York University, 1960.
14. *Ibid.,* p. 334.
15. Dow, K. K. W. "A Tool for Management Evaluation of Library Services." *Special Libraries,* 48: 378–82 (Oct. 1957).
16. Morelock, M. and Leimkuhler, F. F. "Library Operations Research and Systems Engineering Studies." *College and Research Libraries.* 25: 501–03 (Nov. 1964).
17. Shaw, R. R., "Scientific Management in Libraries." *Library Trends,* 2: 359 (Jan. 1954).
18. Howard, P. "Consequences of Management Surveys." *Library Trends,* 2: 428–36 (Jan. 1954).
19. Morris, T. D. "The Management Consultant in the Library." *College and Research Libraries,* 15: 196–201 (April 1954).
20. Kingery, R. E. "What Happens When the Management Engineers Leave?" *College and Research Libraries,* 15: 202–04 (April 1954).

# 10  Academic Libraries

MARK M. GORMLEY

IN CONSIDERING the special problems attending the survey process in academic and research libraries, it is necessary to realize that no guideline could possibly exist which would apply uniformly to all such libraries. *La raison d'être* of an academic library is to serve a particular institution in accomplishing its basic objectives, plus encouraging students to develop the life-long habit of self-education.

This paper will focus briefly upon topics which tend to be common to most academic libraries:

1. The attitude of the governing board.
2. Relationships of the librarian with administration, faculty, and student body.
3. Personnel.
4. The applicability of ALA Standards in survey work.

It is axiomatic that a favorable climate must be created for a survey to be efficiently accomplished. Realization that something is amiss and needs improving is often indicated through a library self-survey of present conditions, or self-conducted surveys concerning long-term growth. The various regional accrediting agencies have formulated criteria to aid libraries in these self-surveys. An excellent example of a self-survey is the 1961 University of Michigan *Faculty Appraisal of a University Library*.[1] The 1962 Florida State University summary report entitled *The Future of Florida State University*[2] introduces the section on the library thus, "A good library is the heart of a good university," and then goes into detail in describing what needs to be done to vitalize that heart.

Recognition of the need for library improvement often comes from an officer of a college, from a faculty committee, from a regional accrediting agency, or from the librarian.

Whether the actual survey contract is negotiated directly between an institution and the surveyor, or through an intermediary, such as ALA, it is imperative that the nature and scope of the survey to be conducted be clearly defined.

In approaching the actual survey process in an academic library, one is well served if he has been able to become acquainted with the total concept of the college or university. For example, the surveyors of the Sioux Falls College library had available to them not only the college catalogs, Governing Board Minutes, and a history of the college but also a copy of the North Central Association accrediting team's report [3] which had been finished a number of weeks previously. By the time they arrived in Sioux Falls, the surveyors already knew much about the college and its library.

## ADMINISTRATIVE RELATIONSHIPS OF THE LIBRARIAN

An understanding of the attitude toward the library by the governing board of the institution to which the library belongs is vital. While I know of no situation where an academic librarian reports directly to a board of regents, overseers, or governors, it is encouraging that one of the first appointments made by some boards of newly established institutions is the librarian. Specific examples include California at Santa Cruz, Florida Atlantic University, and the University of South Florida.

Governing agencies have been known to extend their influence in such a way as to impede the growth of libraries. The stringent budget restrictions of depression years are legend. More recently, in 1962, the Joint Budget Committee of the Colorado General Assembly exercised its prerogative to review all line items in the State budget. It reduced the allocation for materials at Colorado State University.[4]

Since the board determines policy and controls the purse strings it is well to understand its attitude about the library and its role in the teaching, research, and service functions of the college or university. Paul Buck speaks of this concept in his "A Credo Reconsidered." [5]

Patterns of organization in academe vary widely. The surveyor must accurately and quickly find the true locus of power within the structure. The relationship of the librarian to that locus is critical. The librarian may not report directly to the president or chancellor, nor do I think that it is necessary that he do so—what *is* important is the relative position, authority, and influence of the officer to whom the librarian does report, and the sympathy and rapport between that officer and the librarian.

The librarian's status in the total hierarchy of deans and directors is important. It is absolutely necessary to know the relative respect and position enjoyed by the librarian and his staff, not only among the administration but in the total academic community.

FACULTY RELATIONSHIPS

One factor unique in librarianship is the relationship of the faculty library committee to the academic librarian. The compilers of the ALA Standards for College Libraries recommend "as a rule, there should be a faculty library committee. The Committee should act strictly in an advisory capacity." [6] Erickson found that in some places such a committee does not exist.[7] Erickson and Anderson, in 1962, found that the Library Committee at Western Washington State College had spent four years in meeting ". . . irregularly . . . trying to define its function and seeking ways to help in the development of a library program . . . the committee has no clearly defined duties but considers itself advisory in function." [8] Harwell and Moore, in 1959, in their survey at Arizona State University, detected a deviation from the suggested purpose of the committee. "A faculty library committee has been appointed and holds regular meetings. There is now, however, some uncertainty within the library committee concerning its functions. The committee should be . . . an advisory body. It should concern itself with library policies and not with the details of library administration." [9]

The strong role of the elected faculty committees in the government of certain universities is exemplified in the University of Wisconsin-Milwaukee statute concerning the faculty library committee. "The Library Committee will represent the interest and authority of the Faculty in library affairs. The Committee will serve as both an advisory and a policy-making group, as the importance and nature of issues concerned indicate on all matters pertaining to the library." [10]

The understanding of this concept of democratic power is all important to those who would seek to evaluate certain academic institutions. Equally important as the library surveyor's ability to determine the total relationship between librarian and administration is the ability to determine librarian relationships with the faculty.

STUDENT RELATIONSHIPS

The largest group on the academic scene with which the surveyor will be concerned is the student body. It must be determined if undergraduate as well as graduate students feel that they are being fairly dealt with, if the library is providing the materials needed, if the hours of public service are sufficient, and if the library staff is helping all patrons to fully utilize total resources. The surveyors at Arizona State University stated:

Student . . . interest in the welfare of the library is a very healthy thing. But such interest is not always accompanied by a full cognizance of library problems, and the present criticism of the library has not always been completely valid. . . . student criticism . . . has been sometimes based on isolated incidents and sometimes even on misinformation. But criticism, however ill-founded, is real and must be taken account of, both as it relates to library service and to the public . . . relations of the library.[11]

The report suggests the publication of guidebooks, an effort to orient students to library procedures and flexibility in interpretation of rules, among other measures to improve relationships between students and the library staff.

Scanning various reports reveals many suggestions leading to the improvement of service to students. Various universities, including the University of Wisconsin-Milwaukee, make use of student library committees to increase liaison between library and student body.

## PERSONNEL

As Paul Buck said, "Special education preparation fits the librarian for his profession. Careers in librarianship have their own distinctive patterns, and the librarian's contribution to his university is one that only he can make." [12]

It is a fact that the character of the educational and research programs of the college or university depends principally on the quality of the faculty and the library, and that the library is, in fact, one of the primary teaching agencies of the college or university. Professional librarians contribute to the teaching, research, and service functions of the college or university, not only by making available materials for both assigned study and independent research, but by individual teaching contact with professors and students alike. The practice of accepting librarians as members of academic faculties is becoming common. Librarians are recognized as eligible for membership in AAUP and for NDEA Loans to teachers.

In spite of the fact that conditions of employment and salaries are improving in librarianship, personnel problems continue to be vexing. Indeed, the ranks seem to be thinning. Erickson [13] found in 1961 that in all of the surveys he analyzed, personnel problems came under the scrutiny of all surveyors. Jerrold Orne, in his *Survey of Facilities for the Sciences and Social Sciences*, published in 1965, states, "Our responses on personnel needs tell us no more than we already know. . . . We appear to be losing, rather than gaining ground. Current needs are even larger than four years ago." [14] ". . . our personnel adequacy has depreciated by about 30% in four years." [15] Helen Wheeler calls our attention to the disquieting fact that in 1930 the Junior College Round Table of ALA set a minimum standard of two professional librarians per library. That standard is still waiting for recognition. [16]

An inspection of the texts of Wilson and Tauber and Lyle will indicate a variety of organizational pattterns. The surveyor must determine if the one existing in the library under survey is the most efficient for *that* library. Does it make the best possible use of existing staff? Does it get the job done most efficiently? Does it allow for growth? Does it provide for emergencies and contingencies?

A surveyor can do tremendous service by aiding in the development of a personnel policy statement, a personnel program, and an organizational chart. Each position must be scrutinized. Any upgrading of professional assignments must be accomplished. Any possible tasks which can be assigned to clericals, or possibly to machines, must be so assigned.

APPLICABILITY OF STANDARDS IN SURVEY WORK

Concerning published library standards Tauber has observed:

In any profession which seeks to raise the level of work of its craftsmen, it is essential that guiding principles and standards, so far as they can be derived, be identified and made available to the practitioners. Surveyors, if they are conscious of the existence of principles or standards, should use them when appropriate. . . . Standards represent guides, and must be applied with caution. [17]

*The ALA Standards for College Libraries* [18] were published in 1959. They were designed to provide a guide for the evaluation of libraries which emphasize four-year undergraduate instruction. Reprints of the Standards have been distributed by the ACRL office. The use made of those standards has been varied, and general acceptance by the profession has, in my experience, been favorable.

The first direct application of the Standards in a college survey occurred at Sioux Fall College in 1961.[19]

Painstaking analysis of the particular situation indicated an ideal laboratory situation in which to interpret the document. Felix Hirsch, then chairman of the ACRL Standards Committee, lent his aid and advice. The Standards were used with the full understanding and cooperation of the college officials.

Surveyors, including Robert Downs [20] in 1963, have since cited sections of the Standards in actual survey situations.

The *ALA Standards for Junior College Libraries* [21] were published in May, 1960. It would seem that this set of Standards has not enjoyed the same acceptance as have the college Standards. B. Lamar Johnson has stated:

Because of the qualitative and subjective nature of most of the criteria included in Standards for Junior College Libraries, difficulties will inevitably be encountered in applying the criteria to specific libraries. Conclusions regarding the *quality* of the book collection and of its relevance to the educational program of a particular college must, for example, largely be based upon subjective judgment. Likewise standards for evaluating the effectiveness of library service are not objectively defined.[22]

Helen Wheeler's study indicates that, while the Standards are accepted and used by a large number of librarians, they have not been accepted wholeheartedly by Junior College Administrators:

The Association of College and Research Libraries has published ALA Standards for Junior College Libraries, designed to provide a guide for junior colleges, including community college libraries. They cover functions, structure and government, budget, staff, collections (including audio visual materials), building, quality of service and its evaluation and inter-library cooperation. The concepts are those of the library as the intellectual powerhouse of the junior college and the junior college librarian as an educator. But, The (American Association of Junior Colleges') Commission on Administration does not approve of these statements as *standards* for junior college libraries, since these statements so labeled will undoubtedly be used for accreditation purposes.

· · ·

The Commission is in general agreement with the purpose and functions of junior college libraries as stated by the American Library Association. It finds itself in disagreement. . . .

· · ·

with the *Standards'* recommendations that the library director report to the president, the library budget consist of at least 5% of the college budget, there be at least two librarians, the library director have faculty status, the need for a collection of at least 20,000 titles is crucial and the library seating facilities provide for at least 25% of the total enrollment.

· · ·

At this writing (March 14,1963) the Association has determined that it will engage someone in the junior college field to develop a set of guidelines for junior college libraries.

· · ·

No further effort to aid progress in junior college library programing has been announced by the American Association of Junior Colleges. This fact and the specialized nature of the community junior college and its library have produced *The Community College Library; A Plan for Action.*[23]

This comprehensive survey should be required reading for anyone concerned with community colleges and their libraries. The continuing development of standards pertaining to various aspects of librarianship should be of increasing value to surveyors.

## COLLECTIONS

In the final analysis, it is the quality of its collections by which a library is judged. It is axiomatic that a critic does not damn an academic library for what is found in it as often as what is not found in it.

It is true that a small liberal arts college could admirably serve its purpose if it has a large percentage of the items listed in the Shaw, Lamont, and Michigan lists, a generous input from such a current aid as *Choice*, and additional items to satisfy its unique demands, with a quality staff to interpret those collections.

The development of excellent collections for the university library entails much more involved planning. Intelligent collection development can result only from a comprehensive study of past and present publications in the many subject fields for which the library is responsible.

The age of the institution should indicate strength in certain disciplines. Such is not always the case. As years have passed, and with no definite acquisitions policy, very spotty collections may have resulted.

The role of the library being surveyed in regional or national cooperative efforts, and its relation with other research libraries must be analyzed in trying to determine adequacy of total collections. Verner Clapp gives us much food for thought on this matter in *The Future of the Research Library*.[24]

## BUILDINGS

Of the three essentials of library operation, collections, staff, and building, I would suggest that a building is essential only to the extent that it *efficiently* brings into a close and harmonious relationship patrons, staff, and materials. It might be that a surveyor finds that a library operation has simply outgrown its physical plant. Need for extensive remodeling, additions, transfer of part of the operation into some type of branch library, or a completely new building may be necessary. The surveyor should not hesitate to make his recommendation. In his report, he should further suggest the retention of a competent library building consultant to aid the institution, its engineers, and architects in programing a solution to the particular problem.

REFERENCES

1. Michigan. University. Survey Research Center, *Faculty Appraisal of a University Library*, Ann Arbor, University of Michigan Library, 1961.
2. Florida. University. Steering Committee of the University Self Study, *The Future of Florida State University*, Tallahassee, Florida State University, 1962.
3. North Central Association of Colleges and Secondary Schools. Commission on Colleges and Universities, *Report of an Accrediting Examination of Sioux Falls College, Sioux Falls, South Dakota, December 19–20, 1960*. The Association [1961].
4. Anderson, LeMoyne W., telephone interview by Gormley, Mark M., June 9, 1965.
5. Buck, Paul, *Libraries and Universities*, Cambridge, Massachusetts, Harvard University Press, 1964. p. 149.
6. ACRL Committee on Standards, "Standards for College Libraries," *College and Research Libraries*, 20: 275 (1959).
7. Erickson, Ernst Walfred, *College and University Library Surveys 1938–1952*, Chicago, American Library Association, 1961. p. 27.
8. Erickson, Ernst Walfred, and Anderson, LeMoyne W. *Report of a Survey of the Western Washington State College Library, May 21–25, 1962*, Chicago, American Library Association, 1962. p. 5.
9. Harwell, Richard and Moore, Everett T., *The Arizona State University Library: Report of a Survey of the Library*, Chicago, American Library Association, 1959. p. 1.

10. Wisconsin. University. Secretary of the Faculty, *Rules and Regulations Governing the University of Wisconsin-Milwaukee*, Milwaukee, University of Wisconsin-Milwaukee, 1959. p. 31.
11. Harwell and Moore, *The Arizona State University Library*, p. 17.
12. Buck, Paul, "A New Personnel Program for Harvard Librarians," *The Status of American College and University Librarians*, ACRL Monographs, No. 22, American Library Association, 1958. p. 8.
13. Erickson, *College and University Library Surveys 1938–1952*, p. 76.
14. Orne, Jerrold, *A Survey of Facilities for the Sciences and Social Sciences in Academic Libraries of the United States*, Chapel Hill, University of North Carolina, 1965. p. 5.
15. *Ibid.*, p. 3.
16. Wheeler, Helen Rippier, *The Community College Library, A Plan for Action*, Hamden, Connecticut, Shoe String Press, 1965. p. 5.
17. Tauber, Maurice F., "Survey Method in Approaching Library Problems," *Library Trends*, 13: 22 (July 1964).
18. ACRL Committee on Standards, "Standards for College Libraries," pp. 274–80.
19. Gormley, Mark M. and Hopp, Ralph H., *The Sioux Falls College Library: A Survey*, Chicago, American Library Association, 1961.
20. Downs, Robert B., *Report on a Survey of the Libraries of the Arkansas Foundation of Associated Colleges*, Little Rock, The Foundation, 1963. 44 pp.
21. ACRL Committee on Standards, "Standards for Junior College Libraries," *College and Research Libraries*, 21: 200–6 (1960).
22. Johnson, B. Lamar, "The New Junior College Library Standards: An Analysis and Critique," *ALA Bulletin*, 55: 159 (February 1961).
23. Wheeler, *The Community College Library*, pp. 5, 6.
24. Clapp, Verner W., *The Future of the Research Library*, Urbana, University of Illinois Press, 1964.

# 11 Public Libraries

ANDREW GEDDES

M Y first reaction when asked to write on the topic of special approaches and special problems of public library surveys was to say that there really are none—at least none that differ radically from other types of library surveys. One approaches a survey of a public library in a fashion no different from that used to approach a study of any problem whether it be a public library, a school library, or the local shoe factory. By that I mean one finds out what the problems are, seeks facts related to particular areas, analyzes those problems in relation to the facts and goals of the organization, tests conclusions, and then makes recommendations. This procedure is basic to any study, for a sound analytic approach is essential.

However, when recommendations and their possible effects are considered, one begins to realize that while the differences may not seem great in terms of approach to the problem, significant differences exist which must be constantly weighed and which constantly influence a public library study. Let me share some of my feelings about these significant areas of difference in approach, and some problems which must be considered which, I believe, are unique to the field of public library surveying. I would also like to share some of my feelings about surveying in general.

First of all, what kinds of public library surveys are being conducted? The scope is tremendous and the variety is infinite. Surveys range from broad studies of technical services such as the Tauber-Kingery analysis of the central technical processing service of the Nassau Library System [1] to studies of small

aspects of technical services such as catalog-card production or
serials cataloging. The need for expansion of branch library
service in a metropolitan area is another favorite subject. An
excellent example of such a study is Martin's report for the
Dallas Public Library.[2] Of equal importance are studies of individual branches or a segment of a branch operation such as the
book collection.

Community analysis is usually undertaken as part of any
public library study and many reports could be cited. Studies
have also been done on limited segments of the community such
as Bundy's study of voter reaction to a library issue in Illinois.[3]
In general, however, most public library studies fall into a
pattern which involves research to develop chapters on the
history of the community and the library, analysis of the
community with a projection of trends, analysis of present
services and the budget, study of the book collection, evaluation
measured by acceptable standards, and finally a series of conclusions and recommendations. If problems related to the choice of
site for a building are involved, then, of course, a detailed
analysis is required of transportation, traffic patterns, and similar
related factors. Joseph Wheeler's report on "The Effective
Location of Public Library Buildings" is an excellent summary
of the factors to be considered in conducting a site survey.[4]

Most certainly the surveyor should in the course of his study
determine the attitudes of the community toward the library in
deciding, at least in part, the approach he will use in his reporting. While a survey may be directed toward solving particular
problems such as financing or the location of a branch library, a
surveyor is rarely called upon to do a community survey as
such. Yet this is invariably the first step in any public library
survey. Before any determination of need can be made, there
must be a clear-cut knowledge of what the community has been,
what it is, and, most particularly, what it will be. Here, then, is
another dissimilarity between a public library survey and other
types of surveys. The other types of libraries offer a relatively
homogeneous community for study—limited in size, limited in
interests, limited in composition. This is not true of the public

library. Communities served by public libraries are in a state of constant change and recommendations must be built into any public library survey providing for ease of adjustment to this continually changing situation.

While the data required by a surveyor, such as collection, use, staff, budgets, do not vary greatly with the type of library, the problems of amassing that data can be enormous. Data for public libraries, simply because of the volume dealt with, are greater, more complex, and, unfortunately, more difficult to locate. The inability of the library, and frequently the governmental units, to provide the sort of data necessary to conduct a competent survey is a problem. Libraries just don't keep good records in some cases or their records will be at a variance with records kept elsewhere by another department or governmental unit. Nothing leaves a surveyor as far out on a limb as sets of conflicting statistics and the need to make a choice.

The college or special library community is more easily defined and the required data more easily obtained. The non-public library is generally a single institution whose clientele is required to use its facilities. The public library is not a single institution but is closely aligned with many other facets of the community and, unfortunately, a major part of its public is largely uninvolved with its program of library service. These are a few of the factors which make a survey infinitely more complex for public libraries. In fact, only in the public library field is a surveyor faced with such complexity—complexity of clientele, complexity of programing and services, complexity of financing, complexity of organizational structuring, and complexity of legal and political structures.

Clientele in public libraries nowadays ranges from the pre-school child all the way through our most advanced-in-age-senior citizens. Any evaluation of a public library, therefore, must consider collections and services in terms of these age levels. But of even greater consideration is the fact that within this wide spectrum there are intermediate segments of population such as children, young adults, adult and senior citizens, and these can be further subdivided ad infinitum. Within each of these age groupings there are persons who want only light fiction or just a superficial treatment of a subject, but also there are those who want to explore in considerable depth an area of some obscure subject. This complexity of clientele is found in no other library situation and creates one of the initial problems confronting a consultant who seeks to evaluate a library and its service program.

Stemming from the variety of clientele the public library must serve are the programs which the community expects of it such as book discussion groups, film discussions, story hours, musical evenings, and many more activities that confront a surveyor in his efforts to evaluate the needs of a community and to judge the relative merits of each of these programs. How are questions answered such as: Is a separate young adult room needed? Should we have microfilms? Do we need photocopiers? What about records? This series of questions requires much analysis of the community before legitimate answers can be given.

The complexity of financing is an ever-growing problem that sometimes defies understanding, and legislators are constantly reviewing old bases for financing and devising new ones—per capita levies, mill levies, levies based on complicated formulas, state-aid, federal funds, private funds, fines and fees. A surveyor attempting to work in different states must plan to spend considerable time and effort learning the financing patterns of library support. While the surveyor, wending his way through the maze of public and private financing which exists in many public libraries today, will have a challenge and may find public financing confusing, he will seldom find cause to worry about regional or community planning. Libraries are rarely considered in such long-range planning; there are only a few major instances of such consideration. The proposals recently made for East Orange, N.J., and the J.F.K. Center in Nassau County [5] are notable for their uniqueness in this respect. If such long-range community planning included libraries, many of the problems which at present require a survey might be eliminated.

If all of these complexities of clientele, financing, and services are not enough to scare all but the bravest from undertaking a survey of public libraries, let me add a complexity which, while still fairly new, nevertheless promises to be most bothersome: systems. School-district libraries, village libraries, city libraries, county libraries, association libraries, and special-library district libraries had certain complexities which at times posed real problems of structure and relationship, but today we have regional libraries, cooperative systems, federated systems, and area libraries. Who knows what the newest term will be? *Each* of these concepts is so new and its service goals are defined in such general terms that it is difficult to determine the relationship of a given library to its community, parent body, and fellow system members. The laws which have established these networks of libraries are many and varied, and are confusing even to a legal mind let alone a poor librarian. Such a network of libraries, understood by relatively few librarians even in terms of service program, poses a real test for any hardy soul seeking to clarify a muddy library situation.

There are very few guidelines or standards for this type of interdependent service. Each decision a director makes becomes the latest standard, and the areas of comparability from one system to another are small because of the tremendous variations among them. This is true even in New York State where twenty-two systems operate under a general law. It will be interesting to see the results of the evaluation of these systems being conducted under the general direction of Lowell Martin.[6] How much the New York systems differ from one another will be small compared to the differences which would become apparent if nationwide surveys were attempted. A surveyor who has always explored consolidated-type branch systems will find the subtle nuances of studying a cooperative or federated system unique. He will find the usual approaches to solving the problem can not be used, for his previous experience no longer applies.

So far I've discussed the problems facing the surveyor but not the surveyor himself. The surveyor unquestionably is hired as *the* authority; it is expected that he will cure all of the ills of the library. Yet, in fact, many of the problems he will face will be new to him. Unfortunately, few library boards when hiring surveyors really understand that they are hiring part-time consultants who have full-time jobs. They believe, despite all explanations to the contrary, that they are hiring specialists. That most surveys turn out so well is a tribute to the profession in general. But as time goes by the availability of more federal money will result in more studies being undertaken. Unless standards for consultants are drawn money is going to be wasted. Too much money is around; too few competent surveyors exist. The profession, it would seem, has an obligation to the taxpayers, governmental agencies, and boards of trustees to ensure that they get competent advice and guidance. The difficulty, of course, is how to set such standards, how to transmit the information about competent surveyors to interested groups, and how to police the practitioner.

I also believe that large amounts of federal money will make library consulting work more attractive to management firms and more firms will move into this area. Some have already done so, but not always with satisfactory results. A study [7] conducted in Nassau County has led the Nassau Library System Board of Trustees to issue an eighteen page rebuttal [8] to the firm's recommendations. Another study, done by the Little Hoover Committee of the state library of Ohio, made drastic recommendations for change and the reverberations are still being felt in that state.

I strongly urge that we do not entirely relinquish to management firms, composed of nonlibrarians, the responsibility for evaluating our problems and making recommendations. Such a course of action could result in some questionable conclusions affecting the service program of public libraries for years to come. In a way, librarians are at the same point in relation to management firms as they are to data-processing specialists. If librarians do not seize opportunities and widen their vision others, less competent, or at least less service-oriented, will take over and make the decisions determining the future course of librarianship.

This means that librarians must become more adept at handling their own problems and evaluating their own needs. They must also be more dynamic in their leadership roles. When a board of trustees brings in an expert to confirm an opinion already expressed by the director, one can not but wonder about the relationship existing between the librarian, his board, and the community which produces such a situation. There are always times when an outside opinion is helpful, but surveys should not be asked for to avoid decision-making or to sidestep taking a stand. Surveys should not be undertaken simply to achieve status by use of the newest status symbol. Librarians must assert the leadership necessary to move librarianship ahead; no better way can be found than to have their professional opinion honored. Therefore, librarians are urged to resist the temptation to ask for a survey before making every effort to solve their own problems.

It is true that public librarianship is becoming more and more complex administratively. Computers have arrived on some doorsteps and are just around the corner elsewhere. New media, new nonbook forms, new concepts, new services are here, and demanding attention. We cannot constantly turn to others for the decisions. We must find the answers among our own staff. If this sounds antisurveys, it is because I believe the competent, practicing librarian can find answers as good as those any survey can suggest.

Too often surveys are undertaken to find answers known before the surveyor arrived on the scene. But the director, the board, or the public were unwilling to admit they knew the answers or to make the effort needed to sell the right solution. Undertaking such surveys seems to me an unjustifiable expenditure of taxpayer's money. Legitimate surveys have a place, but, just as there are unethical doctors who operate on a patient when no real need exists, there are unethical surveyors. I once read a survey and called the surveyor long-distance to discuss some standards he quoted. They fitted quite well into a study I was doing and I wanted to indicate their source. After some discussion the surveyor finally admitted he had made up the standards to fit the situation! Is a survey ever turned down? Has anyone ever said: It doesn't need to be done. I haven't the time to do it well. I don't feel competent to do this study. Or, is it ever suggested that a study be combined with another project already underway? I'm afraid that with so much federal money around for the asking, unethical or at least unqualified people will not be able to resist the urge to survey. If surveys are to have any meaning in the library field they will be only as valid as the people who are doing them are competent.

Hopefully, librarians will work more and more as consulting teams to bring the widest possible experience to problems in public librarianship. The team approach can also be used to help develop competent surveyors, if experienced surveyors will use neophytes as assistants. This, in a sense, could become a trainee program for apprentice surveyors.

At the present time most surveys are being done by a limited number of firms and professional librarians. If public libraries are to be a dynamic force in the community we must avoid stereotyping of solutions to problems; we must advance the art of surveying; we must create more competent surveyors. Library schools can play an important role in this through developing research centers similar to that at the University of Illinois. State library agencies also have a responsibility for such centers. No business firm in this country today would expect to progress and grow without a large investment in research and development. With the library movement approaching the billion dollar expenditure category, the failure to analyze systematically where we are and where we should be going seems inconceivable to me. By holding this conference, Columbia has taken an important first step. I sincerely hope that there is not only a second and a third step but a tenth and a twentieth as well.

REFERENCES

1. Tauber, Maurice F., and Kingery, R. E. *The Central Technical Processing of the Nassau Library System; A Report on the Organization, Facilities, Operations and Problems.* Hempstead, N.Y., Nassau Library System, 1962.

2. Martin, Lowell A. *Branch Library Service for Dallas, a Report Sponsored by the Friends of the Dallas Public Library.* New Brunswick, N.J., 1958.

3. Bundy, Mary Lee. *An Analysis of Voter Reaction to a Proposal to Form a Library District in LaSalle and Bureau Counties, Illinois.* ("Illinois State Library Research Series," No. 1.) Springfield, 1960.

4. Wheeler, Joseph L. *The Effective Location of Public Library Buildings.* (University of Illinois Library School Occasional Papers, No. 52) Urbana, University of Illinois Library School, 1958.

5. Becket, Welton. *Technical Report for the Master Plan Concept of the John F. Kennedy Educational, Civic and Cultural Center Proposed for Mitchel Field in the County of Nassau.* New York, 1964.

6. Prentiss, S. Gilbert. "Public Library System Program to be Evaluated," *The Bookmark* 23:277–78 (July 1964).

7. Nelson Associates, Inc. *A Proposed Governing Structure for the Mitchel Field Library.* New York, 1965.

8. Nassau Library System Board of Trustees. *An Analysis of the Nelson Associates Report: A Proposed Governing Structure for the Mitchel Field Library.* Hempstead, N.Y., 1965.

# 12  School Libraries

### FRANCES E. HENNE

THE word *survey*, as used in this conference, covers other related terms commonly used in the educational field. As far as school libraries are concerned, the term *evaluation* appears more frequently than *survey*, probably because evaluations—which are common occurrences in schools—employ survey techniques as one phase of a broader endeavor. Evaluation denotes probing, interpreting, and planning in greater depth than does the typical survey. Furthermore, evaluations generally involve a single school library or a small number of libraries, whereas the survey's coverage embraces larger areas—a state, a region, or the nation. The *status study*, a popular form of survey today, usually follows a four-part process: collecting facts about school libraries in a given region, comparing these facts with standards, indicating what the libraries need to reach the standards, and constructing a planning program whereby goals can be achieved. *Planning* is currently stressed at all levels and forms an integral part of evaluation. *School library statistics*, another commonly found term, refers to those statistics compiled from national, regional, or state surveys of school library facilities and practices.

In collecting the literature on surveys and surveying in the school library field, the inquirer finds it necessary to follow these many avenues of terminology. In addition, the area of evaluation and measurement in education applies to the school library in innumerable respects, as do surveys of reading, instructional methods, and other related educational and social topics.

Whatever the term, the survey is more than a simple technique. The instruments and methodology are designed on a basis of a sound knowledge of the objectives and programs of schools and school libraries; the evaluation of the data thus collected and the subsequent planning program also reflect this knowledge.

## TYPES OF SCHOOL LIBRARY SURVEYS

A three-part classification of school library surveys can be noted. In the first category, the surveys or evaluations fall within the following groups:

*Local Surveys: The Single School Library:* The school library may be evaluated separately or as one part of a total school evaluation. It may be evaluated by the school librarian with or without the assistance of members of the faculty, or by accrediting teams, or by other outside specialists. Scores of such evaluations take place yearly. In other instances, the librarian may elect to evaluate only one part of the school library program, such as the materials collections or student use, and spread the evaluation of the total program over a period of several years.

An informal, albeit very important, process of evaluation of individual school libraries goes on continuously in many states, cities, towns, and counties—the advisory visits of school library supervisors.

*Local Surveys: School Libraries in a School System:* Again, these surveys may be self-evaluations or conducted by outside specialists; and they may be of the school libraries only, or of the school libraries in total school evaluations. They tend not to have the detail of many single building evaluations because of the time involved in making depth studies. Their scope covers the libraries in the schools and also the system-level office or center for instructional materials and centralized school library services (supervisory, advisory, technical, and other).

*State Surveys:* Several kinds of state surveys exist. In recent years, many events and activities have motivated or launched, on a rather widespread scale, status studies or surveys of school library facilities and services—among them, the publication and implementation of the national standards for school library programs (2),* the work of the School Library Development Project of the American Association of School Librarians (4), the promotion of school library programs by National Library Week committees and staff, the interest of professional organizations and citizen groups, and federal and state legislation. Many of these studies are not statewide in scope, but cover several counties or a cluster of school systems scattered throughout a state. Most of them are made through the professional interest of school librarians (who give considerable "spare" time to these enterprises), and usually are undertaken as projects of local, regional, or state professional associations of school librarians. An important part of these activities is the frequent involvement of school administrators, teachers, parents with children in school, and other citizens.

Some state surveys of school libraries constitute status studies in a sense, but are much more systematic, comprehensive, and far-reaching in their planning, support, coverage, and depth. Qualitative as well as quantitative features of school library programs are presented. Examples of recently completed studies are the Puerto Rico (9), Washington (1,34), and Maryland (23) surveys. California is currently conducting a comprehensive survey and evaluation of school libraries, and other states have indicated their intent of undertaking similar projects.

The annual statistics about school library services and facilities that are collected and compiled by state departments of education or other state agencies represent another source of survey information on the state level.

A burgeoning form of evaluation, which falls more accurately within the bounds of planning than within those of systematic surveying, consists of the state plans or area studies for cooperative library services. Their nature and extent can be ascertained from a list that appeared in a recent issue of the *ALA Bulletin* (6). Among those projecting future plans are the Rhode Island

* The numbers in parentheses refer to the references at the end of this chapter.

(13), New York (26,27,29,30), and New Jersey (28) reports. Some problems connected with projecting plans for library cooperation, as they affect school libraries, are noted in the last section of this paper.

*Regional Surveys:* Not many regional surveys of school libraries have been made. The Pacific Northwest survey of libraries contains a volume on school libraries in that region (31), and a study dealing with elementary school libraries in the Southern states has recently been made (33). Collections of facts by regional accrediting associations and the major role played by these associations in school library evaluations for accrediting purposes should also be noted.

*National Surveys:* National surveys of school libraries include statistics of public school libraries compiled by the United States Office of Education (21,22); the survey of school libraries as instructional materials centers, conducted by Alice Lohrer for the United States Office of Education (19,20); and a tabulated but unpublished survey that led to the national standards for school library programs. The standards were evolved from a comprehensive survey of the best school library programs throughout the nation. Facts about existing facilities plus information about what was needed to achieve the school's objectives were obtained, and from the combination of these data the quantitative standards were derived. A preliminary survey, of course, identified the sample of good school libraries. A battery of questionnaires, covering many aspects of school library programs, yielded materials used as guidelines in formulating the qualitative standards.

The five types of surveys described above are taken from the first of three categories of school library surveys. The second category covers surveys that do not deal with school library facilities and services in general, but explore special aspects that have been isolated for particular scrutiny: student use of school libraries, student use of public libraries, centralized processing costs and procedures, school library architecture, use of school libraries by teachers, the prospective teacher's knowledge of school libraries and their resources, and others. Since these surveys represent topics discussed in other papers, they will not be discussed here. Let it be said, however, that there is great need for more studies or surveys about the actual use made of libraries by students and teachers, about the materials used, and about the nature and requirements of school assignments. Such inquiries are among the most important to be undertaken in the school library field at this time. Without the essential data that such studies would provide, multischool district centers for school library services and resources, state plans, and cooperative library resource centers cannot be reliably constructed or even validly discussed.

The third and final category has been judged to fall without the scope of this conference, although in some respects it is the most important of all: the special studies, demonstration projects, and other investigations that frequently employ some survey techniques but that have broader purposes and classify as pure research.

GENERAL PRINCIPLES

General principles and procedures for conducting school library evaluations have been described at some length and for some time in professional literature. In 1943 *The Library In General Education* (11) contained a critique of evaluative techniques and an analysis of surveys. A later summary of developments and writings on the subject appeared in 1953 in *Current Trends in School Libraries* (10). The introductions to several basic tools used in evaluating school libraries (to be mentioned later) present objectives, criteria, and methodology in considerable detail.

Only a few of the many general principles shaping school library evaluations can be presented here. The ones mentioned pertain to the types of surveys noted in category one in the preceding section, and have been selected primarily on the basis of their being more characteristic of school library evaluations than of surveys of other types of libraries.

School library evaluation consists of four main parts: (1) critical study of the library's objectives and of the objectives and characteristics of the school of which it is an integral part; (2) measurement or survey of the quantitative and qualitative aspects of the school library program (facilities and services), a process that employs a variety of fact-finding devices as well as many evaluative techniques; (3) evaluation and interpretation of the findings in relation to the extent that the school library is helping to achieve the objectives of the school and in relation to standards; and (4) formulation of the planning program.

These depth evaluations, generally done at the individual level and occasionally at the system level, require time and effort, and, not infrequently, they are done by degrees, extending over an academic year or a longer period of time. Even in the case of visits by accrediting teams, which cover a short but action-packed time span, preliminary preparations and post-implementations represent an expenditure of time and energy on the part of the school involved.

Another principle followed in school library evaluations recommends that evaluations, whether self-survey or conducted by outside specialists, involve not only the school librarians but also the administration, faculty, and, not infrequently, students and parents. The pattern of having some person or persons "blow in, blow off, and blow out," although not unknown in the annals of school library evaluation, has little, if anything, to commend it. Under any circumstances evaluations should be constructive in design and intent, with the primary purpose of working with and assisting the school and the librarians to effect improvements in the library benefiting students and teachers. The school librarian quaking in his boots before, during, or after an evaluation may be confronted and affronted with poor evaluative techniques. This fact holds true even in those situations where the school librarians are the blocks impeding the progress of the library program.

As already stated, planning programs constitute one of the key parts of school library evaluation. Such programs consist of spelling out in detail the services, personnel, funds, resources, and facilities needed by the school library for optimum development (also any recommended eliminations of outmoded facilities, creaking procedures, and faulty services). Specific time periods in which the various parts of the proposed planning program should be accomplished are generally indicated. (Examples of forms used in constructing planning programs will be shown later.)

One of the most important principles centers in the emphasis placed on conducting and interpreting evaluations and constructing planning programs in terms of benefits to be gained for the students and the teachers, not in terms of gains for the library or the librarians—hence the stressing of the library's role in helping to achieve the school's objectives. A recommendation for additional staff is not made to save the librarian from collapse through overwork, but on the basis of providing the improved library services needed by students and teachers.

Another characteristic of school library evaluations is that they are ongoing and continuous. Reevaluation at specified intervals of time is required in many states, and is a common practice in innumerable building and system situations. Schools, standards, and numerous other factors constantly change, and reevaluations, taking these changes into consideration, become imperative. Thus, a decade ago, demands came from school administrators and librarians for the revision of national school library standards to reflect the current educational scene and to meet the needs of the modern school, so that the standards would provide a realistic, workable tool for use in reevaluations. Similar requests are now being made for a revision of the 1960 standards.


METHODOLOGY

The techniques employed in surveying and evaluating school libraries vary. A commonly used procedure is to compare the facilities existing in a school library with the recommendations incorporated in state, regional, or national standards. These studies are primarily concerned with quantitative standards for staff, funds, the materials collections, quarters, and equipment.

For state-level and other surveys cited in this paper, more sophisticated methods have been employed, with techniques and instruments devised and used to meet particular purposes. The normative survey approach, with specially constructed questionnaires, prevails.

With the current emphasis on developing and strengthening elementary school libraries, two recently published tools have been indeed helpful: Gaver's rating scale (8) for the accessibility of learning materials, and the evaluation guide (32) released by the Southern Association of Colleges and Schools.

The methodological techniques employed in some of the tools are rather intricate in design, and stress qualitative as well as quantitative features of the library program. Other tools are reduced to minimum essentials. In order to show variations in methodology, four examples have been selected from the general evaluative instruments. Since the brief descriptions that follow do not show fully the purposes, scope, and coverage of the tools, they should in no way serve as a substitute for an examination of the original works. (Sample pages, shown on transparencies during the original presentation of this material, are appended.)

*A Planning Guide for the High School Library Program* (12) covers both library services and facilities in detail, listing items to be evaluated and including for each item not only a measurement symbol but also guidelines for measurement, ranging from a sentence to several paragraphs, that give recommended conditions or practices and thus provide directives to assist the evaluator. In addition, many tables are provided for the recording of facts needed to make evaluations requiring ratings. National and regional standards are quoted and space provided for the recording of state standards, with measurement devices to show the school library's development in relation to the achievement of these standards. The volume is designed for use in a long-range evaluation. Although some parts are very much out of date, basic techniques remain sound, and hence the tool is still used.

The devices used for measurement throughout the *Planning Guide* employ two criteria: the extent to which certain facilities or services can be found in the school library or the degree of quality of these services or facilities, and the relative importance of the individual items being evaluated in the total school library program. The code for the symbols to be used by the evaluators follows:

| How good? | To what extent? | Yes or No? | Degree of importance |
|---|---|---|---|
| A. Excellent | A. Very extensively | A. Yes | 1. Of utmost importance |
| B. Good | (or completely) | F. No | |
| C. Fair | B. Considerably | X. Does not | 2. Of considerable importance |
| D. Poor | C. Some | apply | |
| F. Not at all | D. Very little | | 3. Of some importance |
| X. Does not apply | F. Not at all | | |
| | X. Does not apply | | 0. Of no importance |

The Illinois Area Consensus Studies (14), constructed for the purpose of evaluating separate curriculum and service areas in the secondary school, have several unique features. The project as a whole involved the cooperation and advisory services of the professional associations and professional education agencies in the state. For each area, the evaluative tools, called "inventories," were constructed by "juries" composed of school administrators and specialists in the subject or service; for the school library field, the specialists included librarians in schools, school library supervisors, and library school faculty members. Special characteristics of the evaluative design are the recommendations that no more than two areas, and preferably only one, be evaluated in a school during each phase, that one year be devoted to evaluating the area selected for evaluation, and that the entire faculty, some students, some parents, and some other citizens in the community participate in the evaluation (with group dynamics much in evidence).

Inventory A (15) consists of forty-one principles that deal with objectives, services, facilities, and standards for school libraries. For each principle, three questions are asked, obtaining from the participant his judgment as to whether he believes in the principle, how he rates the principle in importance, and to what extent he believes the library in the school is achieving the principle. A guide (18) is provided for the group discussions that follow the administering and tabulation of Inventory A. Inventory B (16) is then presented to the group. This inventory is exactly the same as the first one but has a fourth question added to each of the principles, asking whether the school should make specific plans for improving that particular feature of the library program. Following this, a committee is appointed and given the responsibility of designing a planning program that will put the improvements recommended by the group into operation. Inventory C (17) contains directives for assisting the committee in collecting essential data about the library, evaluating the library program, and constructing the plan.

The Evaluative Criteria (24,25) are probably the best known evaluative instruments and are widely used for school accreditation and for other purposes. These are fundamentally tools for all-school evaluations, and, if separate parts are isolated for evaluation, those general sections of the Criteria that cover objectives, philosophy, and characteristics of the school must be carefully considered. The section on "Instructional Materials Services" deals with the school library. For the different sections, there are checklists of facilities and services to be rated (E for extensive provision or condition, S for moderate, and L for limited or missing), evaluations, with a rating scale from 5 (excellent) to 1 (poor), and space for recording supplementary data. The checklists and evaluations also have the symbols of M (missing but questionable need) and N (does not apply). These tools are essentially qualitative measurements. When they are used by visiting committees who are evaluating the school for accreditation, there are additional important activities in the evaluative process, such as conferences with faculty members and students and visits to the classrooms as well as observation in the library.

Simplified forms for the evaluation of the school library in the individual school (3) and on the school system level (5) were made and distributed by the School Library Development Project. These tools are designed to help schools measure their school library facilities and services in relation to national standards, and provide space for charting a three-year planning program.

## SPECIAL PROBLEMS

A brief summary of some of the problems existing in the field of evaluating and surveying school libraries follows:

1. Although geared to school objectives, most evaluations and evaluative techniques fail to measure adequately or with sufficient refinement such basic factors affecting library programs as instructional methods, curriculum content, the nature of assignments, and classroom motivation of library use.

2. Many qualitative elements of school library programs do not lend themselves to precise measurement, and these elements are among those that form the most important parts of school library services. For example, it is impossible to measure accurately and comprehensively the effects of the library program on the reading patterns of children and young people unless very complicated and expensive research studies are conducted (and even then it is difficult to control the many variables in any given situation).

3. Schools, curricula, students, and society itself are constantly subject to change, and hence tools and techniques used for evaluation must be frequently reappraised and revised. Measuring instruments used to survey materials collections in high-school libraries today, for example, bear little resemblance to those used even five years ago. The use of library resources by students provides another instance where evaluative measures have assumed new forms. School library standards, commonly used as a measure in surveys, require continuous revision, too, and this precept applies to both quantitative and qualitative standards.

4. Surveys that amass quantitative data about school library

facilities do not, at times, report in sufficient refinement all the factors and variables needed for complete and accurate interpretation of the statistics. They are more apt to err on the side of overestimating, rather than underestimating, existing conditions. These surveys also have the obvious limitation of all surveys that report only quantitative, and not qualitative, aspects of school library programs. The old, old problem arises of ascertaining not just "how many?" or "how much?" but also "how good?"

5. School situations vary and so do school library practices and hence comparative studies are difficult to make. It is usually hazardous to make comparisons among school libraries on the sole basis of quantitative evidence reported in two or more surveys conducted under different auspices. Variables cannot be easily controlled in a survey dealing with any sizable number of schools.

6. Evaluations in depth employ subjective appraisals, even when the techniques used may be quite precise. Some aspects of school library programs can best be judged on the basis of expert opinion, and the degree of expertness may affect the nature, even the validity, of the findings.

7. Because standards for size of the library staff are seldom met, few school library programs have reached an optimum level in this country. The reliability and validity of measuring instruments and evaluative process have therefore rarely been tested adequately and established with certainty.

8. The danger exists that evaluations may on occasion lead to undue smugness on the part of the individuals connected with the school or systems being evaluated. Statistical surveys covering broad geographical areas may cause personnel in some high-ranking schools to view with contentment their comparative advancement over schools in other localities, and see no need to make plans for further improvements in their own situations. Quantitative standards have always had the built-in limitation of being misused to perpetuate an undesirable status quo.

9. Some of the area studies or planning proposals, particularly those that incorporate or project cooperative measures for different types of libraries—school libraries among them—suffer from

two major drawbacks: they are frequently made on purely subjective and theoretical bases and not on a reliable body of evidence, and they are sometimes formulated by surveyors without specialized knowledge of all the types of libraries represented. The imminent danger here is that new plans may be proposed which, if adopted, would keep individual libraries at a functionally substandard level.

10. In the school library field, surveys are sometimes made or recommended unnecessarily and become, in effect, a form of beating down open doors. The need to have good school libraries should not, in an enlightened democratic society, have to be proved by tons of statistics. Structuring plans and procedures to obtain such libraries may require statistical data for guidelines.

11. On the other hand, the school library field today stands greatly in need of the collection of data based on surveys, feasibility studies, evaluations, and other inquiries. The changes within the last five years—all those explosions in population, communications, knowledge, and technology that we hear about wherever we go and witness ourselves—have created an almost new world for school library programs and planning at all levels, and we need, sometimes desperately, a great body of new information.

The seven pages that have been drawn from four important texts are illustrative of good survey technique.

From *A Planning Guide for the High School Library Program* (12

THE READING GUIDANCE PROGRAM OF THE SCHOOL LIBRARY

A.  Information background needed by the school librarian

The school librarian needs a knowledge of all of the factors listed below in order to participate effectively in the reading program of the
school. The first five statements should be measured on the basis of
quality, and the last two statements should be measured on the basis
of quantity.

ABCDF      1. The librarian has an understanding of the methods of teach-
1230          ing reading.

ABCDF      2. The librarian knows what are the standard reading achieve-
1230          .ments that can be expected of students, from the first grade
              through college.

ABCDF      3. The librarian is familiar with the reading program in his
1230          school.

ABCDF      4. The librarian is familiar with the types and nature of read-
1230          ing tests, their scope, purpose, and use, and he knows how
              to interpret the scores made by students on tests.

ABCDF      5. The librarian is familiar with the types of reading records
1230          that are used in the school. He knows the scope, nature,
              purpose, and uses of these records, and he knows how to
              interpret the records that are kept of the reading of students.

ABCDF      6. The librarian is familiar with the backgrounds and abilities
1230          of as many students as possible.

ABCDF      7. The librarian keeps informed about recent investigations,
1230          research, and other developments in the field of reading,
              and knows the basic books about the reading of young people.

B.  Reading guidance activities performed by the librarian.

The activities listed below form a basic reading guidance program
which should be carried on by the school librarian. The first eight
statements should be measured on the basis of the extent to which the
librarian performs these services.

ABCDF      1. The librarian cooperates with all teachers in the school in
1230          any aspect of the reading program with which they may be
              concerned.

From *A Planning Guide for the High School Library Program* (12)

ANALYSIS OF LIBRARY SERVICES TO MEET TEACHER REQUESTS

Fill in the following chart on the basis of an <u>average week</u>:

| | | | Number not answered, distributed by reason why request could not be answered | | | |
|---|---|---|---|---|---|---|
| Types of requests | Number answered | Lack of time on part of librarian | Needed materials not in the library collection | Needed materials already in circulation | Other reasons | Total |
| Fact questions | | | | | | |
| Material for class assignments | | | | | | |
| Material for cur-riculum planning | | | | | | |
| Material for extra-curricular activities | | | | | | |
| Compilation of reading lists | | | | | | |
| Remedial reading material | | | | | | |
| Other (describe) | | | | | | |

## From *Inventory A of the Illinois Area Consensus Study* (15)

1a. Do you believe that the teaching methods used in our school should encourage students to use a wide variety of library resources? (Check one)

    ____ 1) Yes
    ____ 2) No
    ____ 3) No opinion

b. If your answer is "yes," how do you rate the importance of this principle? (Check one)

    ____ 1) Of utmost importance
    ____ 2) Of considerable importance
    ____ 3) Of some importance
    ____ 4) Of no importance
    ____ 5) No opinion

c. To what extent do you think our school is actually using teaching methods that encourage students to use a wide variety of library resources? (Check one)

    ____ 1) Fully
    ____ 2) To a considerable extent
    ____ 3) To some extent
    ____ 4) Not at all
    ____ 5) I don't know

2a. Do you believe that our school librarian should participate actively in curriculum planning? (Check one)

    ____ 1) Yes
    ____ 2) No
    ____ 3) No opinion

b. If your answer is "yes," how do you rate the importance of this principle? (Check one)

    ____ 1) Of utmost importance
    ____ 2) Of considerable importance
    ____ 3) Of some importance
    ____ 4) Of no importance
    ____ 5) No opinion

c. To what extent do you think our school librarian does participate actively in curriculum planning in our school? (Check one)

    ____ 1) Fully
    ____ 2) To a considerable extent
    ____ 3) To some extent
    ____ 4) Not at all
    ____ 5) I don't know

## From *Inventory B of the Illinois Area Consensus Study* (16)

1a. Do you believe that the teaching methods used in our school
should encourage students to use a wide variety of library resources? (Check one)
_____1) Yes
_____2) No
_____3) No opinion

b. If your answer is "yes," how do you rate the importance of this
principle? (Check one)
_____1) Of utmost importance
_____2) Of considerable importance
_____3) Of some importance
_____4) Of no importance
_____5) No opinion

c. To what extent do you think our school is actually using teaching
methods that encourage students to use a wide variety of library
resources? (Check one)
_____1) Fully
_____2) To a considerable extent
_____3) To some extent
_____4) Not at all
_____5) I don't know

d. Should we make specific plans for improving our school in this
respect? (Check one)
_____1) Yes
_____2) No

2a. Do you believe that our school librarian should participate actively in curriculum planning? (Check one)
_____1) Yes
_____2) No
_____3) No opinion

b. If your answer is "yes," how do you rate the importance of this
principle? (Check one)
_____1) Of utmost importance
_____2) Of considerable importance
_____3) Of some importance
_____4) Of no importance
_____5) No opinion

c. To what extent do you think our school librarian does participate
actively in curriculum planning in our school? (Check one)
_____1) Fully
_____2) To a considerable extent
_____3) To some extent
_____4) Not at all
_____5) I don't know

d. Should we make specific plans for improving our school in this
respect? (Check one)
_____1) Yes
_____2) No

From *Evaluation Criteria* (24)

## SERVICES

1. Services for Teachers and Administrators:

CHECKLIST

Members of the instructional materials staff:

( )   1. Share with teachers the indexes and published bibliographies of instructional materials and assist teachers in selecting printed and audiovisual materials for classroom planning.

( )   2. Systematically inform teachers of new materials and equipment that have been acquired.

( )   3. Assist in planning for effective use of instructional materials and equipment.

( )   4. Inform teachers systematically of student interests and needs as observed in the use of instructional materials.

( )   5. Assist teachers in the development of reading lists.

( )   6. Cooperate with teachers in providing materials and preparing exhibits for bulletin boards and other displays.

( )   7. Provide professional materials.

( )   8. Provide facilities and assistance in the production of simple and inexpensive instructional materials.

( )   9. Order and schedule the use of instructional materials rented or borrowed.

( ) 10. Train and schedule projectionists for audiovisual equipment.

( ) 11.

( ) 12.

From *Evaluation Criteria* (24)

**2. Services for Students:**

CHECKLIST

Members of the instructional materials staff:
( )  1. Cooperate with other members of the instructional staff in systematically acquainting students with the proper and effective use of instructional materials.
( )  2. Guide students in their selection of books and other instructional materials in terms of their abilities and interests.
( )  3. Assist students to develop discrimination in reading, viewing, and listening.
( )  4. Provide educational and vocational experience for students through an organized student-assistant program.
( )  5. Help to develop desirable attitudes in the care of school property.
( )  6. Assist student organizations to use resources of center in the promotion of their projects.
( )  7.

( )  8.


SUPPLEMENTARY DATA

1. Average daily attendance (number of students) in the library _____

EVALUATIONS

( ) a. How adequately do members of the instructional materials staff aid teachers and administrators in the effective use of instructional materials and equipment?
( ) b. How adequately do members of the instructional materials staff work with teachers in selecting materials for use?
( ) c. How adequately do members of the staff keep teachers and administrators informed of the status of and the need for instructional materials services?
( ) d. How adequately do members of the staff help in the production of appropriate instructional materials?
( ) e. How adequately do members of the instructional materials staff help students make effective use of instructional materials?
( ) f. How cooperative are students and teachers in the care and maintenance of instructional materials and equipment?
( ) g. How effectively do students use the materials and facilities for leisure activities?

From *Individual School Guide for Planning*
*School Library Development* (3)

### ACTION AREAS

Policies for Library Operation

"Optimum use of school library materials and good library service for students and teachers depend in large measure on having the resources of the school library easily accessible within the school." *Standards*, p. 87

Steps

Plan with librarians and teachers the policies and procedures that will enable maximum use of library resources (see *Standards*, pp. 87-94)

> Library available for use by individuals and groups throughout the school day

> Flexible scheduling of class groups to library (school schedule and library schedule promoting flexible use by class groups)

> Library open before and after school (at least 30 minutes before school; at least 1 hour after school)

> Library open for extended service (afternoons, evenings, weekends, summer) where conditions permit

> Centralization of all instructional materials in library

> Functional arrangement of library quarters and equipment

> Continuous short-term and long-term loans of all types of materials furnished to classrooms

> Library resources easily accessible and available for home use

> Efficient procedures for cataloging, classification, and arrangement of materials

REFERENCES

1. Ahlers, Eleanor E. "Story of a Survey." *School Libraries* 13:19–29 (May 1964).
2. American Association of School Librarians. *Standards for School Library Programs*. The American Association of School Librarians in cooperation with the American Association of Colleges for Teacher Education and others. Chicago, American Library Association, 1960.
3. American Association of School Librarians: School Library Development Project. *Individual School Guide for Planning School Library Development*. Chicago, American Association of School Librarians, 1962.
4. —— *Planning School Library Development*. Report by Mary Frances Kennon and Leila Ann Doyle. Chicago, American Library Association, 1962.
5. —— *School District Guide for Planning School Library Development*. Chicago, American Association of School Librarians, 1962.
6. Bunge, Charles A. "Statewide Public Library Surveys and Plans: 1944–1964." *ALA Bulletin* 59:364–74 (May 1965).
7. Darling, Richard L. *Survey of School Library Standards*. Washington, D.C., U.S. Government Printing Office, 1964.
8. Gaver, Mary Virginia. *The Accessibility of Learning Materials: A Rating Scale* (Elementary School Library Series No. 2). East Brunswick, N.J., SSH Press, 1962.
9. Gaver, Mary Virginia, and Velázquez, Gonzalo. *School Libraries of Puerto Rico: A Survey and Plan for Development*. San Juan, Puerto Rico, 1963.
10. Hayes, Margaret. "Evaluating School Library Services." *Library Trends* 1:372–85 (January 1953).
11. Henne, Frances. "The Evaluation of School Libraries." *Forty-Second Yearbook of the National Society for the Study of Education. Part II: The Library in General Education*, pp. 333–49. Nelson B. Henry (ed.). Chicago, University of Chicago, Department of Education, 1943.
12. Henne, Frances, Ersted, Ruth, and Lohrer, Alice. *A Planning Guide for the High School Library Program*. Chicago, American Library Association, 1951.

13. Humphry, John. *Library Cooperation: The Brown University Study of University-School-Community Library Coordination in The State of Rhode Island*. Providence, Brown University Press, 1963.

14. Illinois Secondary School Curriculum Program. *Prospectus of the Local Area Consensus Studies*. Prepared by Harold C. Hand. Circular Series A, No. 51. *Bulletin* No. 15. Springfield, Illinois, Department of Public Instruction, 1951.

15. —— Consensus Study Number 6, Inventory A: *What Do You Think About Our School Library Program?* Prepared by Alice Lohrer. Springfield, Department of Public Instruction, 1951.

16. Consensus Study Number 6, Inventory B: *In What Respects Should We Strengthen Our School Library Program?* Prepared by Alice Lohrer. Springfield, Department of Public Instruction, 1951.

17. Consensus Study Number 6, Inventory C: *What Should We Do to Strengthen our School Library Program?* Prepared by Alice Lohrer. Springfield, Department of Public Instruction, 1953.

18. Consensus Study Number 6, Manual for Discussion Leaders: *Why Are These Principles Important in Our School Library Program?* Prepared by Alice Lohrer. Springfield, Department of Public Instruction, 1953.

19. Lohrer, Alice. "Future Possibilities in the Development of the School Library Materials Center." *The School Library Materials Center: Its Resources and Their Utilization*, pp. 101–7. Alice Lohrer (ed.). Champaign, Ill., The Illini Union Bookstore, 1964.

20. —— "School Libraries as Instructional Materials Centers, with Implications for Training: A Progress Report of This Study Under Title VII, National Defense Education Act." *The School Library as a Materials Center: Educational Needs of Librarians and Teachers in Its Administration and Use*, pp. 12–18. Mary Helen Mahar (ed.). Washington, D.C., U.S. Government Printing Office, 1963.

21. Mahar, Mary Helen. *Statistics of Public School Libraries, 1960–61*. Part II: *Analysis and Interpretation*. Washington, D.C., U.S. Government Printing Office, no date.

22. Mahar, Mary Helen, and Holladay, Doris C. *Statistics of Public School Libraries, 1960–61*. Part I: *Basic Tables*. Washington, D.C., U.S. Government Printing Office, 1964.

23. Maryland State Department of Education. *School Libraries in Maryland.* Baltimore, Maryland State Department of Education, 1964.

24. National Study of Secondary School Evaluation. *Evaluative Criteria.* Washington, D.C., National Study of Secondary School Evaluation, 1960.

25. —— *Evaluative Criteria for Junior High Schools.* Washington, D.C., National Study of Secondary School Evaluation, 1963.

26. Nelson Associates, Inc. *A Reference and Research Library Resources Plan for the Rochester Area.* Prepared for the New York State Education Department. New York, Nelson Associates, Inc., 1962.

27. —— *Strengthening and Coordinating Reference and Research Library Resources in New York State.* Prepared for the New York State Education Department. New York, Nelson Associates, Inc., 1963.

28. New Jersey Library Association. Library Development Committee. *Libraries for the People of New Jersey: or Knowledge for All.* By Lowell A. Martin and Mary Virginia Gaver. New Brunswick, N.J., 1964.

29. New York (State University). The State Education Department. The New York State Library. Library Extension Division. *Improving Reference and Research Library Resources in New York State.* Albany, N.Y., The State Library, 1965.

30. —— *Report of the Commissioner's Committee on Reference and Research Library Resources.* Albany, N.Y., The State Library, 1961.

31. Pacific Northwest Library Association. *Library Development Project Reports.* Volume 2: *Elementary and Secondary School Libraries of the Pacific Northwest.* Seattle, University of Washington Press, 1960.

32. Southern Association of Colleges and Schools. Committee on Elementary Education. *Evaluating the Elementary School Library Program.* Atlanta, The Association, 1964.

33. Srygley, Sara K. "A Study of Selected Elementary School Libraries in the Southern Region." *Progress in Southern Elementary Schools,* 2 (April 1964), no paging.

34. Washington State Office of Public Instruction. *School Library and Audio-Visual Survey.* Research Report 06–01. Olympia, State Office of Public Instruction, 1964.

# 13 Special Libraries

JANET BOGARDUS

WHEN we consider the application of any phase of librarianship to special libraries, we are always faced with the difficulty of applying principles to the whole due to the extraordinary diversity of its parts. In the latest annual volume of *Library Literature*, under "Special Libraries," there are *see also* references to sixty different types of libraries, all, apparently, presumed to be special.

The Special Libraries Association has grouped more or less like with like, but still has twenty-three subject divisions and sections. In addition, law, medical, and music librarians each have their own professional association.

However, we can rule out university departmental libraries, business branches of public libraries, and government libraries, which so far as surveys are concerned, present rather different problems from the libraries of corporations and other private business institutions. Once a division by size of municipality served has been made, public libraries do have certain common denominators of operation, circulation, readers advisory and community services, per capita financial support, and so on. University libraries, once division by size of university faculty and student body has been made, while still in many respects diverse, do have certain common characteristics of purposes served, place in the instructional complex, and type of materials. School libraries, once sorted by size of school and age of child served, do have standards applicable on a wide basis for book collections, services, staffing, and use.

Special libraries have much less of a recognizable essential core of likeness. As a whole, their distinguishing features are, perhaps, (1) the nonlibrary environment in which the library is situated, (2) intensive subject specialization, (3) the nonbook character of much of the collection, and (4) the variety of services offered, hand-tailored to serve the purposes of the firm, some of which are rather far out if judged by traditional library concepts. All four of these common characteristics actually emphasize the diversity of the individual situation, and defy the application of common standards. In this sense a special library has less of a life of its own than does a university or public library. Services and procedures may be instituted or dispensed with purely on the basis of present value to the current work of the firm. The library operations can be judged only as they serve the purposes of the particular firm of which the library is a part. The nonlibrary management does not greatly care by what means the library produces information—so long as it produces to the satisfaction of the user, and so contributes to good management of the business. Fortunately, good library practices do provide better services. Special libraries are expected to produce information, rather than the sources of information; success in producing information is rather harder to measure than success in producing sources, which is hard enough. Undeniably it is on this information service that the special library stands or falls. There is a great diversity in the information services called for. Some special libraries engage in abstracting and indexing; some provide translations. Literature searching, public relations activities, and editorial work may or may not be within the province of the library. The extent to which mechanized information storage and retrieval contributes service runs the gamut from zero to a high degree of automation in some technical information centers.

I have belabored this point about the diversity of special libraries because I think it is the outstanding reason, although not the only one, why the library survey as a technique to improve operations and provide for orderly development is so much further advanced in its application to university, public, and school libraries than to special libraries. And as a direct result of their diversity, special libraries have lagged far behind university and public libraries in the production of usable standards to serve as guidelines or benchmarks in evaluating library service and operation. Without this means of comparability, a survey is a much more subjective procedure and, however much it hits the mark, lacks the means to get the message across. A consultant, if an *experienced* librarian in the same specialized subject field— banking for instance—can often, after no more than a day's visit to a small special library, judge with some accuracy whether the collection is good, poor, or indifferent, the cataloging operation economic or wasteful, the reference services elementary or expert, the staff qualified; but if there is no norm, it is difficult to make the point with management. The findings of library surveys in turn tend to help build up, or at least influence, standards of judgment for the next survey.

Another factor which has discouraged the use of the survey in a special library is the character of its environment. I have already mentioned the diversity of that environment. But, in addition, the firm or institution is a nonlibrary organization, generally with a nonlibrary-conscious management. While it is not likely that management would object to a self-survey, and while it may include the library in an overall management survey, it generally does not look with favor on comparisons of any of the firm's operations with similar operations in other businesses, competing or not. If any such survey is undertaken, the report will likely be held confidential, so that it does not serve as a source of information for the formulation of standards or as a guide for later surveys.

All too often the surveys that have been made have left special librarians in no frame of mind to encourage their use. The survey may have occurred as part of a package-deal cost survey of the parent organization by outside management consultants. Rarely has such a survey been conducted by a library expert; usually, the most junior member of the management team is assigned to the library. The horror stories of these ordeals are part of the folklore of special librarianship—the young man who assured the catalog librarian if she'd just learn shorthand he felt sure she could in time get on the secretarial staff; the extra points on the evaluation sheet when it was learned the order librarian handled "cash" (a responsibility not lightly regarded in a bank) even though the cash was only the change for messenger carfare and for postage for free materials; the final admission by the management expert, after hours of patient explanation by the librarian, that "Well, I can see the reference librarian is no ordinary file clerk." A classic example was described with remarkable good nature in "Survey of Slurvey?" by Gertrude Annan, librarian of the Academy of Medicine, in the *Library Journal*, June 1, 1960. However, her sad story had a happy ending. The Library Commission of the Academy, recognizing the inadequacy and distortions of the survey report, later called for a second survey to be made by a competent librarian who was also an experienced consultant.

It is not surprising then that reports of findings on special library surveys are conspicuous by their absence. For the past ten years (according to a quick check I made of library literature) the *printed* record of surveys (omitting library school SLA theses) seems to be approximately 90 references to public library surveys, 38 to university surveys, 20 to governmental, 28 to schools, and 10 to special libraries. Of these ten, four were references to ASLIB publications and probably did not concern U.S. libraries. Of the remaining six, three referred to across-the-board surveys and one to an article on the use of statistics in surveys. Only two citations were to individual library surveys, and these referred to remarks about the surveys rather than reports on the findings.

The case seems well documented that at present there is too little intelligent application of library surveys to special libraries and that reports of such that have been undertaken have not generally found their way into our professional literature.

However, with all these factors operating against the use of surveys, special libraries are making some progress in establishing standards and in the use of the survey method for evaluating library performance. Most of the progress has been through the Special Libraries Association, and in a less-wide application, through the American Association of Law Libraries and the Medical Library Association.

The Special Libraries Association Personnel Survey in 1959, although it was not intended to determine standards, did provide quite a lot of basic information on personnel. The questionnaire was sent to all libraries represented by SLA membership and, with a 55.5 percent return, reported on 1137 special libraries and on 2,311 special librarians. Part of the questionnaire's success, it may be instructive to note, was due to the great care taken in its introduction to management and in its provision for strict confidence. The mailing, receipt, and tabulation were handled entirely by an outside accounting firm, Price Waterhouse, and at no time were the completed questionnaires in the hands of the SLA sponsoring committee. While the librarians were the first to be apprised of the coming survey and their cooperation requested, Price Waterhouse dealt directly with management.

At the Special Libraries Association annual convention in 1959, the Professional Standards Committee took initial steps toward the provision of standards and five years later, after considerable laying of groundwork by successive Standards Committees, the *Objectives and Standards for Special Libraries* was published. A background fact-finding survey of selected libraries had been conducted, and the questionnaire was a detailed and searching one expertly compiled by knowledgeable, experienced librarians. Many SLA division and group members worked on preliminary drafts, or served on fact-finding committees within their own geographical or subject areas, under the guidance of the national committee. Even so, I understand, it was very difficult to get meaningful measures from the results, due to the great diversity in operations. The final draft of the *Standards*, and the intensive preparatory work for it, was done by Professor Ruth S. Leonard of the School of Library Service at Simmons College, Boston. The result, in my opinion, is a big step forward. In addition, the Committee and Miss Leonard are now engaged in writing "profiles" of specific types of libraries, e.g., banking, manufacturing, chemical, etc., as supplements to the *Standards*. This should do much to meet the criticism that the *Standards* are too general to be useful.

The SLA Consultation Committee maintains a roster of approved special-library consultants in various subject fields. In addition, each chapter appoints a chapter consultation officer from its membership who, in answer to requests from firms and institutions for information, tries to recommend a competent consultant in the area. On the whole, I think the Consultation Committee has done a useful job, mostly because it has maintained very high standards for the consultants it has recommended to the board of directors for certification. How consistently well this is managed at the chapter level I do not know. The original concept of the consultation service was "to encourage the establishment of new special libraries and to enhance the professional reputation of the Special Library Association." Since its establishment in 1957, the chapters have reported 745 inquiries, which resulted in 395 consultations and in the establishment of 124 new libraries, the Committee's 1963–64 annual report notes. It goes on to say:

Briefly, these past six years have marked the establishment of a workable, working group of Chapter personnel, designated by their Chapter Presidents to be Chapter Consultation Officers, and a roster of Professional Consultants approved by the Committee and ratified by the Board of Directors, all headed by the appointed SLA Consultation Service Committee, which has as its Association Headquarters liaison, the Executive Director.

To have the Consultation Service operate in a uniform manner throughout the United States and Canada, the Chapter Consultation Officers are provided with a Consultation Service Manual, the most recent revision having been issued during the past year. In addition, a *Consultation Service Newsletter* . . . acts as a liaison between the Chapter Consultant, the Professional Consultant, and the Committee.

Some SLA Divisions have made sporadic attempts at establishing standards. Due to the similar nature of the member libraries, these group efforts, if engaged in more diligently and seriously, might be the best hope for practical standards.

So much for the two recent across-the-board surveys and

present efforts to formulate standards. Considering the lack of available data on individual library surveys, can we make any valid points as to the methodology used in such surveys?

The self-survey, whether by the librarian or by the planning or other management division within the firm, is not, I think, likely to be very productive in the small special library. If the librarian had new or better ideas, presumably he would have tried them. Attention from the management is likely to revolve around cost-cutting or space-saving objectives.

Outside management consultant surveys are satisfactory only when the management consultants provide personnel really knowledgeable in library practices. This has happened, but not often.

The most useful special-library surveys are those made by an outside consultant librarian, experienced not only in the subject field but also in the techniques of library surveys. Because special libraries are small, it is usual to have only a single consultant, and because of the lack of printed guidelines and standards, the method used will necessarily be rather subjective—I believe "impressionistic" is the proper term. However, I think procedures need not differ greatly from the usual sequence followed. In brief, the consultant may survey:

(1) *The environment in which the library is situated.* This includes, through interview and the scanning of files and records, a description of the firm, its purposes, size, organization, type of personnel, and any other pertinent characteristics which may influence library objectives, policies, and procedures. Particular attention is paid to that part of the firm population which can be expected to be regular library users and to the character of their work. This first part of the survey may account for as much as 30 percent of the survey time. Incidentally, it has been my experience that the consultant, in interviews with management, often has unusual opportunity to explain good library practice in a receptive setting and throw some weight behind the librarian's efforts, which may be just what is needed rather than an internal survey.

(2) *The Collection.* Appraisal is likely to be based partly on

bibliographies and partly on the knowledge of the consultant. Particular attention is paid to the currency of the materials, the depth of the subject coverage, the strength of the periodical subscription list, the availability of unpublished materials (working papers, technical reports, etc.), and the quality of the reference collection. Analysis should be qualitative rather than quantitative.

(*3*) *Selection Policies.* This is important and is usually a purely qualitative analysis based largely on the consultant's conversations with the chief librarian, who is responsible for the selection.

(*4*) *Acquisition, Processing, Cataloging, and Classification.* It is a brave special librarian who would presume to sketch a general profile in this area, in this time of amazing change and rapid development of automated procedures.

(*5*) *Reference and Information Services.* In considering reference work and literature searching, the quantity is not so important, of course, as the quality, which submits only to subjective judgment based on observation and interviews with both those dispensing service and those receiving it. The efficiency of the circulation of materials, including the routing of periodicals and reports, is much more easily gauged. Special services to be evaluated for efficiency will likely include selected news clipping, indexing, abstracting, scanning, and individual bibliographic service. The kind of other services offered will depend on the type of library. Evaluation of the number and character of the special services offered and the efficiency with which they are performed is a very important part of the survey.

(*6*) *Staffing.* The structure of staffing, the use of job classifications and job descriptions, the provision for supervision and training, and the adequacy of staff size are reviewed. The qualifications for the positions and the extent to which they are met by the staff are matters for particular emphasis in the survey. Personnel policies of the firm and their application in the library are reviewed, and, of course, the salary structure. Comparison of the status of library positions with comparable positions elsewhere in the firm can be revealing.

(7) *Physical Facilities; Space; Equipment.* Character and sufficiency of the facilities; adequacy of the space; nature and up-to-dateness of the equipment.

(8) *Library Finance: Budget.* The adequacy of the appropriations and the extent to which the librarian controls expenditures are important indications of management's view of the library's efficiency.

(9) *Library Administration.* The library is generally small enough so that it is not difficult to get an accurate picture of the efficiency of the librarian's administration. An accurate picture of the place of the library within the company's organization and administration is sometimes not so easily come by, but is just as important.

This is the barest of outlines. If I were applying it to a business-financial library, I could amplify and detail it considerably: other librarians in other special fields could do the same. At any rate, my struggle to find documentation to back up my remarks has made me aware that we who conduct surveys must see to it that the report in full gets in the public record.

# 14  State Libraries

WALTER T. BRAHM

SURVEYS of the library agencies of state governments have been few, so few that a great need exists for turning the spotlight of examination on the administration of state libraries. Such a statement may come as a distinct surprise in view of the fact that professional literature seems to abound with surveys of state library service. A brief review of the number made in the past twenty years may provide some background for discussion.

There have been two studies of state libraries as a group or type of library.

The Public Library Inquiry conducted by the Social Science Research Council in 1949, after strong urging by state librarians, sampled the library agencies of some twenty states. State agencies were not included in the Inquiry's original assignment. Garceau reported its brief observations on the "States as promoters of library extension." [1] We would hesitate to classify such observations as a survey.

Perhaps the first survey aimed at state libraries as a group came in 1952. The National Association of State Libraries' Committee on "Organization of State Library Agencies in the Structure of State Government," reported the functions performed by the various state agencies, and the particular unit of government under which each function was performed in the states. [2] The information was gathered by questionnaire and findings submitted to the state agencies for verification before publication. It was entirely a quantitative survey but it did indicate that state agencies could be observed on a comparative basis to a limited extent. It also laid the groundwork for later efforts to establish standards for state library agencies. Based on the functions enumerated in the report the National Association of State Libraries issued its statement in 1956, *The Role of the State Library*.[3]

Using the Committee's report as a guide Alabama's Legislative Reference Service in 1954 in *A Study of State Library Systems*[4] listed the functions, and the agencies responsible for them. It duplicated the Committee's work to some extent, updating it a year.

Shortly thereafter state librarians working as a committee of the American Library Association, began efforts to secure funds for a comprehensive study of their agencies to serve as a basis for establishing standards for functions of state libraries. Their efforts culminated in a grant of $45,000 by the Carnegie Corporation in 1960 for a survey conducted by Phillip Monypenny and a team of three distinguished, competent surveyors. Every state agency was visited and interviewed, correlating information supplied in a detailed questionnaire. Although the report of the survey will not be available in published form until some time this year (1965) standards for library functions at the state level based on the report have been prepared and printed.[5]

Two specific functions of state library service have also been isolated and studied on a national basis, extension and archives.

Morin and Cohen studied state library extension services in 1955, using information provided in a questionnaire and from administrative reports.[6] They related the historical and legislative development of this function with statistical information on resources of the state agencies administering this service.

Ernst Posner's thorough study of state archival agencies conducted in 1962–63 was published in 1964.[7] An individual and comparative study of the states, it produced specific recommendations for each state and included national standards for this function.

The number of administrative or management surveys of individual state library agencies is relatively as few as for group surveys. Only seven states (Illinois, Missouri, New York, Oklahoma, Oregon, Texas, and Wisconsin) report such a type of survey in the past twenty years.

This is the extent of surveys of state library agencies. Why the states have made so little use of the management review is difficult to say. Certainly in this area they have not yet been oversurveyed. For that reason they might profit by inviting management studies of their libraries.

A third type of state-related survey can be identified. Studies of library service on a statewide or even regional basis have come into favor in the last ten years, particularly since the advent of the Library Services Act. For the most part, they are, in reality, surveys of local library facilities and not of state libraries. A further distinguishing characteristic is that they are studies of libraries as a composite or group. However, because they usually are studied in relation to the state agency and the state program, most librarians probably assign them to the category of state-library surveys. For that reason they should be discussed here.

In the past twenty years a majority of the states have conducted statewide library studies of some magnitude or sufficient formality to classify them as surveys. A number of states within this period have been surveyed a second, third, or even fourth time. Five states have surveys now in progress. A sixth has just completed a comprehensive study of library resources. Two states are projecting surveys.

A rather complete list of statewide surveys and plans appears in the *ALA Bulletin* for May 1965.[8]

The first statewide surveys concerned themselves almost entirely with public libraries. Succeeding and current surveys continue the public library as a major area of study but include other types of libraries in an effort to present a total picture of the statewide library situation. The inclusion of school, academic, and special libraries has been a notable trend of recent years; there has been a trend also to isolate and study certain library functions on a statewide basis. Reference service has received the most emphasis along with centralized processing. There is also a significant trend to identify and locate total library resources, perhaps another reason for the inclusion of all types of libraries in any statewide study.

Many fringe, near-surveys, or *ad hoc* type studies are referred to in library literature such as a committee report on library needs of state health agencies, or institutions. No attempt is made here to analyze them.

If we add up the surveys enumerated, we have two group-studies on a national scale, two of a specific function on a national scale, seven individual management studies, and a number of statewide studies of local libraries or specific library functions. Certainly not many, but perhaps enough to raise questions whose answers may be helpful to those considering future surveys.

How did the surveys originate? Who energized them? Evidence seems clear that they originated exclusively from action of either the state library agency or the state library association, or their combined efforts. Without the motivating force of at least one of these agencies a survey is not likely to be made.

What did the surveys study? Why were they conducted? Were there faulty situations? In most cases no, at least none that could be pinpointed. Coordination of library services as a positive approach rather than fault-finding has been their greatest selling point. Surveys on a national basis were intended to provide information leading to the establishment of standards. The primary purpose of statewide studies has been to assist in the development of a comprehensive plan designed to meet one or more of the following needs:

(1) The compilation and availability of statistical or other information for an area of library service for which no such information in a particular state has been available (number of schools with libraries, number of books and staff).

(2) A guide for identifying the total library resources within a state (all libraries—state, public, school, and special).

(3) A guide for organizing either a specific library facility or all library facilities of a state to make the most efficient

use of those resources or specific services (regional reference service, centralized processing).

(4) A guide for amending or enacting legislation to permit such organization.

(5) A guide for wise expenditure of funds available from all sources but particularly federal funds provided by the Library Service and Construction Act.

(6) A means of communication with the library profession, public officials, and the public in securing the passage of such legislation or the acceptance of the wisdom of such expenditures.

How were the surveys conducted? An individual, a committee of librarians of the state library association, or even of the legislature, a research bureau of the legislature or of the state university have been and continue to be major sources from which surveyors are recruited. Until recently selection of a person or agency appears to have been made on a rather opportunistic basis to meet conditions of a small budget, or of convenience, or perhaps the practical politics of employing a local or state-related person. However, with the availability of federal funds a number of state library agencies have embarked on full-scale reviews of their library situations and moved toward the team survey or consultant-office approach such as the recent surveys in New York and Pennsylvania and the current surveys in California and Oklahoma.

The method used in most surveys has been the traditional pattern of gathering information by questionnaire, lists of book and periodical holdings, personal visits, and interviews with participants or a sample of them, then compiling and analyzing the information and writing and presenting a report. State agencies, library associations, or other sponsors also have established advisory committees to assist the surveyor in preplanning and for consultation while the survey is in progress.

With the publication of *Standards for Library Functions at the State Level* in 1963, the future method and technique of surveying state libraries and planning for statewide library organization and development might appear self-evident and routine. If information could be collected relating to the sixty-two standards enumerated and a technique developed for evaluating the degree of attainment of each standard, a perfect survey should result. However, there are several problems that make this difficult.

A special problem of state library surveys and for those who evaluate them is the great variability of organization of library agencies in the fifty states; there is little valid uniformity with which to measure individual states. Within a state, selection of public or other libraries for comparison with the state agency must be made on an arbitrary basis. Another difficulty is that effective library service at the state level is often a result of intangible qualities that do not lend themselves to statistical or objective measurement. Leadership, legislative know-how, imagination, personality, truly important in local library situations, have a rippling effect when they originate at the state agency. How can the art of practicing those qualities be judged? Expert surveyors advise us to avoid subjective measurement, but this may not be possible. At least a fifth of the *Standards for Library Functions at the State Level* have subjective aspects. Somewhere in the process judgments have to be made and conclusions drawn.

An additional problem arises in that the best measurement, subjective or objective, requires that all agencies be visited personally. Time and distance, therefore, is a problem on a national or statewide basis, affecting the cost of the survey and its scheduling.

Geography is a special problem which must be taken into account. Librarians are usually well aware of the manner in which geography has shaped their own community library development but on a statewide basis it assumes even greater importance. Contrast, for instance, Pennsylvania and New Jersey, New York and Rhode Island, Michigan and Ohio.

The historical traditions of a state which account for the organizational setup of the state or local library agencies and which will hinder or aid new changes should be taken into account. Their possible effect must be determined exactly, neither underestimated nor overestimated. They can be disregarded in describing the ideal situation sought but not in promoting or accomplishing it.

Timing the survey is another special problem. From the date when it is first proposed, the determination of the scope of the survey, finding a competent surveyor, and conducting the survey, two years may elapse before the survey is complete. Sometimes a longer period elapses. With legislative sessions in many states on a biennial basis and with the absolute necessity of explaining the survey recommendations thoroughly to the library profession for its support prior to a legislative session, the time schedule of the survey must be carefully planned and met.

A basic attribute of the statewide survey is that it involves more institutions and more people than other surveys. For its successful implementation, particularly where legislation is concerned, usually a long period of involving these institutions and people is required. This can be accomplished by stretching out the time schedule of the survey so that the survey itself becomes an explanation to the profession. My personal experience is that the same result can be achieved by shortening the survey schedule to the minimum time necessary to do a complete job, but requiring sufficient time between its completion and a legislative session so that the program can be taken into every community of the state, explained and discussed with librarians and officials, and objections overcome or compromised. A solid basis of support can usually be assured with such procedure.

Strength of statewide surveys lies in the opportunity to exercise imagination, creativeness, and bold solutions in solving complex problems and involving great numbers of people. The New York and Pennsylvania surveys are excellent examples of such features. The weakness of statewide surveys seems to be that solutions proposed may also be complex, resulting in the inability of legislators, trustees, and even librarians to grasp the idea. Networks of library service, systems, and New York's 3R program probably fall in this category.

Partisan politics may become a problem at any stage of a state library or statewide library survey but the probabilities of this happening are low. We mention this here because local librarians may feel that any program connected with the state is "political." Political problems are most likely to develop at the legislative stage when efforts are made to pass legislation effecting survey recommendations.

What have been the results of surveys? This is impossible to measure statistically and accurately with such a widely divergent group of library agencies existing in the fifty states. Who can say that any particular action or effect could not or would not have been accomplished without a survey. Acquaintance with results stemming from surveys in California, Connecticut, Illinois, New Hampshire, New York, Ohio, and Pennsylvania supports the opinion that surveys on a statewide basis have been abundantly productive of results. They may not have produced the results they recommended but without their energizing effect, there would have been no results. It is precisely in this area of statewide service that the need for focusing attention, and for communication is so great. The survey is an excellent tool for doing these things.

However, a word of caution. Are libraries in danger of becoming survey sick? It is becoming a fashionable status symbol to have a survey. Are we using the survey as a means of postponing an obvious decision, because we fear the uncertainty of its effect? I have seen more than one community and state go through a series of surveys because the librarians wouldn't accept or activate the recommendations of previous surveys which they had sponsored. Repeated surveys become delaying tactics, are useless and expensive, and produce only negativism.

Suspicion also exists that state agencies and library associations, with the sudden increase in Library Services Act funds, unable to spend such funds within the fiscal year, may be tempted to propose unnecessary and useless surveys merely to encumber the money.

Let me add a positive note to this recommendation. Perhaps surveys in some situations are not needed. However, what is needed, whenever there is a survey, is the ability to effect the recommendations of that study. Tauber sometime ago commented that "in the last analysis the character of the implementation will determine whether or not surveys are effective, working blueprints." [9] Surveys might be much more productive of results if the surveyor, usually selected because of his ability, did not conclude his work with the presentation of a report. If he were employed to stay on the job for a period of time to accomplish what he recommended, either more recommendations would be effected or fewer of them would be made. Those proposing a survey might well include such a condition, as well as funds for it in the prospectus and budget. This is a novel approach, perhaps impractical, but it might be worth trying.

Beyond the special problems of variability or lack of uniformity, personal visits rather than sampling, geography and distance, historical tradition, and timing, survey approaches for state libraries should be basically similar to any other type of survey— determining what the ideal situation should be, finding out what it actually is, and then deciding how best the situation can be changed from what it is to what it should be. In other words, what do we need? What do we have? How do we change what we have to what we need?

REFERENCES

1. Garceau, O. Public Library in the Political Process. New York, Columbia University Press, 1949.
2. National Association of State Libraries. Committee on Organization of State Library Agencies in the Structure of State Government, Tentative Report. 1953.
3. National Association of State Libraries. Role of the State Library. Columbus, Ohio, Stoneman Press, 1956.
4. Legislative Reference Service. A Study of State Library Systems. Montgomery, Alabama, 1954 (mimeographed).
5. American Library Association. Standards for Library Functions at the State Level. Chicago, American Library Association, 1963.
6. Morin, A. L., and Cohen, N. M. State Library Extension Services. Washington, D. C., U.S. Government Printing Office, 1960.

7. Posner, Ernst. *American State Archives.* Chicago, University of Chicago Press, 1964.
8. Bunge, C. A. "Statewide Public Library Surveys and Plans, 1944–64." *American Library Association Bulletin* 59:364–74 (May 1965).
9. Tauber, M. F. "Survey Method in Approaching Library Problems." *Library Trends* 13:29 (July 1964).

## 15 The Library Survey: Its Value, Effectiveness, and Use as an Instrument of Administration

E. W. ERICKSON

THIS paper discusses the value and effectiveness of the library survey, and its use as an instrument of administration. In short, it seeks to answer the cynic—often a member of the staff of a surveyed library—who says, "What's the good of it? Why bother to spend money and waste our time?" In answering this question, the broader values of the academic library survey, not only the value it has for the surveyed library, are considered.

No matter what may be said, it may be hard to convince the cynic that the library survey has value, is effective, and is used.

The basic idea behind a library survey is that a specialist is called upon for advice so that a situation can be improved. There is nothing new about this idea, nor is it limited to the library profession. For many years the special consultant has been used by government, business, and industry to examine ailing operations and suggest more efficient procedures. The public schools have long utilized the services of consultants in curriculum development, building programs, or in the general improvement of school systems. The medical doctor, skilled as he may be, calls in another specialist for advice in a doubtful situation.

Speaking of the medical doctor, it is difficult to resist using that battered cliché, that timeworn anatomical metaphor: the library is the "heart" of the university. This is how it goes: the university suffers a cardiac problem and threatens to collapse unless it gets help. A competent specialist is brought in; the patient is examined carefully, and remedies are recommended. If the specialist is competent and the prescribed treatment followed, the patient improves. This pat analogy breaks down in one vital respect, however. The human patient could die while following the good specialists' advice. The so-called "heart" of the university, no matter how sick, never stops beating completely, and the university somehow manages to continue functioning.

Trite as the analogy is it does make a point. The library whose problems have become serious enough to alarm the administration, the librarian, and faculty perhaps needs the help of a specialist. The value and effectiveness of the library survey depend so much on the competence of the surveyor and the willingness of the librarian, library staff, faculty, and university administration to follow the advice of the expert. In one case where a good deal of money was spent to employ a surveyor and after a great deal of work on his part and the library staff the survey was completed, a report written, and subsequently ignored, allegedly because the surveyor was considered incompetent, a fact which should have been ascertained before he was employed.

Happily, however, research shows, at least so far as academic libraries are concerned, that library surveys that have been done by recognized outside experts are not generally filed away and ignored. In an examination of a dozen academic libraries, following surveys of them during the period 1938 to 1952, considerable evidence was found that the survey was effective and well used as an instrument of administration.[1] The same appraisal cannot be made specifically for the surveys done since that time, but there is no reason to believe that results would be greatly different now than for those surveys done during the earlier period.

The librarians at the institutions included in my study used the survey reports as guides to systematically improve their libraries. When I visited five of the libraries personally I found the survey reports, marked up and dog-eared, on the librarians' desks with recommendations ticked off showing stages of implementation or indicating disagreement. It was clear to me that the reports were being used in the administration of the libraries.

But how effective are these surveys? What results come of them? Of the 775 recommendations made in twelve library surveys the librarians whose business it was to implement the survey recommendations said that more than half of them had been carried out completely or to a large degree. In only about 25 percent of the cases was nothing accomplished. Also, these same librarians believed that slightly more than two-thirds of those recommendations were carried out as a result of the survey, either directly or indirectly, and of these a little more than half were direct results.

I realize that subjective judgment is involved when we try to measure survey results and establish causal relationships, but until someone devises a way to measure the value of surveys more precisely we are going to have to depend largely on the judgment of individuals for an estimate of the effectiveness of a survey. Swank in discussing the Stanford University survey said:

> One thing is clear, however, in the case of Stanford. The survey did set forth a program which in large was promptly effected. There is no question about results, whether direct or indirect, and there is no doubt that the survey was an effective instrument in helping to bring about those results.[2]

I do not intend to restate in detail what has already been published regarding the results of surveys I examined, but a few examples are in order of significant achievements following surveys, which were considered by the librarians to be direct results. Within one year after the survey of the Indiana University Library, all the libraries of the University were integrated into a unified system under the director of libraries. Within four years after a survey of Texas A & M College, centralized direction of libraries was achieved and a policy was established requiring approval by the president, the librarian, the library committee, and the head of the unit concerned before a new departmental library could be established. At the University of Georgia, centralized administration came within two years after a survey—a direct result according to the director of libraries.

At Cornell University reclassification of the collection was begun as a direct result of the survey, a project nearly completed and described so well by Felix Reichmann in *College and Research Libraries*, September, 1962. At the University of South Carolina, the survey resulted in the completion of a reclassification project; this project had been begun eight years before the survey, but had bogged down for lack of funds. Both the librarian and the head cataloger concluded that without the support of recommendations by outside experts they could not have obtained a foundation grant and matching funds from the university for the reclassification project.

Personnel was increased in most libraries following the surveys, as direct results in some cases, but more often as indirect results. In most instances the financial picture brightened for the library following the survey, again more often as an indirect result. Routines in technical processes were changed for the better in most of the libraries, as direct or indirect results of the surveys. Readers' services were improved in many respects at the various libraries by following the recommendations of the surveyors. In short, either as direct or indirect results of the surveys, the libraries became stronger and more efficient arms of instruction within their university organizations.

How do we know that the survey brought about these results? Might not these results have come regardless of the survey, given strong, competent leadership in the library? In answer to these questions, I can only accept the judgment of the librarian and his staff who, it seems to me, are in the best position to assess the role of the survey in the development of the library. I realize that there are many factors that may bear on the situation. A new university administration may be a stimulus. Perhaps a resurgence of faculty interest in the library occurs, or it may be that pressures of accrediting agencies have brought about increased support. Perhaps the overall economy improved so that the total university suddenly became more prosperous. I believe that the librarian makes an honest judgment with all of these factors in mind and decides to what extent the survey was an effective tool. And in the case of the librarians at the surveyed libraries I examined, there was general agreement that the surveys were decidedly worth while and brought good results.

The related question is an interesting one: given good leadership in the library, might not these same good results have come without a survey? The level of leadership varies greatly in libraries, and in some cases librarians and their staffs are simply not competent to identify and solve their problems without outside help. However, some librarians are not only competent to recognize their own problems and to have good ideas for their solution, but they are often asked for advice by other librarians. Stephen McCarthy, director of libraries at Cornell University, had had excellent experience before assuming that position and indeed was the surveyor of one of the libraries in my study. Yet, as director of libraries, he requested that a survey be made of Cornell; he was aware of the problems that existed and together with his staff had ideas for their solution. McCarthy wanted technical advice, of course, on some phases of the operation, but more than that felt that he needed corroboration and support from outside experts, and with a team like Wilson, Downs, and Tauber he got it! The university administration was greatly impressed by these experts and their recommendations were taken seriously. The old saying is still true: "A prophet is not without honour, save in his own country, and his own house."

A by-product of the library survey which lends itself even less to measurement than the carrying out of recommendations is the good that accrues from the involvement of the university administration, faculty, student body, and library staff in the survey process. In the properly conducted survey most campus groups get involved in some way and a healthy attention is focused on library problems and needs. There is generally a sincere interest at this time on the part of everyone to help identify library weaknesses and strengths and an eagerness to assist in improving the situation. In my own experience as a surveyor I have found willing cooperation on the part of the administration, faculty, students, and library staff as I have sought information from various campus sources. This involvement can become burdensome for everyone, and the late Seymour Robb was speaking not only for himself when he said:

> . . . I know of no other ordeal which can at the same time do so much potential good and be so nerve-wracking.
>
> Sixteen hours a day seems to have become the absolute minimum for arranging conferences, compiling statistics, running down obscure references, and explaining routines or the lack of them.[3]

Another by-product of the library survey is the development of written survey reports. It is hard to tell how many formal surveys of academic libraries have been made and reports written, for in many cases reports are not indexed in *Library Literature*. A good indication of the volume of these publications is the fact that the ALA headquarters library has reports of fifty-eight academic library surveys, half of them done since 1952. How many others exist is not known.

As these reports have become a part of library science literature they have been used extensively in the various library schools. In an attempt to ascertain the extent and nature of their use I polled the thirty-six accredited library schools listed in *The Bowker Annual* for 1964. Thirty-six persons from thirty library schools responded to the questionnaire.

In answer to my first question, "To what extent do you use reports of surveys of academic libraries in your library science courses?" I learned that 11 schools use them regularly and at times intensively; 12 use them regularly but not intensively; 9 make use of them but only on an incidental basis; 4 seldom use them. No one checked the alternative "do not use them."

In sending the questionnaires to the deans of the library schools, I asked in each case that it be referred to the person teaching the course dealing with college and university library problems. I was interested in noting that, in answer to my second question "If you make use of the reports, what is the course in which you use them?" the reports were being used in a great variety of courses. Although courses in college and university library administration (with considerable variation in specific title) led the list, I found that survey reports were being used in such courses as bibliography and reference materials, cataloging, library collections, technical services in libraries, library literature and research, methods of investigation, introduction to librarianship, fields and functions of library services, and reader services.

A third question was directed at identifying the reasons the instructors thought library survey reports were useful in the classroom. I listed three likely reasons for their consideration and invited additional comments or negative reactions. Thirteen persons checked the statement, "they are a means of showing the 'inside story' of libraries"; 26 indicated that they were useful because "they describe practical problems of library organization and suggest solutions," and another 25 checked the statement, "They provide examples of the technique of evaluation." Most of the respondents checked more than one of the statements.

Among the additional comments were the following:

They provide suggestions of comparisons that may lead to generalizations for certain problems, in respect to solutions.

They indicate sets of unsolved problems in varying degrees.

They demonstrate what can go wrong in a library and why.

Useful in the study of the research potential of the survey method.

Excellent in showing "non-ideal" situations, to give students an idea of problems they may face in a library situation.

They show up the results of bad planning, organization and decision making techniques; they are often examples of poor line-staff relations; show up lack of clear-cut goals and objectives and of policies in most libraries.

For the final question of the brief questionnaire, I asked the instructors to check statements that best described the kind of use they made of survey reports in their classes. Sixteen indicated that they use them as general collateral reading, and twelve said that a student is assigned a problem which he studies through examination of a number of survey reports. Eleven checked the statement: "Student is assigned a particular library and he uses the report as a basis for a case study."

Among the additional comments regarding the use made of the survey reports were the following:

The teaching staff use library surveys to keep up with current trends in administration and technical processes.

They are a reference in considering book selection.

May be used in connection with the study of a particular library and other sources about the library; either in a term paper, or as a special oral class report.

Each student is assigned one library survey (not necessarily an academic library survey) to read and prepare a paper. Surveys are used to illustrate particular aspects of college library problems, e.g., subject departments, organizational patterns, etc. Sometimes a student is asked to select a library to study throughout the course, and libraries with surveys available are particularly useful for this purpose.

Student studies methodology.

There is a unit in the course entitled "evaluation." Here surveys are examined in quantity in an effort to discover methods and objectives.

Are survey reports being used in the library schools? If the statements by these library school professors can be considered an adequate sample one can very well conclude that library survey reports have indeed become an important and useful part of the fast growing body of library literature and are being used by students of library science.

If library schools have found survey reports useful in courses in college and university library administration, as well as in the numerous related courses mentioned earlier, does it not follow that these reports could have utility for the library administrator who is constantly concerned with the improvement of his own library? Although each report is written for a particular library and is focused on a set of problems unique in some respects to that institution there are nevertheless many problems discussed in all of the reports which are common to various libraries. The solution offered in the case of one library may not be right for another, but it may suggest a solution for the problem facing a third.

With new four-year and community colleges springing up all around us to meet the increasing pressures, new library administrators are being appointed in great numbers, some with previous administrative experience, but many, if not most, with very little. The newly appointed head librarian would do well to examine the various survey reports with special reference to those of libraries similar to his. The survey reports can serve as case studies in library administration, laying a sound foundation for the organization and development of a library. Whether it be administrative organization, handling of technical processes, development of the book collection, improvement of public services, or any other aspect of the operation of the library, the reports could be a source of sound suggestions. On the negative side, the librarian can certainly profit from mistakes made over the years in some of the surveyed libraries.

The use of survey reports in the administration of libraries need not be confined to the neophyte in library administration. In all libraries solutions are being sought to common problems; the experienced administrator can draw on his experience and theoretical knowledge, but he should be constantly alert to the experience of others. The survey report is an important source to which the well-read library administrator can go for ideas. He may not find every survey useful to him, but neither does he find every article he reads of pertinent interest.

At the conference, discussion was confined pretty much to surveys done by outside experts and little said of the self-survey. This does not mean that the self-survey is not an effective and useful instrument in library administration. The self-survey is conducted, formally and informally, in varying scope, by all good librarians, and often with good results. For the librarian and library committee planning to conduct a self-survey the published reports of library surveys done by outside experts can be most useful; they give ideas for an outline of procedure, suggest devices and tools for evaluation, and provide comparative statistics.

I have no idea to what extent library survey reports are used by library administrators, or even to what extent they are read. Their publication is limited and they are less likely to find their way into the hands of librarians generally than are other books and journals that comprise the literature of library science. This fact was pointed out by one of the respondents to my query regarding library school use of survey reports:

> Is it not the case that many of these reports are for limited circulation only, or are not obtainable in the normal way? For example, those published by ALA are not sent automatically on a standing order, and it has come to my attention that a regular order for Gormley's *Sioux Falls College Library* failed to produce it. How many surveys are listed in periodicals which one normally checks for information about new material in the field of library science? Perhaps a desirable by-product of the Conference might be some improvement in the bibliographical control of this form of publication.[4]

Where does one learn that a college or university library has been surveyed and a report of it published? A careful examination of *Library Literature* reveals that since the mid-thirties twenty-nine academic library survey reports have been published, exclusive of those done as masters theses. Inasmuch as the ALA headquarters library has fifty-eight reports of surveys of academic libraries in its collection we know that at least half of the survey reports published did not get into *Library Literature.* A scattered few are announced in the various journals, but this provides far from complete coverage.

Another respondent suggested that regular distribution to accredited library schools would be very useful. But how do we achieve this if we do not know what surveys are being made? Of the twenty-nine reports in ALA headquarters library bearing imprint dates since 1952 only seven were ALA sponsored. Arrangements could easily be made for standing orders for the library schools for those surveys sponsored by ALA, but if that takes care of only 25 percent (or less) of all survey reports written, it does not solve the problem.

We cannot solve the problem of bibliographical control until we succeed in establishing a kind of clearing house for academic library surveys. If a workable plan could be realized for the organization of survey activities within the official framework of the American Library Association I think we would not only achieve bibliographical control but we would improve the quality of many surveys.

I am not suggesting something new. The American Library Association has been involved in this kind of activity since March 1936 when the following announcement appeared in the *ALA Bulletin:* "In response to requests, the president and secretary of the American Library Association are authorized to cooperate in making official A.L.A. surveys under the following conditions. . . ." [5] Conditions follow stating that the invitation must come from an official body, that costs must be met by the organization requesting the survey, that the president and secretary select the surveyor, or surveyors, and that the findings of the surveyors will be made public.

Through this kind of organized procedure some very fine surveys have been made, and their reports have formed the hard core of survey literature. Established procedure never did preclude the possibility of library surveys outside the aegis of

ALA—nor should this be expected—but over the years it seems that ALA involvement has become less, resulting in more academic library surveys being made without ALA sponsorship than with it. The time has come for ALA to adopt a more aggressive role of leadership in the promotion and sponsorship of library surveys; it should be the clearing house for all types of surveys—public, academic, school, and special. The existing ALA policy for surveys can continue to be used as a basis and the appropriate divisions can be called upon to provide leadership in their special areas. Requests for surveys of academic libraries would naturally be referred to ACRL, as they are now.

What then can be done to foster the development of the academic library survey? Here are five points essential for a strong leadership role in this professional activity:

1. The administrators of colleges and universities, as well as the librarians, must be informed of the value and effectiveness of library surveys and the willingness of ACRL to assist in these surveys. The library journals should, in the normal course of events, publish articles on library surveys, but a special effort should be made to have articles published in journals of higher education which are more likely to be read by college presidents and vice presidents.

2. When a college or university president is referred to ACRL for advice on a possible survey of his library, the executive secretary should suggest an ACRL sponsored survey rather than merely provide him with names of possible surveyors to whom he can write. The latter is a desirable alternative if the former is not possible, but it should be a last resort. Sponsorship of a survey and the handling of all of its details impose a heavy burden on the headquarters staff, but if this is an important and necessary function the staff to do the job must be provided.

3. A corps of trained, competent surveyors who can represent ACRL with uniformly high professional standards must be developed. A step in this direction has been taken by ACRL and the Columbia University School of Library Science in the sponsorship of the Conference on Library Surveys. Survey tech-

niques have been developed over the years which, if learned, make possible more efficient and effective use of the surveyor's time.

The North Central Association saw the need for training consultants in higher education and in 1957, supported by a grant of $147,000 from the Carnegie Corporation, began a leadership training project running for a period of four years.[6] The purpose of the project was "to prepare persons to be generalist consultants—persons who will have an overall grasp of the structure and work of higher educational institutions. . . ."[7] Under this program fifteen persons were selected each year to be trained through conferences, participation in surveys headed by experienced consultants, the writing of reports, and attendance at various meetings. Out of the project has come a corps of trained consultants who not only are better members of accrediting teams because of the experience but are also professionally stimulated and better able to assume roles of leadership in higher education.

4. We must not sell our services cheaply. The institution requesting a survey is in need of a professional service and is generally prepared to pay for expert assistance. A vast amount of work goes into planning, preliminary research and collection of data, the visit itself, and finally the writing of the report. If the honorarium for a typical survey today were reduced to hourly earnings the surveyor would find himself earning student assistant wages or less. A general survey made in the late thirties was budgeted at something under $3000. In 1961 I participated in a two-man ALA-sponsored survey which took one week and was budgeted at $1700. Surveys should not be done as merely a lucrative form of moonlighting. The library consultant has an expert professional service to sell which is certainly worth as much as that offered by the consultant in business, engineering, medicine, or anywhere else. To sell it for less does the profession a disservice.

5. If what I have said about the value of the published survey reports is true, then we should make a greater effort to get these reports into the hands of those who will make use of them. Pro-

vision should be made for standing orders for all ALA-sponsored surveys. Librarians who conduct surveys independently of ALA should be urged to send copies of their reports to ACRL headquarters, and all completed surveys should be listed regularly in *College and Research Libraries* together with information regarding their availability.

If it is agreed that the survey has beneficial results for the library surveyed, desirable side effects within the total college or university, and that the report should become an important part of the literature of library science to be used to advantage by students of library science and practicing librarians, then it has value and we have a responsibility to promote the survey idea. We must make university administrators aware of our willingness to assist in the conduct of library surveys. A corps of trained surveyors from the ranks of competent, experienced librarians to perform these surveys must be developed, preferably under ALA sponsorship. Every effort must be made to achieve bibliographical control of the reports resulting from these surveys so that the benefits from the surveys will not be limited to a few, but will be available throughout the profession.

REFERENCES

1. Erickson, E. Walfred. *College and University Library Surveys, 1938–1952* (ACRL Monograph, No. 25). Chicago, American Library Association, 1961.
2. Letter from Raynard C. Swank to Walfred Erickson, October 10, 1957.
3. Robb, Seymour. "Librarian Looks at His Survey." *Library Journal*, 74: 1712–13 (November 15, 1949).
4. Letter from Effie C. Astbury to E. W. Erickson, March 22, 1965.
5. "Plan for ALA Surveys." *ALA Bulletin*, 30: 191 (March, 1936).
6. Pfnister, Allan O. "A Regional Accrediting Agency Experiments in the Training of Consultants for Higher Educational Institutions." *Educational Record*, 40: 62–68 (January, 1959).
7. *Ibid.*, p. 64.

# The Complete Librarian:
# A Partial View

## AN AFTERWORD BY LEWIS LEARY

WHEN Maurice Tauber suggested that I address myself to the subject of libraries and library surveys, and then when Jack Dalton twisted my arm with leverage such as only a dean can apply, I was momentarily elated. Perhaps, I thought, this was at long last a sign that librarians had conceded the validity of that truth which every professor knows, which is that professors know more about libraries and how they should be managed than librarians do. But then, when I began to cast about for what I really knew about these matters and what my ignorance could with dignity discover to say, my elation became less. For me, as for most of my colleagues, a good library is one which contains the materials which I want; a good librarian is a person who will get for me those materials which he does not have. The more I thought then about my limitations in facing up to the subject assigned me, the more I found myself approaching a condition which may be considered unusual among professors. I found myself becoming somewhat humble, bothered with a sense of guilt because of personal deficiencies. Perhaps that is what Mr. Tauber intended.

At any rate, I come to my subject with an overload of humility, knowing that it is presumptuous, even impertinent, for me to raise my voice on library surveys, where I am by no stretch of definition expert. Yet I am a great admirer of libraries and librarians, and the more eccentric and dusty and fusty they are, the more my admiration goes out to them. I am not comfortable in window-walled or window-less mausoleums, aseptic as hospitals, equipped for every emergency. My preference is for collections which perhaps have grown distorted, but which are the lengthened shadow of the men who made them. Among librarians, one of the loveliest I ever knew was Isadore Gilbert Mudge, who was fierce and frightening, but who knew her business and more besides, and was patiently helpful. Another was Victor Hugo Paltsits, who was so bemused with his own researching that he was even kindly in answering foolish questions. Roger Howson was another, and Earl Swem and Lawrence Wroth, a few among a host of gentlemen scholars, truly secretaries to the mind of man, people on whom we all depended, whom we often abused, and to whom our debt of gratitude is never completely paid. But each of them was more than custodian: each was a contributor also to the substance of which he took effective care.

Of necessity, we are more specialized now, more compulsively efficient, more professionally self-conscious. We depend more, we think, on one another. What gives me some measure of confidence is knowing that library surveying is much the same kind of analysis and self-appraisal which professionals in whatever area at one time or another undertake. Surely many of the same questions which any of the rest of us are serious about will be asked: Where have we been? What have we accomplished or learned or collected by being there? Where are we now? What is the relation of our present position to where we should or might be? And finally, where do we most intelligently and efficiently go from here? How may we most effectively utilize what we have in making the necessary step forward? Does what we have accomplished bear proper relationship to what other people, engaged in other enterprises, have accomplished? Are we in or out of step with progress in other areas?

In my own discipline, which embraces teaching and research in English, American, and comparative literature, we have over the past ten years been strenuously engaged in self-examination, in looking behind and gathering up, in pausing for analytical review of our progress, or lack of it. So much of what is called scholarship is being produced that we are troubled about our ability to digest it, even to taste it all. As more and more people enter seriously into our profession, as we increase in numbers, our voices increase in volume, for we like to talk about what we do. There may not be more thought about literature in our generation, but there is certainly more said than ever before, and publicly said, and in print which we must know about, and librarians must collect and preserve. We have even half-seriously considered imposing some kind of professional injunction against publication, a moratorium of five or ten years, so that we could catch up with ourselves. At Columbia, we even complain, somewhat pridefully, of the difficulty of keeping up even with the writings of our own departmental colleagues.

Meanwhile, faced with so unkempt a situation in our academic household, we enter into small projects in tidiness, often of a kind which we think librarians could do better than we, if they could be relieved of some of the other problems and responsibilities which burden them, so that they could have time for these little jobs of cleaning up which they could accomplish with really expert housewifery. Recognizing, however, the avalanche of information—to be consistent in imagery, I should call it debris or dust—under which any of us is likely to be buried, we put together what we hope can be helpful surveys of what we in our discipline have been up to—books like the problematic one which we called *Contemporary Literary Scholarship: A Critical Review*, in which is set forth and analyzed, area by area, period by period, what has been said, and by whom, about literature or literary figures over the preceding twenty-five years; or periodicals like our *Abstracts of English Studies;* or reviews of research which focus on a single period or area, like *The English Romantic Poets*, edited by Thomas M. Raysor, or *Eight American Authors*, edited by Floyd Stovall. Sometimes we have concentrated in other directions, as in the survey called *The Teacher and American Literature*, which makes available approaches to literature and new attitudes toward literature which can be useful to the beleaguered classroom teacher.

We have even attempted library surveys, like our checklist of the location of *American Literary Manuscripts*, a project which did not do as well as it should, partly because many large libraries which had an equivalently large share of literary manuscripts were too busy with other things to reply more than perfunctorily to our questionnaires. This was so discouraging to us that we have held up a revised second edition of the volume we published. But it was no more discouraging, I am sure, than the lack of response which librarians have had to questionnaires directed to faculty members concerning what should or should not be in your collections. Perhaps we depend too much on each other. Perhaps we should have waited until librarians, with more professional skill and better entree to the cooperation of other librarians, had done the job. But librarians did not do it; therefore we did, and not very well.

These are not all precisely the kind of surveys that are being considered. But we have nonetheless been busy squirrels hoarding information, someone has unkindly said, against the long winter of our mediocrity. We pile up our acorns of bibliographical fact in compilations like our listing, we say, of all *Articles on American Literature* appearing in periodicals from 1900 to 1950, and we continue to pile them in checklists which regularly appear in most of our professional journals, and then once a year we collect them into our giant *PMLA* bibliography, quarreling all the while among ourselves as to whether we are to be inclusive or selective, and according to what criteria, responsive to whose judgment. We are never quite complete, and we are often not accurate, for most of us in tasks like these are amateurs, fumbling about in our small competencies, and not always able to see them objectively in relation to other exercises in inquiry—indeed, so engaged with our own problems of survey that we do not always remember that other people, in other disciplines, have similar problems and work toward their solutions as assiduously and as ineptly as we. Sometimes librarians tell us that we are encroaching, and I suspect them to be correct.

But our situation is disturbing to us on other counts. We are concerned because we sometimes also suspect that our pausing for self-analysis or stocktaking, for surveys of where we have been, where we now stand, or of how we can be most useful or most practical or most efficient in changing, may be a symptom of something like malaise in that part of our profession which I know best, in the humanities, more specifically in talking, whether as teacher or scholar, about literature. We are retrospective and prospective at the same time. Poets and philosophers among us are not to be blamed for looking with austere suspicion on assembly-line machinations. Our individualists remind us that Henry David Thoreau, who is an effective teacher and was a great scholar, but a surveyor also, has cautioned us that "we must first succeed alone, that we may enjoy our success together."

Being what we are and living when we do, unable, we think, to afford the creative individualism of our forebears, we become convinced of the pragmatic necessity for self-analysis, inventories, and surveys. Things *are* in the saddle. The world is so much with us that we are likely to be tempted to lay waste certain of our powers. The national Association of Departments of English, with the concurrence of officials of the Modern Language Association, the College English Association, and the National Council of Teachers of English, has recently applied to the Office of Education for a grant which will allow it to establish a computer-controlled information center where, as a result of surveys carried on by a series of questionnaires, we can provide instant intelligence about curricular procedures, salaries, course loads, subjects most often taught, and books most often read. If we then work at it, we can perhaps convince deans and college presidents that we should teach no more than anyone else teaches, receive no less in compensation than anyone else receives, deal with the same essential subjects, read the same essential books. At Columbia University, at Teachers College, we have entered into an even more far-reaching survey, on an international scale, to discover how literature is taught in France, Russia, Japan, England, Germany, Siam, anywhere, whether with nationalistic, sociological, aesthetic, or whatever emphasis besides. If successful, we can come up with a method,

guaranteed impeccable, which encompasses all of them—an
attractively packaged method which anyone can use. Mark
Hopkins turns uneasily in his grave, but we are of another generation.

Our pause for evaluation certifies that. It has been suggested
to me, and I am tempted to believe it to be true, that the time for
surveys comes at a time of pause, when something is finished,
when progress has been made as far as possible in one direction,
when the end is in sight, and it is clear that one goes no farther
that way; when exciting individual effort is no longer productive, so that one must meet in conference, breaking that greatest
of all the commandments—thou shalt not committee. Men who
go ahead, we have thought, have no time for surveys, no pa-
tience with conference: life is too short for looking behind; the
runner who turns to see how close on his heels the other runners
are is likely to lose the race.

If this is true, it may suggest that we in my profession have
come, or believe that we have come, to the end of an old and
pleasant way of going about our business, and must rethink, re-
vise, retool to a more realistic, more practical and efficient, procedure. We are of divided mind about it. To some of us it seems
inevitable, even good. Others of us are sure that something
honorable and respectworthy is lost. It used to take, shall we
say, an average of eight years to earn the Ph.D. in English. Now
it must take four, and fellowships, which some identify as
fellowship-bribes, are offered to institutions and individuals who
will speed up. We are told that we emphasize process rather than
product. Our concern is increasingly with the mechanics of
production. We resist the temptation of believing that old ways
of doing things are best, and our most effective persuader has
come to be the machine.

Lane Cooper at Cornell used to work leisurely and pain-
stakingly for years, as a gentleman-scholar should, in preparing
his invaluable concordances; now Stephen Parrish with a machine at his command can do concordances, equally invaluable,
in a month. Giant indexes which used to consume most of a
long, hot summer in the making, now can be turned out in

weeks. Information is stored, to be retrieved in minutes. We who have spent years in academic bookkeeping are overjoyed that Lewis Sawin and his associates at the University of Colorado, on another grant from the Office of Education, are proving that it is possible to solve many problems of enumerative bibliography with a computer—and one of the more interesting things which they are finding out is that there is no presently produced computer which will do exactly what they require to be done, so that their project has broadened to include the devising of specifications for a machine of their own.

These are matters quite beyond the comprehension of most of us in the traditional academic disciplines. We even look with suspicion on some of our younger colleagues who pursue them at enthusiastic pace. These are not matters, we think, with which we should concern ourselves, and we are partly right. We tell ourselves that these collecting and sorting and organizing projects with which we have been concerned should not have been attempted by us at all, for we do them ineptly, without the expert experience which library training should provide. Indeed, it is not difficult to look ahead to the time when librarians will have programed all of these things, when every matter of fact, and most matters of opinion, will be stored somewhere in some centrally located giant machine. Then libraries may become small and pleasant places, without books to clean or catalogue, with all knowledge at finger-tip, push-button access. There will no longer then be need for competition among libraries for the acquisition of great collections; libraries instead will cooperate in breaking down the contents of those collections by computor analysis, so that—at a fee—they may be available to all. Books will no longer take up valuable space needed for playing fields or recreational areas, but may be burned with confidence that everything they say or suggest, of content or condition, has been efficiently stored by the Great National (or International) Information Retrieval Center, capable of being piped by direct line or by telestar to any library anywhere.

This is not to me in any sense a nightmare, only an academic's projection of where our surveys which look toward maximum library efficiency must lead. I am confident that some librarians are up to something very much like this even now, having moved beyond the concept of what Robert Downs called "Libraries in Miniscule" through use of microreproduction, which undoubtedly is old hat today, toward a more farsighted concept of libraries by television or electronic tape which transforms print to sound, or sound to print, or either to picture. It will be a short step indeed from computer-controlled catalogs to computer-controlled collections, to computer-controlled librarians and computer-controlled users of libraries. No longer will there be any of those problems of which librarians speak: problems of "dissemination of information that will help scholars to locate materials they need," for it will be there at the turn of a switch; nor will there be further "concern with what is lacking" in any library, because nothing need be lacking. I have great confidence that librarians can do these things for us, for I have enough faith in the resourcefulness of most men to know that there might even be discovered some ingenious method for preserving fiction and drama and poetry intact completely, without the cumbersome old necessity of using ink and paper and space-usurping bindings. What, after all, is sacred about a book, especially a printed book, most especially a modern book, built for disintegration? The printed book is relatively a new thing, hardly more than five hundred years old. Can we not be thought inventive enough to devise more efficient methods for preserving records of the expression of the spirit and knowledge of man?

Though I am confident that librarians can do these things, and though, as I have said, I suspect that some are already up to something of this kind and that surveys will indicate further good opportunities for cooperative ingenuity and mechanized service, I have enough confidence also in the contrariness of individuals, even of librarians, and enough faith in the eternal tug and pull of differing opinions, to know that these things will not go ahead faster than we are ready to have them go, nor without the checks and balances which will insure the library remaining more than just a clean, well-lighted place, and the librarian-in-chief of the Great International Information Retrieval Center something more than an immaculate and well-meaning big brother. I am certain that in setting up this Great Center, or its more humanized equivalent, mistakes will be made, and that when best and biggest they may be good mistakes, errors of commission rather than of omission. I am certain also that I and my colleagues will be shocked at what librarians propose, for we have not been used to thinking of them as initiating people. We will tell them that they cannot do it alone, but will need the help of experts in subject areas, and that help will be hard to come by, for experts who think of themselves as really expert will say that they are too busy at being expert to be able to help.

Where then does this leave us? Surveys, I have suggested, seem to come in my profession, and perhaps also in librarianship, at a time of pause, when things as they have been do not seem exactly to fit the requirements of things as they are. Then I outlined very briefly some of the do-it-yourself kind of information gathering projects which people in my line of business have been up to, projects which I have suggested might have been better managed by librarians than by us. Finally, I have speculated, somewhat naïvely, about certain developments in library procedure which may ultimately become feasible, and I have spoken, briefly again, and perhaps impertinently, about the difficulty of obtaining effective cooperation from people who are, or who think that they are, too busy to pause.

Librarians have too often been too nice, too accommodating. They have been taken advantage of by people like me, who tell them what to do and how to do it, exploring for them possibilities for doing better, explaining the mistakes they have made, the opportunities they have missed.

By and large, there is no group more pampered by the university librarian than the faculty of his university. It may not quite be true, as it was explained to me in my early days as a graduate student, that there are only two kinds of librarians, the fierce and demanding who are helpful, and the pleasantly accommodating who are not, and I should not want my friends who are librarians to become fierce and demanding toward me because I have said it; but it is true, I think, that professors are often spoiled beyond what they deserve, at the same time, in other instances, that they are expected to assume responsibilities beyond those which they are capable of carrying out. Librarians allow us to keep books out too long, without fine or recrimination. Many librarians require departmental committees to order books, knowing all the while that acquisitions librarians are going to have to mop up behind each committee if it is to be certain that essential materials are ordered. We are peppered with questionnaires which we fill out badly, hoping that librarians are too wise to read them with anything but tempered belief.

If total coverage is to be, by any means, complete, we cannot be relied on. We will push librarians about, charging in, each on his own hobbyhorse. The more intelligent our interest is and the more we advise on those small areas which we know, the more collections will bulge. A recent survey of one collection in the Columbia University Library found it:

> . . . comprehensive only in those areas within the specific subjects in which members of the faculty have conducted sustained personal research. The collection's short-comings derive essentially from Columbia's almost complete reliance on the procedure of individual faculty orders in determining additions.

LaFontaine, for example, was well represented; Pascal, not well at all.

This particular surveyor then goes on to suggest that the situation could be improved if more faculty members were involved in collection development:

> Their greatest contribution would be in identifying and helping to fill the existing gaps within their "century," outside the specifics of their current research. In every year at least one incoming faculty member should be given a minimum of one semester course (3 hours) allowance for work in the library. Thus compensated, he could be asked to survey the holdings and submit a written report, with a

detailed list of needed items. Desiderata lists which are currently based on personal research needs could thus be made more comprehensive. A microfilming or Xeroxing program of out-of-print essentials would also be initiated. Beyond the obvious benefits to the Library, such an allowance policy would increase the young scholar's institutional commitment as well as the actual command of his specialty at a crucial point in his career.

Professional librarians will recognize that this survey was made by a professor, not a librarian. His scheme has some merit, but I am not sure that I would want young members of my department to take too much interest in our library, except in their own, usually specialized, areas of research and teaching. I certainly would not want them "compensated" for such interest. But in their own areas, I would have them insist, loudly and angrily, even wrongheadedly, that the materials which they need must be acquired, and at once—no nonsense about it. I would have them beat on librarians' doors with persistent demands, even when the acquiring of what they require must mean that something of equivalent value cannot be acquired. I would have them shout, up with LaFontaine, down with Pascal!

Is it heretical of me to think that there is great charm and usefulness in libraries which are eccentric, which bulge disproportionately, so that one can read in their collections the intellectual history of their institutions, which are, as I have said earlier, lengthened shadows of the men who have made them? We are amused perhaps that the University of Texas boasts ownership of seventeen copies—isn't it?—of the first edition of Whitman's *Leaves of Grass*, that Thoreau's manuscript journals should be housed among the fine medieval collections of the Morgan Library, that Yale should have acquired such a corner on the giveaways of contemporary authors, that Columbia so cherishes its collection of mathematical esoterica.

My hope is that libraries will continue to grow distorted, with personalities of their own. If comprehensiveness is the single goal, professors may be of more hindrance than help, for they are eccentric creatures, sometimes most effective when most fanatic. They will want to help, but will need the help of librarians also, if only in closing the gap which sometimes seems to exist between us. For what many professors miss among many librarians is someone to talk to. They have become accustomed to noticing that too few fine libraries have on their staffs, as librarian, assistant librarian, or librarians of specialized collections, a man or a group of men capable of something more than technical efficiency, who can carry on the dialogue with scholar or teacher which is necessary to successful coordination. Librarians will not, I think, get best results from questionnaires or occasional formal visitation, or through perfunctory establishment of library committees, but through give-and-take so that libraries do contain what librarians' own informed, though perhaps eccentric, opinion tells them are the best things that have been thought and said, or the most unusual artifacts, or the most beautiful.

What experience I have leads me to suspect that a danger which faces librarians may be, not a lack, but rather an excess of efficiency. Surveys can discover what is wrong or wanting, and human determination can make corrections—up to a point, which is determined by one or another, or some combination, of a variety of considerations, including money, space, community approval, and the limitations of human foresight. Tough, shrewd, proficient, energetic, dynamic, skilled in public relations, adept at getting along with people, practiced in flattering members of the faculty, the librarian may become a specialist in management, an administrator who depends, as administrators must, on other people for substantive detail.

As caretaker of other men's thought, the librarian can become finally a substitute, a temporary surrogate, for the machine which will eventually replace him. The man of method only, of neatness, who stretches toward correct completeness as a single goal, is utterly expendable when something even more mechanical than he takes over. Thinking men are likely to distrust a person who knows only how to run a library. There is, as I have suggested, so little for them to talk about together. Perhaps he is necessary, this thoroughly efficient man, as a stopgap house-keeper; but methodism is not finally enough, substantive catholicity is wanted.

I would call on librarians to be prepared to stand on their own feet, wise enough to accept counsel in special areas when they find other people competent to advise them, but ready to advance alone with confidence when necessary. Maurice Tauber, in summing up professorial obligations toward evaluation and maintenance of university libraries, places first on his list the suggestion that "Faculty members, at the time they are recruited by the University, should be selected with some regard for their ability to strengthen library collections." A natural converse of this might be that librarians, at the time they are recruited by the university, should be selected with some regard for their intellectual concern with some substantive area. In this way only can there be maintained a dialogue, which is not between mechanic and inventor, or between caretaker and absentee owner, but between alert and informed, mutually-respected partners in a single enterprise.

My partiality is for the librarian who is learned in more than the mechanics of his profession, just as my preference is for the professor who is concerned, not only with the content, but with the care of books. Each to his own, independent of the other, going about his proper business—up to the point where paths cross. When that meeting will take place, and how often, depends on an erratic combination of variables. But when and wherever it does, my hope is that we shall continue then to have something to talk about together.

*Appendix*

# *Appendix*

## ALA SURVEYS

A SURVEY of a library is widely recognized as a wise procedure for the evaluation of library services, the creation of a basis for planning library development, and the determination of the degree to which a library is achieving its goals. A survey can be appropriate for any type of library: public, college or university, school, or special; or for any aspect of a library's operation: its administration, personnel, specific departments or procedures or collections. A survey by experts not connected with a library's continuing administration has the advantage of bringing expert professional consideration to a library's problems in a manner completely unprejudiced and objective. Such professional objectivity and the authority lent a survey through the opinions and recommendations of thoroughly qualified experts, selected and approved by a national professional organization, make such studies conducted under the auspices of the American Library Association of particular value.

ALA surveys are made only at the request of the official body under which a library functions—a public library board, city council, a county or regional board in the case of public libraries; a college or university library committee or responsible officer of the university in the case of a college or university library; a superintendent of schools; an appropriate officer of a business. The agency making the request for a survey should determine in some detail the purposes for which the survey is made, the areas to be studied and the information it needs to derive. Costs are borne by the agency requesting the survey. Arrangements for it are made by the executive secretary of the most appropriate division of ALA under the direction and with the approval of the Executive Director of ALA. A detailed budget is prepared as part of these arrangements and must be approved by ALA and the agency requesting the survey before a survey is undertaken. The budget provides for honoraria to the surveyors, their travel and living expenses during the period of field work, cost of publication of the report, and lesser sums for clerical work as needed, telephone and telegraph, supplies, and contingencies. It will also include a sum to cover ALA's costs of planning and administration. Surveyors are selected with the approval of the Executive Director of ALA and of the agency requesting the survey. Surveys are usually done by a team of two or more surveyors, the size of the survey team varying according to the size of the library surveyed and to the extent of the work itself. It is strongly recommended that no survey be undertaken by less than two surveyors in order that there be sufficient breadth of view and variety of special competences represented.

A survey team spends one to two weeks at the library being surveyed. The surveyors will ordinarily request certain information from the library staff in advance of this visit, and time should be allowed in scheduling for the information to be collected. It is expected that a written report of the survey will be prepared after its completion and that this report will be published, except in cases where there is agreement otherwise between the agency requesting the survey and ALA. A reasonable number (usually twenty-five) of copies of a published report will be supplied to the agency requesting the survey, which agrees to make the report to its community without deletion. It is assumed that ALA can make additional copies available to the library profession and the public generally by sale. The findings and recommendations in a survey report are those of the surveyors and carry no implication of official endorsement by ALA. In addition to the authority implicit in the qualifications of the surveyors themselves, however, the selection of them through ALA and the publication by ALA of the report gives prestige to it because of the wide acquaintance of public officials and university administrators with the reputation of ALA.

The three questionnaires which follow are excerpted from, respectively, Columbia, McGill, and Southern California surveys. The questions were designed to encourage complete, direct answers and establish good working conditions between surveyors and surveyed.

## A. THE COLUMBIA SURVEY

### Faculty Evaluation of Resources

In its consideration of acquisitional policy, the Subcommittee had available materials which had been prepared by the Library staff during the year 1953–54, supplemented by reports prepared for the present study. However, it appeared to the Subcommittee that it would be important to secure faculty views on the adequacy of the collections, and Part II of the faculty questionnaire (Appendix IV) was devised to give the teaching staff an opportunity to express these views. This appendix summarizes the statements on resources from the faculty members of the various teaching departments. In many areas, the comments are similar to those which have been expressed by the librarians, and it is obvious that the observations have grown out of mutual problems which have been met by both groups.

The following summary statements, arranged alphabetically by field, are given to help further the work of defining an acquisitional policy for the Libraries. Undoubtedly, they need additional refinement, and the Director of Libraries, the supervising librarians, the Library Committee of the University Council, the various library committees of departments and schools, and individual faculty members should give constant attention to this basic problem.

Part II (Evaluation of Resources) of the faculty questionnaire, from which the summary statements have been prepared, is reproduced below. These statements are limited to those fields on which comment was received from the faculty. This does not mean that additional subject areas are not represented in the collections of the Libraries, nor that these other fields do not need similar evaluation. Since many faculty members who returned questionnaires did not complete Part II, the number of individuals reporting for a particular field does not necessarily mean that only that number returned questionnaires in that field.

## Part II: EVALUATION OF RESOURCES

A principal objective of this study is to determine the degree to which the collections of the University Libraries are adequate to meet the instructional and research needs of present programs, and to establish agreement as to appropriate levels of collecting for the future. Part II of this questionnaire is designed to assist you in evaluating the holdings of the Libraries in the fields of your interest, and in presenting your recommendations for the future.

The form which follows has been drawn up to enable you to present your evaluation and recommendations as concisely as possible, and the following instructions are included for your guidance.

*Subject Fields:* Please be as *specific* as possible, and state both inclusions and exclusions. You may include as many subject fields as you desire.

Example: Architecture: its history, philosophy & theory dealing with periods, localities, separate buildings, significant monuments, & individual architects (but *not* naval architecture, primitive architecture, or buildings to house animals).

*Degrees of Coverage:* Five categories have been set up to describe various levels of collecting. Please indicate by the appropriate number your evaluation of the *present* strength of the collection in the subject you are describing, and by the same scale of numbers, please indicate the level which you believe would be reasonable and desirable for the *future*.

1. A BASIC INFORMATION COLLECTION is one in a subject area which falls outside the scope of the Libraries, yet within which readers may need minimum service to aid their immediate understanding or use of material which is properly within scope. Such a collection consists of a dictionary, encyclopedia, handbook, or texts, or a combination of these, in the minimum number which will serve the purpose. It is not sufficiently intensive to support any courses in the subject area involved. (Note that this type of collection may be present in various of the departmental libraries where a more intensive collection in the same subject area is located in another of the Libraries.)

2. A WORKING COLLECTION is one which is adequate to determine the current knowledge of a subject in broad outline, and the most important historical aspects of the area. It consists of one or more dictionaries, an encyclopedia, handbooks, yearbooks, a reasonable selection of monographs in the best editions, and several of the basic journals. Such a collection will support undergraduate courses in the subject.

3. A GENERAL RESEARCH COLLECTION is one adequate for the needs of graduate students of the subject, and includes the major portion of materials required for dissertations and independent research. It includes dictionaries and encyclopedias, the most important handbooks, books, periodicals and journals, and other publications in the languages usually associated with the subject, and in the latest and best editions, as well as comprehensive bibliographies, and indexing and abstracting journals. Some weeding of obsolescent material may take place.

4. A COMPREHENSIVE COLLECTION is a General Research Collection having all the material in the above category, plus a wider selection of books and periodicals having value for current research, and additional works for historical research in the subject, in all pertinent languages, though not necessarily in all editions, or in translation. Considerable documentary and original source material is included. Little or no weeding is undertaken.

5. AN EXHAUSTIVE COLLECTION is one which endeavors, so far as is reasonably possible, to include everything written on the subject, in all languages of all time, in all editions and translations. Under the prevailing conditions of library finance and the proliferation of publishing

throughout the world, the responsibilities of an exhaustive collection can be assumed only in the most exceptional circumstances.

*Languages:* Please name the languages which should be included or *excluded* in a desirable collecting policy for the future. To the extent possible, list the languages in the order of their importance in your field here in the University Libraries. In most cases, collecting in the English language is assumed.

*Country of Origin of Publications:* Please specify the countries which should be included or *excluded* in the collecting policy for the future. Note that this refers to the country from which the publications emanate, and *not* the country as a subject. In most cases, collecting from the United States is assumed.

*Type of Material:* This refers to the *form* in which the information appears, e.g., books, periodicals, annuals, yearbooks, memoirs, dissertations, maps, newspapers, manuscripts, government documents, research reports, pamphlets, clippings, etc. please indicate your desires as to inclusion and *exclusion*—particularly these types of materials which need *not* be acquired.

In making these recommendations for future policy, please do not feel that you are committing yourself or the Libraries irrevocably. Such policies have in the past and will in the future change as the University changes. Please note also that in individual instances involving particular titles, exceptions may be made in any of the above categories. The aim is not an ironclad statement with no deviations, but rather some general agreement which may serve as guidance for both the faculty and the Libraries.

EVALUATION OF RESOURCES

| Specific Subject Field | Estimated Degree of Coverage | | Future Collecting Policy | | | | | |
|---|---|---|---|---|---|---|---|---|
| | | | Languages | | Country of Origin of Publications | | Type of Material | |
| | Present | Future | Include | Exclude | Include | Exclude | Include | Exclude |
| | | | | | | | | |

## Questionnaire to Faculty Members

Name —————————————————
Title —————————————————
Department ——————————————
Field(s) of Specialization —————

*President's Committee on the Educational Future of the University*
SUBCOMMITTEE ON THE UNIVERSITY LIBRARIES

Columbia University, in the next decade or so, will continue to find itself considering the problems of changes in enrollment, curricula, and research programs anticipated by many academic departments. Preparation for such changes is a major undertaking, and requires the most considered planning by all concerned in order to share responsibility constructively in the educational aspects of these problems at Columbia.

At the request of the Director of Libraries, the Subcommittee on the University Libraries has been created as a part of the study of Columbia being undertaken by the President's Committee on the Educational Future of the University. It is anticipated that the results of the Subcommittee's study will provide a basis for planning for the Columbia Libraries for the future.

May we have your suggestions as to how the University Libraries, as a major support of the educational process, may most effectively perform their services? Our hope is that your observations on the items below may take into account the Libraries' responsibilities in connection with both *present* and *future* problems.

Where appropriate, please distinguish between an individual departmental or school library and the library system as a whole. *Please feel free to extend your comments on the back of these pages,* if you so desire. Should you have any questions regarding the interpretation of the questionnaire, please call Prof. Tauber or Mr. Cook at University 5-4000, Extension 666. If you would like a duplicate copy of the questionnaire for your files, one may be obtained from the Subcommittee.

Please return the completed questionnaire to the Subcommittee on the University Libraries, Room 611 Butler Library, Columbia University, New York 27, N.Y., by or before *November 21, 1956.* A self-addressed envelope is enclosed for your convenience. Because of the limited time available for the study, it will not be possible for the Subcommittee to send you a follow-up letter as a reminder.

*The questionnaire is to be returned by or before November 21.*

Subcommittee on the University Libraries

*Part I*

## A. FACULTY USE OF THE LIBRARIES

1. With what approximate frequency do you use the resources of the University Libraries? (Please check one.)
   _____ Daily       _____ Monthly
   _____ Three times weekly   _____ Less than twice a semester
   _____ Weekly      _____ Never
   _____ Every two weeks

2. Is this use of the Libraries *primarily* (Please check one.)
   _____ by yourself personally?
   _____ by telephone?
   _____ through a secretary, or a research or other assistant?

3. Which of the University Libraries do you use? (Please list in the order of estimated frequency of use.)
   (a) _____   (d) _____
   (b) _____   (e) _____
   (c) _____   (f) _____

4. Do you consider the dispersal of the Columbia Libraries a handicap in your use of their resources?
   _____ Yes       _____ No
   If so, what suggestions would you have for improving this situation in the future?

5. Are you satisfied with the faculty borrowing regulations in effect in the Libraries?
   _____ Yes       _____ No
   If not, please indicate in what ways you feel these might be improved:

6. Do afternoon and evening classes affect your use of the Libraries?
   _____ Yes       _____ No
   If so, please indicate in what particular ways:

7. Do you use, with any degree of frequency, other libraries in New York City (or elsewhere)?
   _____ Yes       _____ No
   If so, please indicate:

| *Libraries Used* | *Frequency of Use* | *For What Purposes?* |
| --- | --- | --- |
| _____ | _____ | _____ |
| _____ | _____ | _____ |
| _____ | _____ | _____ |

## B. INSTRUCTIONAL AND STUDENT USE OF THE LIBRARIES

1. Which of the University Libraries do you normally expect your students to use? (Please list in the order of estimated frequency of use.)

   (a) _____         (d) _____
   (b) _____         (e) _____
   (c) _____         (f) _____

2. Have your students complained to you of inadequacies in seating, lighting, other physical facilities, or library services?

   _____ Yes                          _____ No

   If so, please indicate what these complaints have been:

3. Do you expect to have library materials available at hand in your laboratory or classroom as instructional "exhibits" in your teaching?

   _____ Yes                          _____ No

   If so, please indicate the type(s) of material involved, and the frequency with which this kind of use usually occurs, or would be desirable in the future.

4. Do you believe that all the library materials *relating to your courses* should be in one place?

   _____ Yes                          _____ No

   If so, please indicate how this might be done where it is not now the case:

5. Are you satisfied with the present system of handling "reserved" and assigned readings (e.g., Are enough copies available? Are the required materials ordered promptly?)?

   _____ Yes                          _____ No

   If not, what improvements would you suggest?

6. Do you frequently find it necessary to lend to students materials from your office which are from the University Libraries?

   _____ Yes                          _____ No

   If so, please indicate the kind(s) of material involved, the frequency with which this occurs, and the reasons this is necessary (e.g., too few copies in the Libraries):

7. What procedures do you believe might be necessary to provide additional materials if there should be an increase in the number of students in your courses?

8. Do you feel obliged to restrict any assignments because of any inadequacy in the University Libraries (e.g., too few copies, unavailable materials, etc.)?

   _____ Yes                          _____ No

   If so, please indicate the reasons why this occurs:

9. How do you go about evaluating needed library materials before approving topics for doctoral dissertations and research?

10. Do you expect your students to use other library resources in New York City (or elsewhere) in addition to or instead of the Columbia collections?

   _____ Yes                    _____ No

   If so, please indicate:

   *Level of Study:*

   _____ Doctoral     _____ Master's     _____ Undergraduate

   | *Libraries Used* | *Frequency of Use* | *For What Purposes?* |
   | --- | --- | --- |
   |  |  |  |
   |  |  |  |

11. Do you feel that this student use (if any) of libraries other than Columbia is desirable from an educational and/or research point of view?

   _____ Yes                    _____ No

   Please comment:

12. Should members of the library staff have any responsibility in developing the personal, non-curricular reading habits of students?

   _____ Yes                    _____ No

   If so, in what ways might this be done?

13. What is your opinion as to the value of the Libraries' developing house (dormitory) libraries for students? (Please check one.)

   _____ Essential                    _____ Desirable

   _____ Needed                       _____ Not needed

   If you believe that this type of library should be established, what types of materials should be in these collections (e.g., additional copies of reserved readings, extra-curricular reading, etc.)?

14. Do you believe that the undergraduate students would benefit educationally if there were at Columbia a separate library building for all undergraduates similar to the Lamont Library at Harvard?

   _____ Yes                    _____ No

   Please comment:

15. Do you anticipate any changes or developments in your *teaching methods* which would affect students' use of the Libraries?

   _____ Yes                    _____ No

   If so, please explain in what ways:

## C. INSTRUCTIONAL AND RESEARCH PLANNING

1. What, if any, new *programs of instruction* are you planning which will involve library
   Resources?

Facilities?

Services?

2. Are you *currently* engaged in any research at Columbia which is hampered by any lack of library resources, services or facilities?

_____ Yes _____ No

If so, please specify in what ways:

3. Would any of your *projected* research be hampered by any lack of library resources, services or facilities (assuming, of course, that the Libraries would be continuing their program substantially as at present)?

_____ Yes _____ No

If so, please specify in what ways:

4. Should research projects supported by outside agencies make *specific provision* for library support for the University in so far as special or additional facilities may be needed?

_____ Yes _____ No

Please comment:

5. Do you in any way include provision for library support in proposals for research grants?

_____ Yes     If so, in what ways?

_____ No      If not, why is this not feasible?

D. RESOURCES (See also PART II of this questionnaire.)

1. To what extent have the resources and facilities of the University Libraries affected your decision     Indicate by numbers:

_____ To join the Columbia faculty?     1—greatly

_____ To remain with Columbia?     2—considerably

3—moderately

4—scarcely

5—not at all

2. Do you believe that the University Libraries should acquire everything needed for library support of your individual research?

_____ Yes _____ No

If not, at what point may the Libraries abstain from collecting when these needed resources are available elsewhere (e.g., other libraries in the New York metropolitan area, interlibrary loan, etc.)?

3. To what extent do you rely on your personal library rather than on the collections of the Libraries? (Please check one.)

_____ Greatly _____ Moderately _____ Not at all

_____ Considerably _____ Scarcely

4. Do you recommend titles for acquisition by the Libraries?

_____ Yes     If so, please give the approximate number of titles annually: _____

_____ No      If not, please comment on the reasons why:

5. To whom do you make these recommendations? (Please check as many as are appropriate.)

    _____ Library representative in your department

    _____ Central acquisitions department of the Libraries

    _____ Other (Please specify:

6. Has the arrangement just mentioned in D5 been satisfactory?

    _____ Yes         _____ No

If not, please comment on the disadvantages:

7. Have the Libraries usually been able to secure the materials you have requested?

    _____ Yes         _____ No

If not, please indicate how often this occurs, and the type(s) of material (or actual titles) involved:

8. What should be the responsibility of the University Libraries to collect materials in fields not now directly (or indirectly) covered by courses and research under way at present (e.g., Should the Libraries collect Africana to any great extent, in anticipation of the possibility that an African Institute might be created in the future?)?

9. What should be the responsibility of the staff of the Libraries in furnishing information on library resources to the faculty when the latter are considering the establishment of new courses, research programs, etc.?

10. Do you see any reason to be disturbed by the fact that from time to time the Libraries, upon the departure of a particular faculty member, find themselves in possession of library materials acquired for and used only or principally by that person, and for which no future utility can realistically be anticipated?

    _____ Yes         _____ No

Please comment:

11. What suggestions would you make as to ways in which the various members of the faculty might assist the staff of the Libraries in weeding obsolete materials from the collections?

12. For what types of materials in your field do (and would) you find microreproductions (e.g., microfilm, microcards, etc.) most useful and desirable? (Please check as many items as are appropriate.)

    _____ Deteriorating materials

    _____ Dissertations and other items which are being published originally on film or cards

    _____ Expensive materials which can be acquired in microreproduction at greatly reduced cost

    _____ Materials which are bulky and for which there is little space

    _____ Older materials which are little used

    _____ Other (Please specify:

13. Do you have any suggestions for facilitating the use of microreproductions in the University Libraries?

14. In order to help to relieve pressure for additional space, it has been suggested that the Libraries might participate in an interlibrary center or create a "storage" library of their own. In such a scheme, little-used materials would be removed from the active collections; these materials would remain available to the faculty and to students, although with some delay. What would your opinion be as to the advantages and disadvantages of such a proposal as applied to your particular field?

## E. SERVICES

1. What improvements would you suggest which might be made in the catalogs in the Libraries?
2. What suggestions would you have for the reclassification of any portion of the collections?
3. Among the University Libraries, the degree of access to the stacks varies considerably, from complete restriction in the Special Collections to completely open access in libraries such as College. Please comment on what you believe to be the advantages (e.g., educational) and disadvantages (e.g., more rapid deterioration, misplacement) of stack access, and the degree to which the University Libraries should grant access in the future:
4. Please indicate the degree to which you believe the University Libraries should assume responsibility for the services listed below.
   Please weight the items as follows:       1—essential     3—desirable
                                             2—needed        4—not needed

   _____ Abstracting of items for faculty use
   _____ Direct distribution to you of bibliographical items and notes in your field
   _____ Exhibits in relation to specific courses
   _____ Indexing (of periodicals received in the Libraries)
   _____ Interlibrary loan service without charge
   _____ Mail service during vacations, sabbaticals, etc.
   _____ Preparation of bibliographies and booklists
   _____ Translations (of materials in the Libraries)
   _____ Other (Please specify:
5. Which of the services just mentioned in E4 do you believe might be offered upon payment of a fee?
6. In view of the pressures from faculty and students in residence, to what extent do you believe that the University Libraries should be available to Columbia alumni? (Please check as many as are appropriate.)
   _____ Not at all

_____ Reference service (i.e., use in the Libraries) only, *with* payment of a fee

_____ Reference service (i.e., use in the Libraries) only, *without* payment of a fee

_____ Full use (including borrowing privileges), *with* payment of a fee

_____ Full use (including borrowing privileges), *without* payment of a fee

_____ Other (Please specify:

## F. PERSONNEL OF THE LIBRARIES

1. What observations would you make on the qualifications and performance of the personnel of the Libraries? To the extent feasible, please distinguish between professional librarians and student and other assistants.

2. Do you find it a handicap that professional librarians are not available during all the hours which the Libraries are open?

_____ Yes  _____ No

If so, please indicate in what ways:

3. Do you believe that the University Libraries are overstaffed at present?

_____ Yes  _____ No

If so, please indicate specific instances where this may be the case:

## G. MISCELLANEOUS

1. Most of the items in the above sections concern matters of interest to all departments. There are, in addition, special problems arising from the different kinds of materials necessary for faculty and student work in some fields (e.g., clippings in the Journalism Library, corporation reports in the Business Library, etc.). In what ways might the Libraries improve their handling and servicing of these special materials in your field of interest?

2. Do you have any additional specific suggestions for the development of the Libraries in the following areas:

Resources? (See also Part II)

Quarters?

Services?

Personnel?

3. Are the conditions in any of the above areas at present such that some curtailment might be considered in view of the program you anticipate for the future?

_____ Yes  _____ No

If so, please specify in what ways:

B. THE McGILL SURVEY

## Library Questionnaire     May 1963

TO: Deans, Directors, and Department Chairmen

As one means of securing information designed to improve and strengthen the Libraries of the University, we ask your cooperation in completing this questionnaire.

It is requested that information be supplied by each department, faculty or college. In special circumstances it may be desirable for a department to submit more than one completed form. Such additional reports will be welcome.

Similarly, if the questions listed do not appear to cover any aspect of the Library on which you wish to comment, please feel free to make your own additions.

Thank you for your assistance.

R. H. Logsdon
S. A. McCarthy

Department or Faculty _____ Name _____

1. On what Library does your department or faculty primarily depend for library service?
2. *Library Services.* What changes or improvements do you suggest in the following library services?
   a. Circulation
   b. Reserve book, i.e., books assigned for required or collateral reading
   c. Reference
   d. Inter-library loan
   e. Microfilm and other microforms
   f. Other
   g. What services not now provided do you consider desirable?
3. *Cataloging and Classification.* If the present system of cataloging and classification does not meet your needs, please indicate the nature and extent of the improvements you consider necessary.
4. *Acquisition and Binding.* What changes and improvements do you suggest?
5. *Library Collections.*

a. Briefly, what do you regard as the *strengths* and the *weaknesses* of the library collection in your field?
b. What is your estimate of the amount required for books, periodicals and binding in order to make up essential deficiencies? (Please attach desiderata lists or cite types of publications required.)
c. What has been the amount of the book fund provided for your department in the past year?
d. What amount do you consider necessary annually to maintain book and periodical purchasing at an appropriate level for your department?
e. If your department requires special types of material not now provided, please indicate the nature and extent of this material.
f. Is your department planning any new academic or research programs that will require special library materials, services or facilities? (Please be as specific as possible.)

6. *Library Facilities and Equipment.* If present library facilties for your department are inadequate for your needs, please indicate the approximate size and nature of the facilities you consider necessary, including any special facilities or equipment required.
7. *Library Staff.* On the assumption that some increase in library staff is desirable, what positions, departments and services do you consider most in need of strengthening?
8. *Public Relations.* Please indicate briefly some of the elements of a public relations program that you consider appropriate for a university library.
9. Other suggestions for improvement of library collections, services and facilities.

Name _____
Department
or Faculty _____
Date _____

Please return to Mr. W. K. Molson, Morrice Hall, 3485 McTavish Street.

## C. THE SOUTHERN CALIFORNIA SURVEY

### Questionnaire on Centralized Technical Processing

The following questionnaire has been developed for the purpose of determining the framework for a centralized technical processing project for libraries included in the program of joint cooperative activities among the public libraries of Los Angeles, Orange, Riverside, and San Bernardino Counties of the Southern California Area. In order to prepare a statement for a potential program, it is important to have the observation of the libraries which may participate in such an enterprise. Your cooperation is essential.

Please return the questionnaire to Dr. Maurice F. Tauber, School of Library Service, Columbia University, New York, N.Y. 10027, by January 28.

1. Name of Library
2. Our library is willing to consider participating in centralized processing.
   _____ Yes                                         _____ No


A. ACQUISITIONS
1. In the development of the cooperative processing system, it is necessary to have a clear understanding as to whether or not the center would do acquisitions work for the participating libraries as well as cataloging.
   a. It is understood that the center would acquire the books (and possibly other materials) for the libraries. Support this view ———. Do not support this view _____.
   b. If this view is supported, it is understood that the service center would be efficient only if the libraries were willing to check, on schedule, for selection purposes, agreed-upon published guides (*Kirkus, ABPR, LJ,* etc.). This would have no restriction of purchasing of materials outside of current guides. Would the administration of your library agree to participate on this basis?
      _____ Yes                                      _____ No
   c. What is the present average time period for the acquisition of books in your library? (Indicate days or weeks.) It is assumed that the service center would acquire books as quickly or sooner than the average time required for an individual library to acquire titles.
   d. Are there any special problems in acquisitions which occur to you that would present problems for your library if books were acquired by a service center? (Please describe, and use extra space on back page if necessary.)


B. CATALOGING

1. In respect to form of main entry, it may be desirable to enter fiction according to title page form and non-fiction according to the *ALA*

*Cataloging Rules for Author and Title Entries.* Would you agree to this procedure?

\_\_\_\_\_ Yes \_\_\_\_\_ No

If no, please explain why not.

2. In the cataloging of fiction, would you want the center to prepare cards for such titles as the following:
   (a) Mysteries. \_\_\_\_\_ Yes \_\_\_\_\_ No
   (b) Science fiction. \_\_\_\_\_ Yes \_\_\_\_\_ No
   (c) Westerns. \_\_\_\_\_ Yes \_\_\_\_\_ No
   (d) Would you object to stopping the cataloging of such works?
   \_\_\_\_\_ Yes \_\_\_\_\_ No
3. Do you object to the omission of place of publication in the imprint, if the title is published in the United States?

   \_\_\_\_\_ Yes \_\_\_\_\_ No
4. It is expected that the cataloging of serials would follow ALA and LC rules, but that simplification would be introduced where necessary. Do you support this procedure?

   \_\_\_\_\_ Yes \_\_\_\_\_ No

   If no, please indicate alternative.
5. Would you like the center to catalog serials from first issue as open entry?

   \_\_\_\_\_ Yes \_\_\_\_\_ No
6. Would you prefer the center to catalog serials as monographic works when possible?

   \_\_\_\_\_ Yes \_\_\_\_\_ No

   If no, please explain why not.
7. It is expected that the service center may eventually acquire documents and other materials for the participating libraries, if feasible. Please list materials that you consider the center might acquire centrally for the individual libraries.
8. Would you expect the center to make cross-references for your catalogs?
   (a) "see" references \_\_\_\_\_ Yes \_\_\_\_\_ No
   (b) "see also" references \_\_\_\_\_ Yes \_\_\_\_\_ No
   (c) At the present time, do you have "see also" references in your catalog? \_\_\_\_\_ Yes \_\_\_\_\_ No
   (d) Would you take the responsibility for making your own cross-references if you belonged to the center?
   \_\_\_\_\_ Yes \_\_\_\_\_ No
   If no, please explain why not.

## C. CLASSIFICATION

1. It is expected that the center would use the centralized services of the LC Dewey Decimal Center (as indicated by class numbers on LC

printed cards, etc.) for classification of books. Do you support this approach?

_____ Yes                                    _____ No

If no, please explain. (An agreement will have to be reached as to expansion beyond the decimal point.)

2. It is expected that there would be no exceptions to the classification designated by the center (i.e., no special assignments for any particular library). Do you support this approach?

_____ Yes                                    _____ No

3. Please make any comments about classification that occur to you in connection with centralized classification services.

## D. CARD REPRODUCTION: BOOK CATALOGS

1. It is expected that mechanical card reproduction will be used in the center. Do you have any comments or suggestions in this regard?
2. The possibility of book catalog production will be explored, although it is not clear just how these might be used in connection with larger libraries in the group.

   (a) Would you object to having a book catalog for your collection, if this were feasible and economic?

   _____ Yes                                    _____ No

   If no, please explain.

   (b) Do you have any suggestions concerning the type of catalog in book form which you might prefer?

   (c) Do you consider that a book catalog would have no use other than supplementing your card catalog?

   _____ Yes                                    _____ No

   Please Comment.

3. Please describe your present method of reproducing cards.

## E. BOOK PROCESSING

1. Please describe your particular procedures in respect to each of the following:

   (a) Book pockets
   (b) Labeling
   (c) Book jackets
   (d) Marks of ownership
   (e) Bookplates
   (f) Other matters

2. Describe your charging system.
3. Do you consider that a uniform charging system should be used by all of the libraries?

   _____ Yes                                    _____ No

   If no, please explain why not.

## F. UNION CATALOG

1. Do you support the possibility that a union catalog might be developed for the libraries in the Southern California area?
   _____ Yes                        _____ No
   If no, please indicate reason.
2. If a union catalog were established, would you send cards regularly?
   _____ Yes                        _____ No

## G. GENERAL COMMENTS

It would be most helpful for any group studying this problem to have your comments, about any matter related to the project, and to review your observations in relation to any point not considered in the above series of questions. The present study is an effort to project a cooperative enterprise, and it is important to have all of your views at this time. We are grateful for your help.

# Index